Russell Thacher Trall

The New Hydropathic Cook-Book

With Recipes for Cooking on Hygienic Principles

Russell Thacher Trall

The New Hydropathic Cook-Book
With Recipes for Cooking on Hygienic Principles

ISBN/EAN: 9783337091507

Printed in Europe, USA, Canada, Australia, Japan

Cover: Foto ©Andreas Hilbeck / pixelio.de

More available books at **www.hansebooks.com**

THE NEW

Hydropathic Cook-Book;

WITH

RECIPES FOR COOKING ON HYGIENIC PRINCIPLES:

CONTAINING ALSO A

PHILOSOPHICAL EXPOSITION OF THE RELATIONS OF FOOD TO HEALTH; THE CHEMICAL ELEMENTS AND PROXIMATE CONSTITUTION OF ALIMENTARY PRINCIPLES; THE NUTRITIVE PROPERTIES OF ALL KINDS OF ALIMENTS; THE RELATIVE VALUE OF VEGETABLE AND ANIMAL SUBSTANCES; THE SELECTION AND PRESERVATION OF DIETETIC MATERIALS, ETC., ETC.

BY R. T. TRALL, M.D.

With Numerous Illustrative Engravings

NEW YORK:
PUBLISHED BY SAMUEL R. WELLS,
No. 389 BROADWAY.
1869.

ENTERED, ACCORDING TO ACT OF CONGRESS, IN THE YEAR 1863, BY
FOWLERS AND WELLS,
IN THE CLERK'S OFFICE OF THE DISTRICT COURT OF THE UNITED STATES
FOR THE SOUTHERN DISTRICT OF NEW YORK.

Preface.

THE leading objects of this work are, to present, in the smallest possible compass, a summary of the principles and facts, in chemistry and physiology, which apply to the philosophy of diet; and to furnish such as are not familiar with the details of cooking on hygienic principles, plain formulas for preparing an ample variety of dishes, with due regard to the laws of life and health.

Food is one of the elements of the *materia medica* in our hydropathic system, and in importance is second to no other—not even water. A vast number of chronic diseases are wholly incurable, however judiciously all the other appliances of Water-Cure are managed, without proper attention to the dietetic part of the general remedial plan. And herein Water-Cure establishments and hydropathic physicians are more at fault than in any other respect.

I trust the time is not far distant, when not only hydropathic practitioners, but the people generally, will make the subject of diet one of their principal studies. It ought to be taught in all our seminaries of learning, for there is more of health and happiness, or of disease and misery, connected with our methods of cooking and eating, than is dreamed of in the philosophy of most persons.

Whether humanity must become good in order to be happy, or must first become happy in order to be good, is a very pretty metaphysical problem for discussion; but, pending its solution, I will undertake to say, that human beings will never be, in an exalted sense, either good or happy, until they shall have obtained that harmonious and healthful play of all the bodily and mental functions which constitute "peace within;" and that such a consummation can never be realized until a thorough and radical reform is effected in the eating habits of the civilized world.

In the arrangement of the work, I have aimed to make it, as far as practicable, also a health-reform educational book. It seems to me there is something peculiarly humanizing, elevating, and refining in the contemplation of fruits and flowers, and the cultivation of grains and roots, for the purposes of a pure and healthful sustenance, drawn directly from the bosom of mother earth. It appears to me, too, that the pictures of animals displayed in the common cook-books, covered over with lines and figures denoting the different parts of the carcass from which to choose the more or less precious morsels, have a brutalizing, sensualizing, and degrading effect on the human being, especially on the impressible mind of childhood.

To counteract, therefore, to some extent, the demoralizing tendency of ordinary cook-book literature, and to aid in a better development of the youthful mind, I have endeavored to render this work attractive as well as instructive to young persons, by embellishing it with engravings which lead the mind away from scenes or thoughts of blood and slaughter, to subjects of botany, natural history, agriculture, horticulture, etc. I trust the time is not far distant when the foundation for a better development of the human race will be established, in "teaching the young idea how to *eat*," so as to secure uniform health, and realize the first and essential condition of universal happiness—"sound minds in healthy bodies."

R. T. T.

HYDROPATHIC AND HYGIENIC INSTITUTE,
15 LAIGHT STREET, NEW YORK.

Introduction.

COOKERY books are plenty enough in our markets; and although their literary excellences may be unquestionable, I can not regard most of them as any thing better than promiscuous medleys of dietetic abominations.

In a majority of the works extant on the subject of preparing food for the table, the strong point of authorship seems to have been, to mix and mingle the greatest possible amount of seasonings, saltings, spicings, and greasings into a single dish; and jumble the greatest possible variety of heterogeneous substances into the stomach at single meal. No wonder the patrons and admirers of such cook-books are full of dyspepsia, and constipation, and hemorrhoids, and biliousness of every degree, and nervousness of every kind!

"Cookery is an art," says Mrs. Sarah Josepha Hale (*New Book of Cookery*, etc.), "belonging to woman's department of knowledge; its importance can hardly be over-estimated, because it acts directly on human health, comfort, and improvement."

It is precisely *because* the art of cookery is so intimately connected with the whole development and improvement, bodily and mentally, of the human being, that I so strongly object to almost all that is taught and recommended in Mrs. Hale's book. The following recipe, copied from page 159, will illustrate my meaning better than a long argument:

"*Pork Cheese.*—Choose the head of a small pig which may weigh about twelve pounds the quarter. Sprinkle over it, and the tongues of four pigs, a little common salt and a very little saltpetre. Let them lie four days; wash them, and tie them in a clean cloth; boil them until the bones will come easily out of the head; take off the skin as whole as possible; place a bowl in hot water and put in the head, cutting it into small pieces. In the bottom of a round tin, shaped like a small cheese, lay two strips of cloth across each other; they must be long enough to fold over the top when the shape is full; place the skin round the tin, and nearly half fill it with the meat, which has been highly seasoned with pepper, cayenne, and salt; put in some tongue cut into slices, then the rest of the meat, and the remainder of the tongue; draw the cloth tightly across the top; put it on a board or a plate that will fit into the shape, and place on it a heavy weight, which must not be taken off till it be quite cold. It is eaten with vinegar and mustard, and served for luncheon or supper."

Whether such cookery is calculated to improve or misimprove the human race need not be argued here. If the trade of butchering animals for food has a tendency to imbrute the minds of those engaged in it, certainly the dressing up of a pig's head for the table, so as to resemble as nearly as possible the shape, form, features, and *expression* of a live pig, is equally vitiating to all true delicacy and refinement. Such cooking is bad enough when the only pretense about it is to gratify an exceedingly depraved appetite; but when it is commended in a book claiming for itself peculiar merit for "setting forth the *true relations of food to health*," it becomes, like vice,

"A monster of such hideous mien,
That to be hated needs but to be seen."

Another popular cook-book is that of Miss Beecher. (*Domestic Receipt Book.*) In her preface she says: "No book of this kind will sell without receipts for the rich articles which custom requires; and in furnishing them, the writer has aimed to follow the example of Providence, which scatters profusely both good and ill, and combines therewith the caution alike of experience, revelation, and conscience, 'Choose ye that which is good, that ye and your seed may live.'"

On looking through Miss Beecher's book, it seems to me the evil is much more profusely scattered than the good; that the wine and brandy she commends in her cakes, and pies, and pudding sauces are better calculated to make men drunkards, than to render them wise in choosing. And I apprehend the world would soon come to a pretty pass, if we should all go to scattering good and evil about us after what Miss Beecher considers to be the example of Providence!

Cook book-makers, like cigar-makers and liquor-compounders, may manufacture an article to suit the demands of traffic. They may pander to vitiated appetite, and help the business of doctors, and nostrum-venders, and undertakers; but I think an educated and literary woman *ought* to be better employed than in compiling voluminous works, wherein almost every vile and filthy thing under the sun is paraded temptingly and recommended authoritatively to appetites already deeply sensualized, if not incorrigibly depraved.

When the women of our country can be made to understand clearly and correctly the relations of food to health, they will repudiate all such "Complete Housekeepers" and "Domestic Guides" as the books I have alluded to. And when our mothers are fully aware of the intimate connection between the health and proper development of their offspring, and their own dietetic habits, they will study rather to avoid all seasonings, than to mingle many; they will seek purity of material and simplicity of preparation, instead of compounding their dishes after the most ridiculous fashions, and the most unnatural tastes.

Ten years' experience in the management of hydropathic establishments has convinced me that the dietetic part of our curative plan is far the most difficult to carry out properly. Among the obstacles we have to contend with are the false habits, perverted tastes, and blind prejudices of the patient; the commerical frauds and adulterations practiced more or less with almost every thing used as food; and the imperfect state of agriculture, especially as relates to the culture of fruits and garden vegetables.

However strange may seem the assertion, it is nevertheless true, that the philosophy of diet has *never been taught in medical schools!.* Physicians generally are as profoundly ignorant of the whole subject as are the great masses of the people. And even many professedly hydropathic doctors give the matter very little attention. Many a Water-Cure house, and not a few "establishments," have "gone down" because there was no competent person found to manage the table.

Bread and fruit, it is, or ought to be, generally known, are, or should be, staple and principal articles of food on all tables for Water-Cure invalids. Yet I have seen on such tables an article of bread more calculated to create dyspepsia than to cure it; and samples of fruit better calculated to excite colic than to relieve constipated bowels. And it is unfortunate for the cause of dietetic reform, that many persons get their impressions of hydropathic diet from witnessing or experiencing its abuse instead of its use.

In the general out-door practice of hydropathic physicians the matter is still worse. We are often called in private families to prescribe a course of home-treatment for some chronic disease. And frequently it happens that bad eating habits are the principal cause of suffering, to remove which the patient seeks our advice. We can tell him what he should eat; but where will he find it? We can explain to him what materials to get, but where will he get them? We can instruct him in the tests of their proper quality and purity, but how will he be able to distinguish by seeing and feeling them? We can talk to him all about the manner of preparing such food as we recommend, and leave him with the consoling reflection that he will very likely spoil the thing in cooking it, and then lay all the blame to our system or our misapplication of it!

All these difficulties exist; and they exist only because the people have never yet given sufficient attention to " the relations of food to health."

Under the auspices of the vegetarian reform movement many improvements have taken place in the manner of preparing a great variety of dishes for the table. But vegetarian diet is not necessarily physiological. The *best* diet contemplates the physiological preparation and use of vegetable food. But most of the vegetarian cook-books thus far are improvements on the ordinary plan of a mixed diet, mainly in excluding " flesh, fish, and fowl," and substituting butter for lard. This *is*, however, an improvement of no small importance; but it recognizes no physiological principle save the preference of vegetable food for flesh meat. The vegetarians, however, are beginning to study the philosophy of diet more thoroughly, and will, no doubt, very soon modify their cook-books accordingly.

I must in this place caution those who undertake to cook after the rules and receipts of this book, against being discouraged if they do not always succeed in their first attempts. I know excellent bread-makers who spoiled many a loaf of Graham bread before they could get the "knack" of producing exactly the right article. Notwithstanding the nicest formularies that can be given, something must always be left to "tact and judgment." All, however, who sincerely desire to become good cooks in accordance with the principles inculcated in this work, will in due time become proficient by practice and experience.

A cockroach crawled o'er a baker's shelf,
Waving his horns and looking for pelf;
The baker, upon his broad board below,
Was kneading and rolling about the dough.

The board received such terrible thumps
As the baker's rolling-pin struck the lumps,
The shelf was shaken, the cockroach fell—
Ah, where? the baker he could not tell!

Into the oven, deep in the dough,
Stern Fate would have the cockroach go—
Dead and buried, his fate unknown,
Perished the cockroach all alone.

*　　　*　　　*　　　*

A napkin lay where a feast was spread,
In its midst a bit of dainty bread;
A lovely lady, with hands most fair,
Unravell'd the napkin lying there.

Soups, fish, and birds, of many a kind,
A pig, with skewers its joints to bind—
A hare, with parsley stuck on its nose—
And snipes and pheasants all laid in rows.

Huge limbs of pork, beef, mutton, and veal
Were sliced by the flourish of sharp-edg'd steel;
The well-charged plates were borne around
By valets, in coats with gilt lace bound.

Many a beggar might live on the steams
That danced in the hall on the wax-light beams,
But he must have a most delicate smell,
Who by its strange odor the dish could tell.

*   *   *   *   *

A terrible shriek stirs the steam and air
That circle around the lady fair:
The guests all about the table rise,
Gaze toward her with dread surprise.

"Pray, sit, my good lords," at length, quoth she,
"And, kindly, I pray, don't question me!"
And glad were they when the fright was o'er,
To turn to the sumptuous feast once more.

In vain did the lady strive to eat
Delicate morsels of richest meat;
A dreadful sight met her constant view—
She had bitten the hateful cockroach through!

Then to her in the steam from a bright tureen
Was the ghost of the luckless cockroach seen;
While confusion in her ears did ring,
The sprite of the cockroach seemed to sing:

"Lady! why gave you that terrible shriek?
Why rolled your eye, and paled your cheek?
Why dread to bite a poor worm like me,
But eat sheep and swine most greedily?

"Oh, delicate lady, oh, sensitive fair,
See the table strewn with carcasses there—
Mangled and torn, all flesh from bone—
Oh, leave such horrible feasts alone!

"The waving corn and fruitful tree,
Bear gracious nourishment for thee;
Live, fair one, as a lady should,
And being beautiful—be good!

"Though lions, tigers, vultures prey,
Be thou more merciful than they;
Thy health will last, thy life be long!"
And thus the cockroach ceased his song.

NOTE.—To those who desire to investigate thoroughly the subject of diet, and especially to those who wish to be well posted in the multitudinous facts and statistics which can be adduced in favor of an exclusively vegetable diet, as derived from history and science, I would earnestly recommend the addition to their libraries of Smith's "Fruits and Farinacea, the Proper Food of Man;" "Alcott's Vegetable Diet;" and Lax's "Organic Laws."

Without involving the reader in difficult physiological problems, they collectively present an array of evidence and principles which, if not conclusive, are at least interesting and instructive.

The former is an English work, now being republished by Messrs. Fowlers and Wells. The other works are published by the same house.

Contents.

Introduction.

Books on Cookery—Medleys of Dietetic Abominations—Sources of Disease—Relations of Food to Health—Commercial Frauds and Adulterations—Philosophy of Diet never taught in Medical Schools—Water-Cure Establishments—Practice of Hydropathic Physicians—Difficulties—Vegetarian Reform—Caution to Bread Makers—An Instructive Poem.. Page vii–xiv

Chapter One.

PHILOSOPHY OF DIET.—A Fundamental Principle—Theory of Vegetarianism—Summary of the Vegetarian System—Organization with regard to Diet—Population with regard to Diet—Nutritive Value of Foods—Illustrative Analysis—All Nutrition is formed in the Vegetable Kingdom... 15–22

Chapter Two.

ELEMENTS OF FOOD.—Alimentary Principles—Errors in Classification—Chemical Elements of Food—Carbon—Hydrogen—Oxygen—Nitrogen—Phosphorus—Sulphur—Iron—Chlorine—Sodium—Calcium—Magnesium—Potassium—Fluorine—Proximate Elements of Food—Water—Filtration—Filtering through Stone—Ascending Filter—Cistern Filtering—Double Cistern Filtering—Cleansing Filtering Apparatus—Cask Filter—Revolving Cask Filter—Box Filtering Apparatus—Jar Filter—Yarn Filter—Stone-ware Filter—Cooling Water—Gum—Sugar—The Sugar-cane Plant—Sirups—Manna—Honey—Starch—Corn Starch—Cassava Bread—Starch Grains Illustrated—Sago—Tapioca—Arrow-Root—Wheat Starch—Lignin—Fungin—Jelly—Organic Acids—Vinegar—Fat—Oleaginous Foods—Volatile Oils—Fibrin—Albumen—Casein—Gluten—Gelatin—Blanc-mange—Glue—Saline Matters—Common Salt—Pereira Controverted... 23–47

Chapter Three.

ALIMENTS, OR FOOD PROPER.—Classification of Aliments—Wheat—Frauds in Flour—Rice—Wild Rice—Oats—Oatmeal—Groats—Barley—Pot Barley—Rye—Schwartzbrot—Ergot—Indian Corn, or Maize—Hominy—Samp—Green Corn—Buckwheat—Millet, or Hirse—Peas—Beans—Lentils—Pea-meal—Parched Peas—Split Peas—Green Peas—Lima Beans—Nuts—Chestnut—Butternut—Almonds—Bitter Al monds—Walnut—Hazel-nut—Filbert—Cocoa-nut—Peanuts—Brazil-nuts—Madeira-nuts—Pistachio-nuts—Acorns—Classification of Fleshy Fruits—Peaches—Nectarines—Plums—Prunes—Apricots—Cherries—Olives—Dates—The Apple—Early Strawberry—Fall Pippin—Pears—Quinces—The Aku, or Aker—The Medlar—Currants—Gooseberries—Whortleberries—The Blueberry—The Barberry—The Buffalo Berry—The Cranberry—Elderberries—Juniper Berries—Scheidam Schnapps—The Grape—Catawbas and Isabellas—Raisins—The Black Currant—The Orange—The Lemon—The Citron—The Shaddock—The Lime—The Pomegranate—The Tomato, or Love Apple—The Okra, or Gambo—Pepones—Melons—Pumpkins—Squashes—Figs—Mulberries—The Pineapple—Strawberries—Raspberries—Blackberries—The Dewberry—Bread Fruit—Durion—Guava—Mammu—Litchi—Jujube—Juvia—Papau—Avocado Pear—Anchovy Pear—Manjo—Banana—Plantain—Mangostan—Turnips—Carrots—Parsneps—Beets—Potatoes—Artichokes—Yams—The Radish—The Skirret—Onions—Leeks—Garlic—Chives—Shallots—Asparagus—Cabbages—Savoy—Cauliflower—Broccoli—Sourkrout—Spinach—Chenopodium—Sorrel—Rhubarb—Seasoning Herbs—Ferns—Lichens—Seaweeds—Mushrooms—Animal Foods—Qualities of Animal Foods—Roman Custom of Killing Animals—Jewish Custom—Composition of Flesh—Methods of Cooking Flesh—Fish Aliment—Insects—Eggs—Milk—Butter—Cream—Cheese—Concentrated or Essence of Milk .... Page 48–108

Chapter Four.

PRESERVATION OF FOODS.—Preservation of Grain, Meal, Seeds, etc.—Preservation of Vegetables—Vegetable Drying Apparatus—Preservation of Fruits—Plan of Mr. Smith—The North American Phalanx Company—Principal Condition for Preserving Perishable Fruits—Undried Grapes—Green Gooseberries and Currants—Scalding Fruit—Peach and Tomato Leather—Preserving Peaches in Tin Cans—Pumpkins and Squashes—Cultivation of Currants and Gooseberries—Preservation with ice—Plan of an Ice House... 109–117

Chapter Five.

THEORY OF NUTRITION.—Prevalent Errors—Stimulating Diet—Tonic Diet—Low Diet—High Living—Rich Food —Definition of Nutrition—The Abdominal Viscera—Dr. Beaumont's Experiments—Summary of the Digestive Processes—Insalivation—Mastication—Deglutition—Chymification—Properties of Bile—Fatty Matters in the Stomach—The Pancreatic Juice—Chylification—Structure of the Alimentary Canal—The Lacteal Vessels—Defecation—Fecal Accumulations—Practical Reflections—Condiments—Catalogue of the Crystal Palace—Fat Persons and Animals—Modus Operandi of the Fattening Process... 118–147

Chapter Six.

BREAD AND BREAD-MAKING.—Different Kinds of Bread—Theory of Fermentation—General Rules for Bread-making—Unleavened Breads—Fermented Breads—Raised Breads—Digestibility of Breads—Quality of Flour and Meal—Bread-making—Setting the Sponge—The Three Essentials—Ferment, Leaven, or Yeast—Original Ferment—Hop-yeast—Potato-yeast—Milk Risings—Yeast Cakes—Yeast-rubs—Ferment without Yeast—Flour-yeast—Yeast of Dried Peas—Unleavened Bread—Raised Bread—Wheat-meal Bread—Graham Bread—Potato Bread—Rye and Indian Bread—Apple Bread—Pumpkin Bread—Rice Bread—Moist Rice Bread—Sweet Brown Bread—Currant Bread—Scalded Bread................................ 148–164

Chapter Seven.

CAKES AND BISCUITS.—Wheat-meal Crackers—Unleavened Bread Cakes—Wheat-meal Wafers—Indian-meal Cake—Johnny Cake—Raised Indian Cake—Rich Corn Cake—Corn Cream Cake—Molasses Cake—Wheat-meal Sweet Cake—Indian Slappers—Wheat-meal Griddle Cake—Buckwheat Griddle Cakes—Rice Griddle Cakes—Wheat and Indian Griddle Cakes—Oatmeal Cake—Potato Cake—Flour and Potato Rolls—Indian Pancakes—Slapjacks—Sour Milk Biscuit—Shortened Biscuit—Rye Drop Cake—Wheat-meal Drop Cake—Corn-meal Muffins—Hydropathic Crumpets—Cocoa-nut Drops—Milk Biscuit—Water-Cure Waffles—Uncooked Bread Cake—Unbaked Bread Cake—Uncooked Fruit Cake—Frost Cakes—Improved Jumballs—Fruit Cake—Wedding Cake—Potato Scones—Dry Toast—Milk Toast—Cream Toast—Wheat-meal Fruit Biscuits..................................Page 165-172

Chapter Eight.

MUSHES AND PORRIDGES.—Cracked Wheat Mush—Hominy—Samp—Rye-meal Mush—Indian-meal Mush—Oatmeal Mush—Wheat-meal Mush—Farina Mush—Rice Mush—Rice and Milk Mush—Corn Starch Blanc-mange—Molded Farinacea—Milk Porridge—Wheat-meal Porridge—Oatmeal Porridge—Hominy Porridge—Sago Porridge—Rice and Sago Porridge—Bean Porridge........................ 173-176

Chapter Nine.

PIES AND PUDDINGS.—Pie Crust—Wheat-meal Pie Crust—Wheat and Potato Crust—Meal and Flour Crust—Raised Pie Crust—Wheat and Rye Crust—Bread Pie Crust—Pumpkin Pie with Eggs—Pumpkin Pie with Cream—Grated Pumpkin Pie—Squash Pie—Green Apple Pie—Dried Apple Pie—Carrot Pie—Potato Pie—Peach Pie—Dried Peach Pie—Rhubarb Pie—Custard Pie—Cranberry Tart—Whortleberry Pie—Blackberry Pie—Raspberry Pie—Strawberry Pie—Strawberry Tart—Green Currant Pie—Gooseberry Pie—Dried Fruit Pies—Rice Puddings—Sago and Apple Pudding—Pearl Barley Pudding—Barley and Apple Pudding—Bread Pudding—Cracked Wheat Pudding—Hominy Pudding—Indian-meal Pudding—Tapioca Pudding—Snow Pudding—Christmas Pudding—Macaroni Snow Pudding—Rice and Apple Pudding—Sweet Apple Pudding—Snow-ball Pudding—Apple Custard—Cottage Pudding—Farina Pudding—Fig and Cocoa-nut Pudding—Baked Apple Pudding—Berry Pudding—Custard Pudding—Green Corn Pudding...... 177-185

Chapter Ten.

WHOLE GRAINS AND SEEDS.—Boiled Wheat—Boiled Rice—Parched Corn—Boiled Chestnuts—Roasted Peanuts—Boiled Green Peas—Boiled Green Beans—Boiled Beans and Peas—Boiled Green Corn—Roasted Green Corn—Succotash.... 186-188

Chapter Eleven.

GRUELS AND SOUPS.—Wheat-meal Gruel—Indian-meal Gruel—Oatmeal Gruel—Farina Gruel—Tapioca Gruel—Sago Gruel—Currant Gruel—Groat Gruel—Arrowroot Gruel—Rice Gruel—Tomato Soup—Rice Soup—Split Peas Soup—Green Peas Soup—Split Peas and Barley Soup—Barley Soup—Green Bean Soup—Vegetable Broth—Barley Broth—Spinach Soup—Vegetable and Rice Soup—Cucumber and Gumbo Soup... 189-193

xviii   CONTENTS.

Chapter Twelve.

ROOTS AND VEGETABLES.—Boiled Potatoes—Boiled Peeled Potatoes—Browned Potatoes—Potato for Shortening—Mashed Potato—Browned Mashed Potato—Potato Flour—Potato Jelly—Roasted Potatoes—Sweet Potatoes—Baked Potatoes—Boiled Turnips—Mashed Turnips—Boiled Parsneps—Stewed Parsneps—Browned Parsneps—Onions—Carrots—Jerusalem Artichokes—Boiled Beet-root—Baked Beets—Stewed Beets—Asparagus—Boiled Cabbage—Boiled Savoys—Stewed Cabbage—Cauliflowers—Broccoli—Stewed Cucumbers—Greens—String Beans—Egg Plant—Vegetable Marrow—Salsify—Oyster Plant... 194–200

Chapter Thirteen.

PREPARED FRUITS.—Baked Apples—Stewed Green Apples—Boiled Apples—Stewed Pippins—Stewed Dried Apples—Pears—Boiled Peaches—Stewed Green Peaches—Stewed Dried Peaches—Uncooked Peaches—Apricots—Cherries—Quinces—Quince Marmalade—Stewed Cranberries—Blackberries—Whortleberries—Raspberries—Strawberries—Gooseberries—Currants—Plums—Grapes—Pineapples—Tomatoes... 201–205

Chapter Fourteen.

PREPARATIONS OF ANIMAL FOOD.—Beef Steak—Mutton Chops—Stewed Mutton—Boiled Mutton—Roast Beef—Corned Beef—Beef Hash—Venison—White Fish—Poultry—Eggs.. 206–208

Chapter Fifteen.

RELISHES AND FANCY DISHES.—Custard without Eggs—Rice Costard—Raspberry Custard—Apple Cream—Snow Cream—Pineapple Ice Cream—Strawberry Cream—Raspberry Ice Cream—Curd Cheese—Pot Cheese—Cherry Jam—Apple Cheese—Grape Sirup—Baked Milk... 209–212

Chapter Sixteen

KITCHEN MISCELLANY.—New Kind of Oven—Steam Cooking—Steaming vs. Baking Bread—Cucumbers in Tubs—Potato Cheese—Roasting Apples, Potatoes, Eggs, etc.—Burns and Scalds—Cockroaches—Rats and Mice—Cracked Iron—Iron Cooking Utensils—Copper Vessels—Leaden Vessels—Tin Cooking Utensils—Zinc Vessels—Brass Cooking Utensils—German Silver—Pewter Dishes—Britannia Metal—Fruit Stains—Iron Mold and Ink Spots—Papered Walls—Painted Wood—Starch and Paste—Trays, Knives and Forks—Frozen Potatoes—Dresses on Fire—Water-proof Cement—Fire-proof Cement—Ready Rat Trap—Cheap Water-proof Paste. 213–219

Hydropathic Cook-Book.

CHAPTER I.

PHILOSOPHY OF DIET.

A FUNDAMENTAL PRINCIPLE.—The single fact, that all nutritive material is formed by vegetables—animals having power to *appropriate*, but never to form nutrition—is proof positive to my mind, that the best food, and that which is most conducive to man's highest development, bodily, spiritually, physiologically, or mentally, is found in the use of those vegetables themselves. Those who eat animal food do not get a single element of nutrition, save what animals obtain from vegetables. Hence man, in taking his nutrition indirectly by the eating of animals, must of necessity get the original nutriment more or less deteriorated from the unhealthy conditions and accidents of the animals he feeds upon, and the impurities, putrescent matters, and excretions always mingled in the blood, the flesh, and the viscera of animal substances.

I regard, therefore, vegetarianism as the true theory of diet; and although I am a vegetarian in practice as well as in theory, I do nevertheless admit or permit, in the cases of many invalids under hydropathic treatment, the moderate use of animal food. This may be said to be in one sense a compromise with error. But the justification is found in the fact that all are not yet sufficiently educated to carry out an exclusively vegetable regimen.

SUMMARY OF THE VEGETARIAN SYSTEM.—An English periodical (Vegetarian Messenger) has happily compressed the leading propositions bearing on the subject in the following manner:

The Principle.—That man, as a physical, intellectual, and moral being, can become most completely developed in all his faculties by subsisting upon the direct productions of the vegetable kingdom.

The Reasons for entertaining this principle are various with different persons, but they are principally based—

I. On the *Anatomical Structure of Man*, as described by Linnæus, Cuvier, and other eminent naturalists, who express their conviction that man was designed to live on the fruits of the earth.

II. On *History*, which shows that this principle was a rule of life at the happiest—the primeval—period of human existence; and that wherever it has been adopted, it has proved itself to be beneficial to the human race.

III. On *Physiology*, which shows that the purest blood, and the most substantial muscle, sinew, and bone are produced by vegetarian diet.

IV. On *Chemistry*, as promulgated by Liebig and other eminent chemists, showing that all nutriment whatever is derived from the vegetable kingdom, where it is found in the most suitable proportions.

V. On *Domestic Economy*, which proves by chemical deduction that more nutriment can be obtained for one penny from farinaceous food, than for one shilling from the flesh of animals.

VI. On *Agriculture*, which shows the vast amount of food obtained in vegetable produce, compared with that of animal produce, on the same extent of land.

Dietetic Character deduced from Organization.

VII. On *Psychology,* proving to every practical investigator, that in proportion as this principle is adhered to for this end, the passions can be kept in subjection to the moral principles of the mind.

VIII. On the *Practical Testimony* of many great and good men in ancient, modern, and present times.

IX. On the *Appointment* of man's food at the Creation.—*Genesis* i. 29.

X. On the *Individual Consciousness* of the truth of the principle which becomes more and more powerful, in proportion as the principle is adhered to in practice.

ORGANIZATION WITH REGARD TO DIET.—We concede of course that human beings can, to a great extent, and that all animals can to some extent, subsist on flesh-meat. But the practical question is, which is the best? All carnivorous animals, we know, have a very low and generally a ferocious organization. Omnivorous animals are less fierce, perhaps, in temper, but hardly less gross in tastes. Herbivorous animals exhibit not only more firmness of fiber and power of endurance—all *working* animals in all parts of the world being herbivorous—but also milder tempers, gentler natures, more amiable dispositions, more governable propensities, and even a higher grade of mental capacity.

These facts have *some* meaning. To my mind they prove that a subsistence wholly on animal food is designed in the order of nature for the lowest, grossest, and most perishable portion of the animal kingdom—for the beasts of prey which answer a temporary purpose in the scale of creation, and then pass away; that a mixed diet is adapted to a higher order of beings, be they human or brutal; and that a diet strictly vegetable is intended to sustain those animals which are longest necessary or useful on the earth, while man, the crowning glory and noblest work of the Almighty Architect, is to subsist eventually, and in his millennial development, on the highest and purest productions of the vegetable kingdom.

POPULATION WITH REGARD TO DIET.—Another argument, and to my mind also a conclusive one, in favor of vegetarianism, is the true theory of population. If ever the earth becomes very densely inhabited with human beings, a great number of such animals as are raised for food can not possibly coexist. And as ten times the number of "rational creatures" can be sustained on the direct productions of the earth, that could subsist indirectly on the flesh of animals, the presumption is at least very strong, that the races of domesticated animals will become extinct as the races of man progress; just as the weaker races of the human family decline before the advancing strides of the stronger. There is certainly something as revolting in the idea of a "feast of blood" in the millennial period, as in that of a "slaughter-house in Eden," or a pigsty in Paradise.

NUTRITIVE VALUE OF FOOD.—The prevalent opinion that flesh-meat is more nutritive than vegetable food, either as supplying matter for the tissues or respiratory material, is shown to be erroneous by chemical analysis. The best analytical chemists, Playfair, Liebig, Boussingault, etc., give us the following statistical illustration of the subject:

Articles of Diet.	Contains—		Supply to the body—		
	Solid matter.	Water.	Blood forming principle.	Heat forming principle.	Ashes.
lb.	lb.	lb.	lb.	lb.	lb.
100 Turnips	11 0	89 0	1 0	9 0	1 0
100 Red Beet Root	11 0	89 0	1 5	8 5	1 0
100 Carrots	13 0	87 1	2 0	10 0	1 0
100 Potatoes	28 0	72 0	2 0	25 0	1 0
100 Butchers' meat	36 0	63 4	21 5	14 3	8
100 Bread (stale)	76 0	24 0	10 7	64 3	2 5
100 Peas	84 0	16 0	29 0	51 5	3 5
100 Lentils	84 0	16 0	33 0	48 0	3 0
100 Barley meal	84 5	15 5	14 0	68 5	2 0
100 Wheat meal	85 5	14 5	21 0	62 0	1 0
100 Beans	86 0	14 0	31 0	51 5	3 5
100 Sago	88 0	12 0	3 4	84 0	6
100 Maize meal	90 0	10 0	11 0	77 0	2 0
100 Oatmeal	91 0	9 0	12 0	77 0	2 0
100 Rice	92 4	7 6	8 4	82 0	2 0

Identity of Elements in Animal and Vegetable Protein.

In view of the foregoing facts, a late English paper (*Liverpool Mercury*) remarks:

In addition to the above interesting facts developed by an examination of the composition of the various articles of food in ordinary consumption, and proclaiming the respective degree in which each can be made useful in the building up of the body, is another argument presented to the attention, by the advocates of the vegetarian practice of diet. It is found that all parts of the food which can form blood, and thus renew the animal structure of the body, are due to the protein compounds, which have their sole origin in the vegetable kingdom; and thus the nutritive parts of vegetables and flesh being identical, that the popular opinion of the peculiar characteristics of the nutriment of the flesh of animals is altogether erroneous, the nutritive particles of flesh being due to the ultimate elements of nutrition derived from the vegetable food on which animals consumed have fed, as shown in the works of Baron Liebig, illustrating the fact in question "Vegetables produce in their organism the blood of all animals for the carnivora, in consuming the blood and flesh of the granivora, consume, strictly speaking, only the vegetable principles which have served for the nutrition of the latter."

NOTE.—For a brief exposition of the various arguments in support of the propositions indicated here, I must refer to another work, "The Hydropathic Encyclopedia;" and for a complete demonstration of the whole subject to Graham's "Science of Human Life," and Smith's "Fruits and Farinacea the Proper Food of Man." Much useful information may also be gathered from a work written a few years ago by William Lambe, M.D., of England, entitled, "Water and Vegetable Regimen in Chronic Diseases." The *Water-Cure Journal* has recently adopted a dietetic department, for the especial discussion of all problems connected with diet, which periodical I would recommend to all who intend to keep along with the progress of the age.

CHAPTER II.

ELEMENTS OF FOOD.

ALIMENTARY PRINCIPLES.—All alimentary substances are composed of certain constituent parts, which may be properly termed *alimentary principles*. These are formed by certain combinations of elementary constituents, which are denominated *chemical* elements. Alimentary principles are often called *proximate elements* or *principles* of food, and chemical elements are frequently termed *ultimate elements* of food. Thus wheat, beef, potato, apple, etc., are aliments or foods proper; and starch, sugar, gum, gluten, fibrin, albumen, casein, gelatin, etc.—their constituents—are proximate elements or principles. The proximate constituents of food are alimentary principles, while oxygen, hydrogen, nitrogen, carbon, etc., into which these alimentary principles are resolvable by analysis, are chemical or ultimate elements. Chemical elements are regarded as simple substances only, because in our present state of chemical knowledge they have never been decomposed. Proximate elements of food are compounds of the simple or chemical elements, and aliments or foods proper are compounds of the proximate principles.

Pareria divides alimentary substances into *chemical elements*, *alimentary principles*, and *compound aliments*. This arrangement is based on a false philosophy, and is very liable to mislead the superficial inquirer. The truth is, all alimentary substances are compounds of alimentary principles; but this does not make them compound aliments. We might as well call the oxygen and hydrogen of water, aqueous principles, and the water itself, *compound drink!* Aliment and food are synonymous terms, but each represents a simple idea. A potato, an apple, or a grain of wheat, is a compound of various alimentary principles; but it is a simple, and in no sense a compound food. Compound wheat, compound potato, etc., would be as appropriate phrases as are compound food, and compound aliments.

The error above alluded to, trivial as it may seem to the casual reader, has caused hundreds of foolish experiments to be tried on dogs, cats, rabbits, hares, hogs, sheep, and even on the human animal, with a view of ascertaining the dietetic virtue of particular alimentary principles. These victims of science have been fed on sugar, gum, starch, butter, cheese, fat, fibrin, albumen, gelatin, etc., exclusively, and with the uniform result of sooner or later starving to death. No animal can sustain prolonged nutrition on any single alimentary principle, though all of them may on a single aliment.

CHEMICAL ELEMENTS OF FOOD.—Chemists reckon, as constituting the ultimate elements of food, thirteen simple substances, viz.: carbon, hydrogen, oxygen, nitrogen, phosphorus, sulphur, iron, chlorine, sodium, calcium, potassium, magnesium, and fluorine; and Pareria, assuming that "a living body has no power of forming elements, or of converting one elementary substance into another," deduces thence the inference that "the thirteen essential constituents of the human body must, therefore, be the elements of our food."

This proposition requires explanation; for although it may be and probably is true that organized bodies have no power of transmuting one actual element into another, or of creating elements, yet it is perfectly demonstrable that the vital energies of both animals and vegetables have power to decompose substances, usually regarded as elementary, and to transmute, and even form, to some extent, what are usually considered to be chemical elements. Thus *lime* is found in the bones of the chick, while no trace of it can be discovered in the fluid of the egg, from which the chick derives its sustenance; and

Carbon—Hydrogen—Oxygen—Nitrogen—Phosphorus—Sulphur.

sugar, taken into the healthy stomach as food, is found again in the secretions, though it can not be discovered in the blood—the only channel through which its elements can reach the secretory organs.

Carbon, hydrogen, oxygen, and *nitrogen* are essential constituents of all living bodies, animal and vegetable. The first three are found in all alimentary substances, and the latter in the majority of all the animal and vegetable substances which are employed as food. Fat, starch, gum, and sugar are the chief alimentary principles which do not contain nitrogen.

Liebig and some other modern chemists have advanced the theory that non-nitrogenized foods do not nourish the tissues; but in affording carbon for oxydation and the consequent evolution of heat, are properly " elements of respiration." Thus they become useful in affording the " heat-forming principle," while the nitrogenized foods, or those aliments which contain nitrogen, furnish the " flesh-forming principle." The theory, however, has no practical value in dietetics, for the reason that all the elements of nutrition, whether heat-forming, or flesh-forming, or bone-forming, are sufficiently distributed, and nearly equally so, throughout all those portions of both the vegetable and animal kingdom that man ever does or can employ as food.

Phosphorus is an ingredient in the bones, brain, nervous structure, and in the albumen and fibrin of the tissues. It also exists in some form or proportion in nearly all vegetable substances.

Sulphur exists, though in much less proportions than phosphorus, in most animal and vegetable substances. It is possible, and I think quite probable, that both sulphur and phosphorus are formed by mere chemical combinations of the decomposed elements of the worn-out tissues. The human body, in many severe and exhausting diseases, and in various conditions of low vitality, frequently exhibits phosphorescent and electrical sparks; and game, when " very high," that is,

Iron—Chlorine—Sodium—Calcium—Magnesium.

tainted and partially putrescent, often produces a sulphurous discoloration to the silver knife or fork employed in carving it.

Iron is found in the *ashes* of many animal and vegetable substances, and is hence inferred to be a constituent of most, if not all, organized beings. But chemists are wholly unable to determine the state in which it exists; and as the quantity is always exceedingly small and very variable, it becomes at least a matter of doubt whether it is really a constituent at all or not. It *may* be, when found, either an accidental impurity or the product of that process of analysis that detected it.

Chlorine is found in the blood, gastric juice, and in various excretions. But how far it may be an indispensable constituent, and to what extent an accidental ingredient, is not well understood. Still greater uncertainty prevails as to its existence as a constituent in alimentary substances. I regard it as one of the supposed elements which are easily formed, decomposed, or transmuted by the organic economy.

Sodium is found in the blood, in most of the tissues, and in the secretions generally. Common salt, however, which is a chloride of sodium, is not, as is usually supposed, an ordinary constituent of vegetables, with the exception of those which grow near the salt water. It is, therefore, in all probability one of the subtances which the vital power can both create and destroy.

Calcium is a component part of the animal tissues. It exists largely in the bones in the form of a subphosphate of lime. It is found in the blood, and in all the solid structures. Nearly all vegetables contain the subphosphates of lime, to a greater or less extent. Liebig thinks that the appetite some children manifest for eating the plaster which covers the walls of the houses they live in, is owing to a deficiency of lime in the food which is given them. I am of opinion that it is owing entirely to a morbid appetite induced by bad feeding generally.

Magnesium exists in small quantities in the blood, bony

structure, and various tissues of the body. It is also found in the cereal grains, potatoes, flesh-meat, eggs, milk, etc.

Potassium is discovered in minute traces in the blood, the solids, and many of the secretions of the human body; and it exists in nearly all inland vegetation.

Fluorine in minute quantities has been detected in the bones and teeth, but has never yet been found in vegetables; hence another presumptive evidence in favor of the ability of the vital powers to transmute supposed elements; provided, however, that fluorine be really a normal constituent of the body.

PROXIMATE ELEMENTS OF FOOD.—The most important proximate elements (alimentary principles) into which those substances used as food can be divided, are—water, gum, sugar, starch, jelly, fat or oil, fibrin, albumen, casein, and gelatin. Various acids and salts are also properly regarded as proximate or alimentary constituents of food, because they are always found, to a greater or less extent, in a great variety of alimentary substances. They are, however, among those elements which are readily increased, diminished, modified, or transmuted by the organic processes. They vary, too, greatly in the different stages of growth, maturity, and decay, of vegetable substances; and are very much modified or changed by the method of cultivation. In fact, some acids and saline matters which are found in the early stages of their growth are not to be found when they are thoroughly matured.

All of these proximate constituents vary exceedingly in their ability to sustain the prolonged nutrition of man or animals; but neither of them alone can supply perfect nutrition, nor sustain the organism for a great length of time. Their power to do so is in the ratio of their complexity. Thus gluten, which combines in itself a greater number of elements, or, in other words, is a more complex substance in its chemical composition than any other alimentary principle, is capable of sustaining the nutrition of animals longer than any other

Water constitutes about three fourths of the entire bulk and weight of the human body. It forms a portion of all the tissues, and exists as a component part of every kind of vegetable. Only a very small quantity of water is necessary as a drink, provided our dietetic and other voluntary habits are physiologically correct. The vast quantity usually taken into the stomach is called for by the feverish and inflammatory state of the system produced by concentrated food, flesh, salt, spices, etc. But it is indispensable to perfect health that all the water drank, and all that is employed in cooking, should be *pure*.

All persons, however, do not know what pure water really is. Many mistake *transparency* for purity ; and others think all water that is *soft* must necessarily be pure. Pure water is always soft; but soft water is not always pure.

Rain water is the purest known. Springs which are formed by rain water percolating through beds of sand or a gravelly soil, are often almost perfectly pure. *River water* is gene-.lly soft; but contains more or less of vegetable and animal impurities. *Well water* is generally very hard, being impregnated with earthy salts, particularly sulphate of lime (plaster of Paris) and bicarbonate of lime. *Marsh* and *lake water* are usually very impure. *Sea water* contains an average of three and a half per cent. of saline impurities. *Mineral waters* are famous for medicinal *virtues*, precisely in proportion to the extent of their *impurities*. Persons are often poisoned by the *medicinal properties* which water, beer, soda, porter, etc., have acquired by standing in metallic vessels or leaden pipes. Water conveyed through metal tubes should always be allowed to run some time before any is drank.

Filtration will remove all the impurities suspended in common water, but not those substances held in solution. A very cheap and efficient filter may be constructed in a few minutes, at the cost of only a few pence, in the following manner:

Procure a clean flower-pot, of the common kind; close the opening in the bottom by a piece of sponge; then place in the inside a layer of small stones, previously well cleaned by washing; this layer may be about two inches deep, the upper stones being very small. Next procure some freshly burnt charcoal, which has not been kept in a damp or foul place, as it rapidly absorbs any strong smells, and so becomes tainted and unfit for such purpose; reduce this to powder, and with it twice its bulk of clear, well-washed, sharp sand; with this mixture fill the pot to within a short distance of the top, covering it with a layer of small stones; or, what is perhaps better, place a piece of thick flannel over it, large enough to tie round the rim of the pot outside, and to form a hollow inside, into which the water to be filtered is to be poured, and which will be found to flow out rapidly through the sponge in an excellent pure state. The flannel removes the grosser impurities floating in the water, but the latter absorbs much of the decaying animal and vegetable bodies actually dissolved in it; when it becomes charged with them, it loses this power, hence the necessity for a supply of fresh charcoal at intervals.

Under different circumstances porous stone, sand, charcoal, sponge, flannel and other cloths, and unsized or bibulous paper, are used for filtering water. As the subject is one of great importance, especially to invalids, I shall dwell on it somewhat lengthily.

On a small scale, water which has not become attainted by the admixture of offensive gases, may be filtered by compressing a piece of sponge into the neck of a bottle or other vessel, and allowing the water to percolate through it.

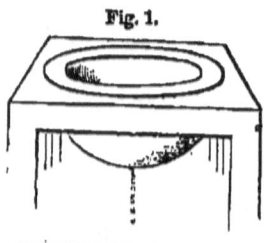

Fig. 1.

FILTERING THROUGH STONE.

Filtering water by passing it through porous stone, hollowed out into the form of a basin (fig. 1), was an ancient method. Filtering through charcoal deprives the water of coloring matter and offensive odors. Sand has been most generally used for filtering on a large scale. In the sand beds constructed by

Nature, the water is more perfectly filtered by an *ascending* motion. In descending, some of the impurities might be forced through the sand by their own gravity; but in ascending, the force of gravitation opposes their farther progress. Fig. 2 is a very simple contrivance illustrative of this principle. Travelers can easily avail themselves of this plan; *a*, *b*, *c* represent a curved tube, round or square, filled with sand or charcoal, or both, up to the level, *c*. A small flannel bag is put in the end of the tube at *a*. The coarsest

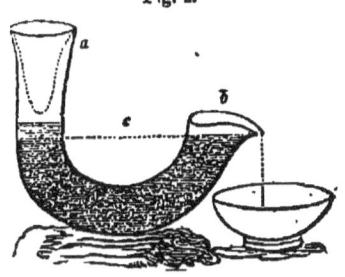

Fig. 2.

ASCENDING FILTER.

impurities are retained by the flannel, the finer by the sand; and in passing upward to *b*, the purification is rendered complete. It should be noticed, that the more compact the sand and the stones the water passes, the more perfect will be the process of purification.

Cisterns are often constructed in cellars, and divided by a partition, reaching nearly to the bottom, into two unequal parts (fig. 3). The largest division, *b*, is half filled with layers of sand, of various degrees of fineness, through which the water passes, and rises perfectly clear into the division, *c*.

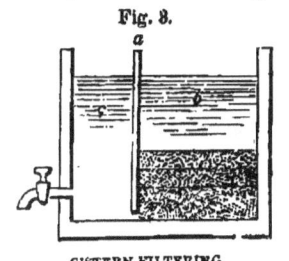

Fig. 3.

CISTERN FILTERING.

A similar cistern with two partitions has been recommended (fig. 4). The partition *a* does not reach quite to the bottom, and the other, *b*, has an aperture. A piece of perforated metal, stone, wood, or a cloth, is fixed in the middle division, a little above the bottom. On this is placed

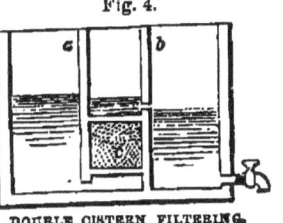

Fig. 4.

DOUBLE CISTERN FILTERING.

a layer of small pebbles, then coarse sand, then layers of charcoal, then fine sand and charcoal, the whole covered by a cloth also fixed just below the aperture *b*. The water is put in the division *a*, passes below the first partition, and by its pressure rises through the perforated plate or cloth, *c*, also through the pebbles, sand, and charcoal, and passing through the cloth above, runs through an aperture in the partition *b*, into the last division, from which it is drawn as wanted.

All kinds of filtering apparatus may be cleansed by making the water pass in the contrary direction. Thus in fig. 4, fill the division *b* with impure water, and it will wash all the accumulated impurities of the filter back to the division *a*, from which they may be drawn off.

An easy method of filtering water coming from a roof or any surface above the apparatus is shown in fig. 5. Two cross partitions made of wood, which is perforated with holes, burnt by a hot iron, are introduced into a cask, as at *a*, *b*. Over each partition is placed a piece of woolen cloth, and between them layers of coarse and fine sand, and of charcoal; *c* is a pipe from the roof, the water from which passes through the filtering materials and may be drawn off at *b*. By placing another cistern on a higher level, as *d*, to receive the water first, it will descend through the pipe, *e*, enter the cask at *b*, and by the pressure of the water in *d* will *ascend* through the filtering materials to *a*, and thus be doubly filtered and more completely purified. By placing a funnel at *f*, water may be poured into and filtered through the cask, independent of any supply from the roof. When the sand requires cleaning it must be taken out and washed

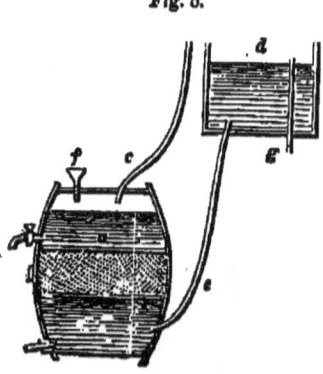

Fig. 5.

CASK FILTER.

Elements of Food.

Revolving Filter—Box Filtering Apparatus—Jar Filter.

A machine, in some respects more convenient than the preceding is represented by fig. 6. A cask is hung on an axis so that it may be turned like a barrel churn. A short, hollow, cylindrical piece, *b*, is fixed on the lower part to contain a piece of sponge. Connect with this, by means of a flange and screws, a pipe, *c*, to supply water from a cistern above. The water will rise through the sponge and sand, and may be drawn off at *d*. The same may be cleaned by taking out the pipe and sponge, stopping up, temporarily, the aperture, and giving the cask, partly filled with water, several turns with the wrench.

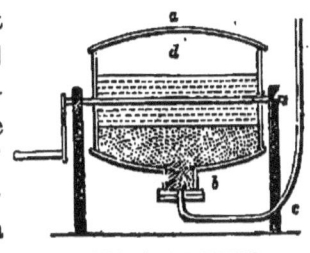

Fig. 6.

REVOLVING CASK FILTER.

A still more simple filtering apparatus is shown in fig. 7. Any convenient vessel, as *a*, *b*, may be fitted with three partitions. The upper one should have an aperture with a sponge stuffed into it, *e*, to retain the coarser impurities; the two lower partitions made of wood and perforated with small holes by a red-hot iron, and covered with woolen cloth. Between these two, sand and coarsely-powdered charcoal are put. A hole is made in the bottom vessel at *c*, through which the filtered water may be caught.

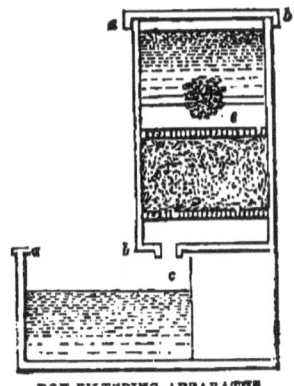

Fig. 7.

BOX FILTERING APPARATUS.

Any jar, watering-pot, or other conveniently shaped vessel may answer for filtering through sand

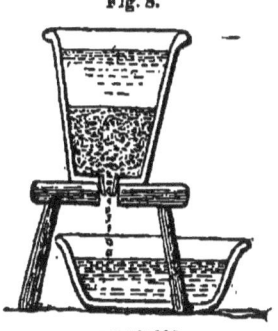

Fig. 8.

JAR FILTER.

and charcoal. Fig. 8 is a large garden-pot with a hole in the bottom, into which is inserted a small tube, or a round bit of wood with a hole in it, through which the filtered water passes into the vessel placed there to receive it.

The most simple, perhaps, of all filtering contrivances is represented in fig. 9. A thick wick or skein of cotton or worsted thread is hung over the edge of a deep basin or jar; and the water follows the course of the threads, by what is called capillary attraction, leaving the impurities behind. The filtration, however, is not as complete as by other methods.

YARN FILTER.

The original London stone-ware filter, of which most of the similar devices seen in the shops are modifications or imitations, is shown in fig. 10. The impure water is put in the vessel at a, passes through the cock, b, and drops into the projecting lip of another vessel at c, which has a movable partition pierced with numerous small holes. A piece of woolen cloth or a slice of sponge is placed on this partition to stop the coarser impurities; the water next passes through the holes into the lower part, which is filled with bruised charcoal.

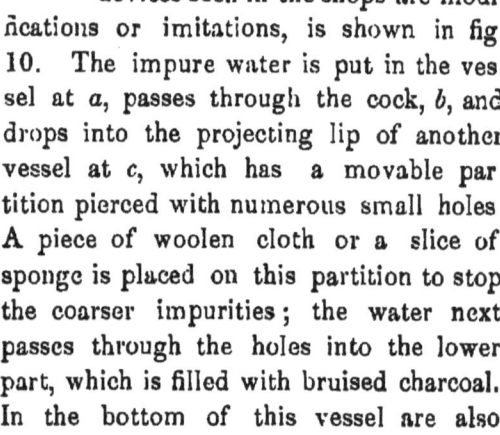

STONE-WARE FILTER.

In the bottom of this vessel are also holes, to enable the water to pass into a third vessel, d, where the water passes through sand, by which the process is completed. All the parts of this apparatus are easily separated and cleansed, which is, indeed, an important consideration in all filters.

ELEMENTS OF FOOD. 35

Waters purified by Filtration—Cooling Water—Gum—Sugar.

The principle of filtration being understood, all persons under almost all circumstances can contrive some plan of procuring a sufficient supply of pure water for drinking purposes. It must be recollected, however, that substances held in solution are not removed in this way. Ordinary well or mineral waters, which, though transparent, are hard, can only be purified by distillation; and this is an expensive and tedious process. But river, brook, rain, or water containing vegetable, animal, and gaseous impurities, which give it a discolored or muddy appearance, can be purified in this way.

Cooling water is, in this climate, generally effected with ice. But when ice is not obtainable, it may be advantageous to many to be reminded that water, in any ordinary earthen or stone pitcher, or other vessel, can be reduced several degrees by evaporation. Place several folds of linen or cotton cloth around the vessel, wet them as often as they become dry, and the constant evaporation will gradually abstract the heat of the water within the vessel. The more porous the vessel is, the more rapidly will the water cool.

Gum, or mucilage, exists almost universally in plants. Barley-meal contains in one hundred parts, 4; oatmeal, 2; wheat-flour, 2 to 5; wheaten bread, 18; rye-meal, 11; corn, 2; rice, 0.1; peas, 6; garden bean, 4; kidney bean, 19; potatoes, 3 to 4; cabbage, 3; sweet almonds, 3; ripe greengage, 5; ripe fresh pears, 3; gooseberries, 0.78; cherries, 3; ripe apricot, 5; ripe peach, 5; linseed, 5; mashmallow root, 35.

Sugar is generally distributed throughout the vegetable kingdom. It is also found in the milk of animals. Wheat flour contains (rejecting fractions) 8 per cent.; wheat bread, 4 to 8; oatmeal, 8; barley-meal, 5; rye-meal, 3; maize, 1 to 2; rice, 0.05 to 0.29; peas, 2; sweet almonds, 6; figs, 62; tamarinds, 12; ripe green-gage, 11; pears, 6; ripe gooseberries, 6; ripe cherries, 18; ripe apricot, 11; ripe peach, 16; melon, 1 to 2; beet root, 5 to 9; milk, 4 to 7.

Sugar-cane—Maple Sugar—Confectionery—Refining Sugar.

The sugar in common use is manufactured from a cane or reed called sugar-cane (fig. 11). The sap of the maple tree of the American forests yields a large amount of sugar in the spring season. Sugar was scarcely known, and certainly not in common use, among the ancient Greeks and Romans; and there can be no question that it is generally used to an injurious excess. Were proper attention paid to the cultivation of the sweet and sub-acid fruits and esculent roots, we should have an abundant supply of saccharine matter in the very best possible state, without resorting to the crystallized product of the expressed juice of plants.

Fig. 11.

THE SUGAR-CANE PLANT.

Sugar is made into an immense variety of candies, confections, lozenges, etc., most of which are poisoned with coloring matters, and many of which are drugged with apothecary stuff. The intelligent physiologist will repudiate their employment in every form or shape.

The raw sugars of commerce contain various impurities; and the refined and very dry sugars tend to constipate the bowels. The best article for dietetical purposes is of a pale yellow color, with large, clear, brilliant crystals.

The art of refining sugar was unknown until the early part of the sixteenth century. Lime and albumen—the latter obtained from the serum of bullock's blood or the white of eggs—are mostly employed in refining. Charcoal is used for bleaching it.

Syrup—Molasses and Treacle—Manna—Honey—Starch.

Sirup is made by dissolving two pounds and a half of sugar in a pint of water. Molasses is the viscid fluid which drains from raw sugar. Treacle is a dark-brown uncrystallized sirup which drains from the molds in which refined sugar concretes. Molasses and treacle can be deprived of their peculiar rank taste by boiling for half an hour with pulverized charcoal.

Sirups made with raw sugar may be bleached by filtration in the following manner (fig. 12.): A A is a wooden funnel lined with tinned copper. Above the bottom is another bottom, *b*, which is movable, supported on feet, and perforated with small holes. Over this a piece of cloth is laid. Animal charcoal, *c*, reduced to grains like gunpowder, is placed on the cloth. Another movable cover, also pierced full of holes, *d*, is placed over the charcoal, and upon this is put the sirup, *e*, which is to be purified. The sirup is drawn off at the spigot.

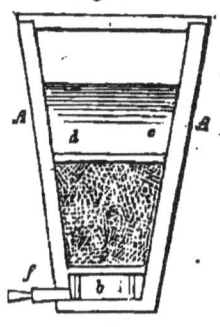

Fig. 12.

MOLASSES FILTERER.

Manna is a saccharine substance, intermediate between cane sugar and honey. It is the concrete juice of a species of ash (*Fraxinus ornus*), which exudes spontaneously, and is obtained by incisions made into the stem of the tree.

Honey is a species of sugar, consisting of a crystallizable portion, and a liquid sirup which can not be solidified. Its nature is much influenced by the flowers on which the bees feed. The best known is said to be from the Peak of Teneriffe. In some localities honey is poisonous, no doubt owing to the nature of the plants or flowers. The bees collect, by means of their proboscis, the sweet juice contained in the nectaries or honey-cups of flowers; and although this juice is somewhat modified by the secretions of the animal, it is still a vegetable substance. Dietetically, however, it is inferior to sugar.

Starch is a constituent of the seeds, fruits, roots, stems, tubers, and mosses of a large portion of the vegetable kingdom. Iceland moss contains 44 parts in 100; tapioca, 7 to 25; arrow-root, 12 to 26; yam, 12; bread-fruit, 3; barley-meal, .67; oatmeal, 59; wheat-flour, 56 to 72; wheat-bread, 53; rye-meal 61; maize, or Indian corn, 80; rice, 32 to 85; peas, 34; beans, 35; potatoes, 9 to 18.

Corn starch is now being extensively manufactured, as it is much used as an article of diet. Of course its nutritive value is far inferior to that of the whole grain. Indeed, the value of all amylaceous preparations as food for invalids is commonly greatly overrated. The different kinds of starch in market are sago, tapioca, arrow-root, rice starch, wheat starch, corn starch, potato starch, and lichenin, or feculoid, obtained from Iceland moss. The *cassava bread*, used in Brazil, Guiana, Jamaica, and other places, is a preparation of the whole roots of the plant which yields the tapioca.

The appearance of starch grains as magnified by the microscope, has attracted much of the attention of analytical chemists, and so far as the investigation of any principle pertaining to the philosophy of eating is concerned, such examinations may be regarded as rather curious than useful. The facts developed are, however, of importance in enabling us to demonstrate with mathematical precision, the principles in physiology which are established by other methods of investigation.

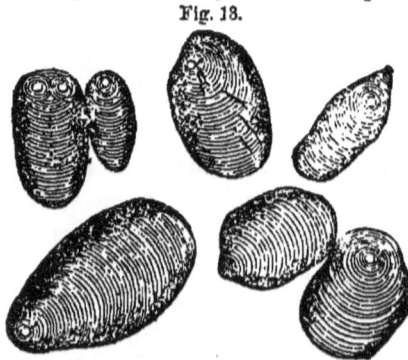

Fig. 13.

GRAINS OF CANNA STARCH.

Fig. 13 represents the grains of the *Tous les Mois*, or canna starch. It is imported from St. Kitts, and is prepared by a troublesome and tedious process from the rhizome of the *canna coccinea* of botanists.

ELEMENTS OF FOOD. 39

Grains of Potato Starch—West Indian Arrow-root—Sago Starch—Grains of Tapioca.

Fig. 14, representing the grains of potato starch, shows the normal starch particle, *a;* irregular starch particle, *b;* particles each having two hila, *c, d;* particles broken by pressure and water (the internal matter remaining solid), *e, f, g.*

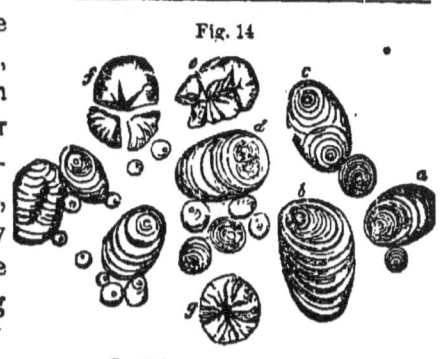

GRAINS OF POTATO STARCH.

Fig. 15 represents the grains of the West Indian arrow-root.

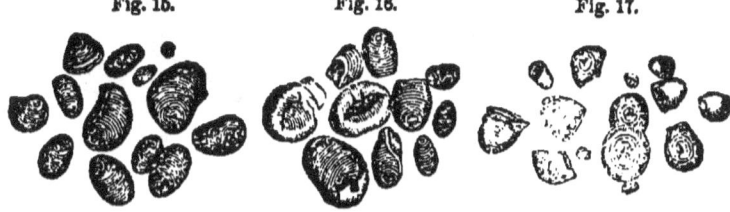

ARROW-ROOT STARCH. SAGO STARCH GRAINS. ENTIRE GRAINS OF TAPIOCA.

In fig. 16 are seen grains of the sago-meal. Sago is the medulla or pith of the stems of various species of palm; it is manufactured principally in the Moluccas, and comes to us in the forms of sago-meal, pearl-sago, and common sago. The first is principally employed in making sago sugar; the second is generally used for domestic purposes. Common or brown sago comes to us in brownish-white grains, varying in size from the grains of pearl barley to those of peas.

Fig. 17 shows the entire grains of tapioca. The Brazilian plant from the roots of which the tapioca is obtained is said to be poisonous. The irregular lumpy form in which the article is found in our market, is owing to its being dried on hot plates.

Fig. 18 exhibits a section of the stem of the sago tree, showing the pith from which the sago is extracted. The tree grows to the height of thirty feet or more, and measures five or six feet in circumference. One large tree will yield from to two to four hundred pounds of sago flour.

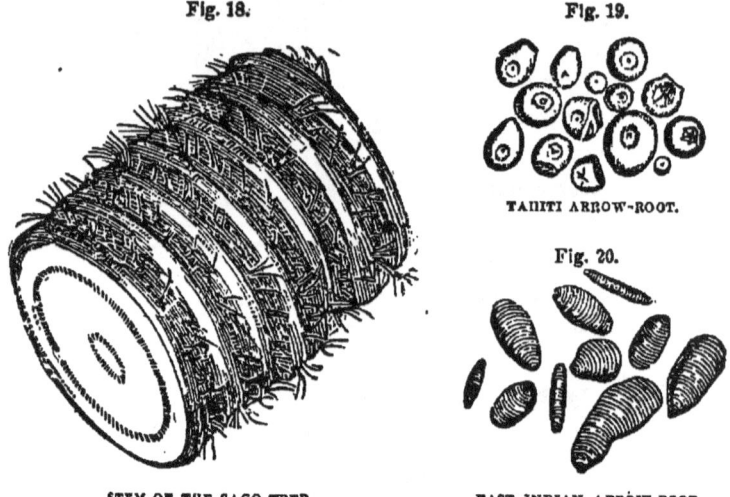

Fig. 18.

Fig. 19.

TAHITI ARROW-ROOT.

Fig. 20.

STEM OF THE SAGO TREE.

EAST INDIAN ARROW-ROOT.

Fig. 19 exhibits the grains of Tahiti arrow-root, or Otaheite t p. It is prepared by the native converts at the missionary stations in the South Sea Islands.

Fig. 20 represents the grains of East Indian arrow-root. It is imported from Calcutta. In Travancore it forms a large proportion of the food of the lower classes.

Fig. 21.

Fig. 22.

GRAINS OF WHEAT STARCH.

PORTLAND ARROW-ROOT.

The grains of wheat starch are seen in fig. 21; a is a particle as seen edgeways.

Fig 22 shows the grains of Portland arrow-root, some

Amylaceous Preparations—Ligneous Matter—Fungin.

times called Portland sago. It is obtained from the roots of the *arum maculatum* (wake-robin, Indian turnip).

An immense variety of starchy or amylaceous preparations have been introduced into our market, under medical and commercial authorities, as light, easily digestible, and highly nutritious food "for children and invalids." They are not, as already intimated, to be compared with more complex aliments, or the whole roots, plants, grains, etc., as principal articles of diet.

Lignin, or woody fiber, is found in every variety of vegetable matter. It forms the skin of potatoes, the husk of various berries, the peel and core of apples, pears, the bran of grains, etc. Rice contains of ligneous matter 4.8 per cent.; barley, 18.75; oats, 34; rye, 24; ripe apricots, 1.86; ripe green-gages, 1.11; ripe peaches, 1.21; ripe gooseberries, 8.01; ripe cherries, 1.12; ripe pears, 2.19; sweet almonds, 9; peas, 21.08; garden bean, 25.94; kidney bean, 18.57; potatoes, 4.03 to 10.05; cocoa-nut kernel, 14.95.

In nothing is the modern act of cooking more mischievous than in rejecting, as innutritious, this alimentary principle. In fact, bran and other forms of lignin are just as indispensable to healthful nutrition, as are starch, gum, sugar, fibrin, etc. Medical writers often recommend its employment as a mechanical irritant "to stimulate the action of the bowels," just as they do gamboge or pulverized glass, forgetful that it is just as much a component part of *all food* as is fibrin, albumen, or casein. To healthy stomachs it is neither irritating nor stimulating.

That ligneous matter is really nutritious, though not usually in the forms of bran, skins, etc., to any great extent assimilated, is proven by direct experiment, for good, wholesome, and palatable bread has been made of solid wood, dried and ground to an impalpable powder.

Fungin, the fleshy part of mushrooms, is a variety of lignin.

Jelly—Organic Acids—Lactic Acid—Vinegar—Fats and Oils.

Jelly is found in both animals and vegetables. It exists in the most pulpy fruits, and in many edible roots. The pulps of fruits and sugar are called jams. The vegetable principle, called jelly, is somewhat analogous to the animal principle, called gelatin, and some dietetical writers confound them. They are, however, essentially different, though dietetically the difference is unimportant, for neither possess much nutritive value, except as they exist in combination with other alimentary principles.

Several *organic acids* which are formed in the process of vegetable growth, are usually regarded as alimentary principles. *Citric, tartaric, malic,* and *oxalic* acids belong to this class. Acetic and lactic acids are also considered to be organic and alimentary by most dietetical writers, but I think erroneously. The former is a product of decomposition instead of formation; and the latter is only found in *unhealthy* stomachs, sour milk, and fermenting vegetables. *Vinegar* is so far from being alimentary, that, like alcohol, it is a product of vegetable decay, and always injurious to the human stomach.

Vegetable acids, it should be remarked, vary greatly in the different stages of the growth of the plant, root, seed, or fruit yielding them. Some are found in much greater proportions during the growth of the plant than in its maturity; and some are lost and others developed in the process of the ripening of fruits—an evidence conclusive that the organic powers of the vegetable kingdom can at least transmute their proximate elements into each other.

Fat comprehends the various oleaginous substances of animals and vegetables, as *suet, lard, tallow, marrow, grease, butter, blubber,* and *almond, olive, walnut,* and other *nut oils.* Animal oils are among the least nutritious and most injurious kinds of alimentary materials. The oils from the vegetable kingdom are far more wholesome, and probably, to a well-trained stomach, perfectly innocuous.

Medical books are full of errors respecting the dietetical

properties of fatty and oily matters. By most medical writers they are said to be "eminently nutritious," though all confess they are very "difficult of digestion." This, to my mind, is a physiological contradiction.

The writers of the Liebig school of chemistry have propagated some very absurd vagaries about the use of oleaginous foods in the animal economy. Upon the well-known facts that carbon exists largely in alimentary substances; that carbon is oxydized in the system; and that the chemical combination (combustion) of oxygen with carbon is attended with the evolution of heat, these chemico-dietetico-physiological philosophers have constructed a *theory*, that a large amount of grease, fat, oil, butter, blubber, or something similar, is necessary to keep the body warm, especially in cold climates. And I hear that certain Water-Cure doctors and professors of hygiene are teaching the same ridiculous notions, as if they were the veritable demonstrations of science.

The volatile oils of several vegetables which are employed chiefly as condiments, are regarded as alimentary by some authors. This is a mistake. Though some vegetables themselves, as radishes, onions, mustard, garlics, leeks, etc., contain alimentary properties with this volatile oil, the oil itself is as destitute of them as alcohol or vinegar.

The quantity of oil or fat in 100 parts of the following substances is: filberts, 60; olives, 32; olive seeds, 54; walnuts, 50; earth nut, 47; cocoa nut, 47; almonds, 46; plums, 33; white mustard, 36; black mustard, 18; grape stones, 11 to 18; maize, 9; dates, 0.2; yolk of eggs, 28; ordinary flesh-meat, 14; ox liver, 4; cow's milk, 3.13; human do., 3.55; ass's do., 0.11; goat's do., 3.32; ewe's do., 4.20; bones of sheep's feet, 5.55; bones of ox head, 11.54.

Though fixed oils or fats are among the most injurious materials of diet, they are rendered still more objectionable by the usual methods of cooking, baking, and frying.

The most objectionable dishes at ordinary tables, on account

Flesh and Fat of Swine—Fibrin—Albumen—Casein.

of their fatty character, or of the grease cooked into them, are *yolk of eggs, livers, brains, strong cheese, butter cakes, pastry, marrow puddings, suet puddings, hashes, stews, broths,* and several kinds of fishes, as *eels, sprats, salmon, herrings,* etc. The greasy parts of that filthy animal, the hog, in the shape of fat pork, bacon, lard, sausages, etc., are prolific sources of scrofula, erysipelas, jaundice, liver diseases, leprosy, scurvy, and a variety of cutaneous blotches, discolorations, and eruptions.

Fibrin, albumen, and *casein* exist alike and are identical in chemical constitution in both animal and vegetable foods. But they are formed *only* in the vegetable kingdom; hence, as heretofore intimated, those who eat flesh get precisely the same nutritive elements as those who eat bread; yet they are always more or less deteriorated by admixtures with morbid secretions, and waste and putrescent animal matters.

Vegetable fibrin is found abundantly in the cereal grains, and in the juice of grapes. It also exists in considerable quantities in the juices of many esculent roots and vegetables, as carrots, turnips, beet-root.

Animal fibrin is the principal constituent of lean muscle or lean flesh. It is also found in fresh blood, from which it can easily be obtained by stirring with a stick until a clot is formed, and then washing the clot repeatedly.

Vegetable albumen exists in the greatest proportion in oily seeds, almonds, and other nuts. It is a constituent of all the grains, and carrots, turnips, asparagus, cabbages, and other esculent roots; fruits and vegetables contain it in considerable quantity. It differs from fibrin in dissolving in water, and from casein in not coagulating when heated.

Animal albumen exists in the solid state in the flesh, glands, and viscera, and in the fluid state in the egg, and in the serum of the blood.

Vegetable casein is found chiefly in leguminous seeds—peas, beans, and lentils—from which circumstance it has been called

Caseum or Curd—Cheese—Gluten—Gelatin.

legumin. Many vegetable juices yield it in small quantities. Almonds, nuts, and oily seeds contain it with albumen. It is soluble in water and its aqueous solution is not coagulated by heat.

Animal casein is the coagulable matter in milk, and forms its *caseum* or *curd*. Heat does not coagulate it in the liquid state. Cheese is the coagulated casein deprived of its whey, and mixed with more or less of butter. Cheese which contains a large proportion of butter—usually called *rich* or *strong cheese*—is very liable to become poisonous by spontaneous decomposition. Old strong cheese is among the vilest of dietetic abominations. Fresh curd and green cheese are comparatively wholesome.

Gluten is a compound of several organic principles, and exists most abundantly in wheat. It is also contained in greater or less proportions in nearly all the cereal grains, and in most edible roots, leaves, stalks, etc. It is the gluten of wheaten flour which renders it elastic and adhesive, and hence conveniently manufactured into maccaroni, vermicelli, and similar pastes. It is the gluten also which retains the carbonic acid evolved in the process of fermentation, and thus enables yeast and acids and alkalis to *raise* bread.

The quantity of gluten yielded by vegetable alimentary substances varies with the soil, climate, mode of cultivation, etc. Chemical analysis has found in wheat, in 100 parts, 12 to 35; barley, 5 to 6; oats, 4 to 8; rye, 7 to 10; rice, 3 to 4; corn, 3 to 6; common beans, 10; dry peas, $3\frac{1}{2}$; potatoes, 3 to 4; red beet, 1.3; common turnips, 0.01; cabbage, 0.08.

Gelatin abounds in the bones, ligaments, tendons, cartilage, integuments, etc., of animals. When boiled with water into a tremulous mass it is called *animal jelly*. Gelatinous substances are moderately nutritious, but their usual preparations in the forms of stews, soups, hashes, etc., are difficult of digestion on account of the fatty matters they contain. *Calf's-foot*

Blanc Mange—Glue—Jellies—Saline Matters—Common Salt.

jelly is a favorite article with physicians and invalids, but is far inferior to simple Indian or wheat-meal gruel.

Muscle yields, of gelatin, in 100 parts, 5 to 7; antlers of stag, 27; caviare (fresh), 0.5; spongy bones, 39; hard bones, 43 to 49; isinglass, 70 to 93.

Blanc Mange is prepared of Russian isinglass dissolved in milk and flavored with sugar, lemon, etc. *Glue* is extensively prepared from the skins, hides, and bones of animals, for both dietetical and commercial purposes. That obtained from cod sounds is often used as a substitute for isinglass. Jellies made from *calves' feet, calves' heads, cows' heels, sheeps' trotters,* and *sucking pigs' feet (petittoes)*, are in great repute as delicate aliments for invalids and epicures. They are miserable trash as compared with vegetable soups or farinaceous gruels.

Various *saline matters* are found to exist in small quantities in fruits and vegetables, the most abundant of which are the earthy phosphates. *Chloride of sodium*, or rather its elements, *salts of potash*, etc., are also generally found and regarded as essential constituents, and therefore alimentary principles. Many physiologists, with singular absurdity, deduce a conclusion in favor of the dietetic employment of common salt, as an external seasoning to our food, from the fact that it exists naturally as a constituent of the vegetables we employ as food. It would be not a whit less absurd to argue that our foods ought to be seasoned with salts of potash, phosphate of lime, carbonate of lime, ferruginous compounds, etc., because these are found among their proximate constituents! Nature must have made a strange blunder, if in compounding the substances destined for human food, she only put in half enough of one of the requisite ingredients, but mixed all the rest in exactly the right proportions!

Pereira says: "Though salt is a constituent in most of our foods and drinks, we do not, in this way, obtain a sufficient supply of it to satisfy the wants of the system; and nature has accordingly furnished us with an appetite for it. The salt

Error with regard to Salt—The Japanese—Useless Experiments.

therefore, which we consume at our table as a condiment, in reality serves other and far more important purposes in the animal economy, than that of merely gratifying the palate. It is a necessary article of food, being essential for the preservation of health and the maintenance of life."

All of the above assertions are purely fictitious. Common salt is in no sense dietetical. It is entirely a foreign irritant, and its free employment renders the blood putrescent, the solids dry and rigid, the muscles inflexible, and the glands obstructed. The notion that it is essential to life or health is positively disproved by the experience of the millions of Japan, who have never yet known its dietetic use.

In all the cook-books I am acquainted with, a great or greater dose of salt is a fixture in every receipt; and hardly a dish or preparation is named in which a "pinch," or "teaspoonful, or "table-spoonful" of salt is not prescribed as one of the ingredients. The "natural appetite," which Pereira supposes nature has furnished us with to secure the salting of our food, is just as natural, and no more so, than that which many persons have for vinegar, pepper, alcohol, and tobacco—a kind of "second nature."

Those who would prepare healthful food, and those who desire to "eat to live," should ever bear in mind that none of the alimentary principles we have been considering is capable of itself of properly nourishing the body. Neither of them, in the proper sense, is food, but merely a constituent part of food. And almost all the aliments or substances used for food contain very nearly, and some of them quite, all of these proximate elements. Hence the futility of all the multitudinous experiments in feeding human beings or animals on a constituent part of an aliment instead of the aliment itself. Such experiments only show the physiological ignorance of the experimenters.

CHAPTER III.

ALIMENTS, OR FOODS PROPER.

TIEDEMAN has arranged the following classification of vegetable aliments, which I shall follow in their description:

I. *Aliments derived from Flowering Plants.*

1. Seeds,
2. Fleshy Fruits,
3. Roots, Subterraneous Stems, and Tubers,
4. Buds, and young Shoots,
5. Leaves, Leaf-stalks, & Flowers,
6. Receptacles and Bracts,
7. Stems.

II. *Aliments derived from Flowerless Plants.*

1. Ferns,
2. Lichens,
3. Algæ, or Sea-weeds,
4. Fungi, or Mushrooms.

§ 1. SEMINA OR SEEDS.—These may be classified in the following manner:

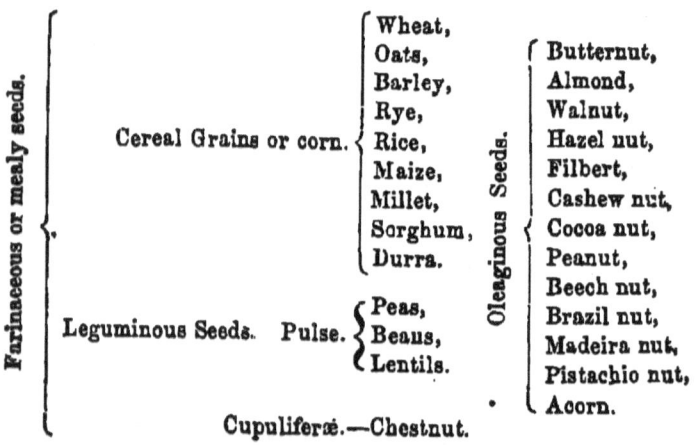

To the above list I must add *vegetable milk;* the juice of the *cow tree,* as it is called, which grows to a vast height amid

Proximate Elements of Cereal Grains—Varieties of Wheat.

the arid mountains of South America, and supplies the Indian of the Cordilleras with a rich, yellowish-white fluid, more nutritive than the milk of any animal we are acquainted with.

CEREAL GRAINS.—The proximate elements of the cereal grains are:

- Starch,
- Vegetable Albumen,
- Vegetable Fibrin, ⎫
- Glutine,   ⎬ Raw or Ordinary Gluten.
- Mucine,   ⎪
- Oily Matter,   ⎭
- Sugar,
- Gum,
- Earthy Phosphates,
- Ligneous Matter (bran, husk, etc.),
- Water.

Wheat, as a leading article of food, is raised in preference to all other grains, wherever it can be conveniently cultivated. Several varieties are known to botanists and agriculturists, but those generally cultivated in this and most European countries are called *winter wheat* (*Triticum hybernicum*), and *spring wheat* (*Triticum cestivum*). The latter is also called *summer wheat*. In fig. 23, *a* represents a head of winter, and *b* one of spring, wheat; the latter differing from the former in having awns, or beards, like barley.

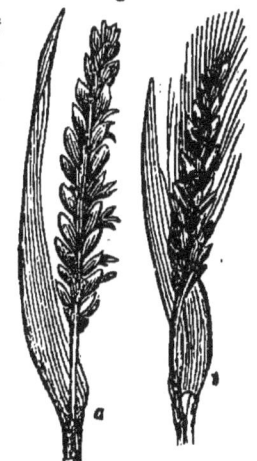

Fig. 23.

HEADS OF WHEAT.

In Europe, wheats are distinguished into *hard* and *soft* varieties; the former growing in the warm regions—Italy, Sicily, Barbary, etc., and the latter in the northern parts of Europe—Belgium, England, Denmark, etc. In this country, the *red*, or *Southern*, wheat corresponds to the hard variety; and the *Western*, or *white*, to the soft. The latter contains more starch, and the former more gluten, which renders it more profitable to the baker, who, for commercial reasons, looks more to the size than quality of his loaf.

Extraordinary Productiveness of Wheat—Frauds and Adulterations.

All the cerealia are remarkable for their extraordinary power of multiplication; a fact to my mind presumptive at least, that *starvation* among the inhabitants of this world is owing, to a great extent, to that abuse of agricultural science which cultivates animals for the butcher, instead of corn for the reaper. A Mr. Miller, of Cambridge, England, once sowed on the 2d of June, a few grains of wheat which produced eighteen stalks. On the 8th of August following he divided the stalks from each other, each having its root, and planted them again separately. Every separate plant then again tilled, threw out fresh roots and stalks. These wer again taken up, divided, and planted as before, and so on several times. By the succeeding April they had multiplied to 800 vigorous plants; the number of ears from them amounted to 21,109, and the grains to 576.840!

Those who superintend the preparation of food for invalids should be careful in selecting wheat whose berries are plump and well cleaned. Millers and provision dealers are doubtless as honest as people in general; but they are not all either intelligent concerning or regardful of the health of their customers. The use of unbolted flour, cracked wheat, etc., opens the way to every species of fraud; for the poorest and dirtiest kinds of wheat may be ground into Graham flour, or broken into wheaten grits without the purchaser being able to tell precisely what the impurities are. Chaff and cockle are common admixtures of the articles which are found in our markets; and stale or sour superfine flour is often mixed with "shorts," and perhaps a little alkali of some kind, and passed off as wheat-meal or Graham flour.

Those who would be sure of a proper article had better trust only themselves. I have long since despaired of being able to get clean and sound grains, or proper farinaceous preparations at our mills in this city and vicinity, and have been compelled, in order to supply my own establishment, to construct a steam-mill on my own premises; so that by grind-

ALIMENTS, OR FOODS PROPER.

Hand-mills—Proper Method of Making Wheat-meal—Rice.

ing our own grain we can have ocular demonstration of its character and quality.

Hand-mills or common coffee mills will answer for making cracked wheat for family use; and enough for an ordinary water-cure establishment may be ground in the largest-sized coffee mills which are kept at the hardware stores.

When wheat-meal is manufactured at the flouring mill, the miller ought to understand that the stones should be well sharpened so as to *cut* the whole grain into fine particles, instead of mashing it, as will happen when the stones are dull. In the former case the bran is cut up and mingled with the fine flour, and in the latter it is separated in flakes or scales. This will never make good bread, for, besides the rough and uneven appearance of the loaf, the particles are not uniformly mixed with the yeast or other risings, the consequence of which is that some parts of the loaf are over-fermented, while others are not fermented enough.

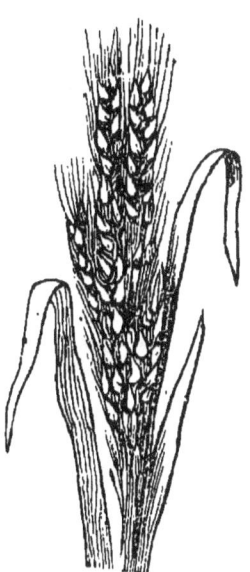

Fig. 24.

Rice (*Oriza Sativa*) probably affords more human beings nourishment than any other aliment in existence. It is a plant of Asiatic origin, and is the principal food of the people of India and China. *Common rice* is a marsh plant, though in some countries a variety called *hill rice* grows on the slopes of hills. *Carolina* rice is the best in the New York and London markets, and the large plump seeds called *head rice* are the most highly prized. In its growth, rice resembles barley very nearly. It rises to the height of about a foot and a half, and then branches into several stems, at the top of which the grains form in clusters, as seen in fig. 24.

Wild rice, called by the Indians *menomeme,* grows abundantly along the branch-

HEAD OF RICE.

es of the Upper Mississippi, and on the marshy margins of the northern lakes, where it rises up from a muddy bottom some six feet under water.

Oats (*Arena Sativa*) have been extensively used as food by the people of Scotland, and to some extent in this and other countries. It is one of the hardiest of the cerealia, and prefers a rather cold climate. The most common variety is the *white oat* (fig. 25). The *black oat* and several other kinds are also more or less cultivated.

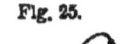

Fig. 25.

HEAD OF OATS.

Oatmeal is prepared by grinding the kiln-dried seeds, deprived of their husks and outer skin. *Groats* are the grains deprived of their integuments. Oatmeal is made into *bread* or *cakes*, *mush*, *porridge*, *stirabout*, etc. As an exclusive diet, it is less constipating than rice, but more so than wheat-meal.

Barley is more easily cultivated, and will mature through a greater range of climate than any other grain. It grows rapidly. In Lapland it is sown and reaped within six weeks, and in Spain two crops are raised in a year.

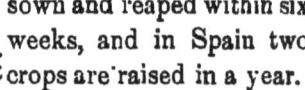

Fig. 26.

HEADS OF BARLEY.

The principal varieties are *spring* or *summer barley* (*Hordeum vulgare*), *winter barley* (*Hordeum hexasticon*), and *common* or *long-eared barley* (*Hordeum distichon*). In fig. 26, *a* represents a head of spring, and *b* one of winter, barley.

Barley is less nutritive than wheat, but probably

nearly equal in dietetical value. It contains more mucilage, and about the same quantity of sugar and starch, and only one third the proportion of gluten. The rapidity with which the seed germinates favors its conversion into malt, and is the chief reason why the brewer has cursed mankind with the abuse of this grain, instead of the baker blessing them with its use.

Pot barley, used for making broth, is the grain of which the outer skin only has been removed. *Pearl barley* is the small round kernel which remains after the skin and a considerable portion of the seed have been ground off. *Patent barley* is the pearl-barley ground to flour.

Rye (Secale Cereale) is much used among the peasantry of Russia, northern Germany, and most parts of northern Europe. It is but little employed in this country, except in some parts of New England. It contains more gluten than any other grain, except wheat, and hence ranks next to wheat for making fermented bread. The amount of saccharine and mucilaginous matters it contains has caused it to be extensively used in the manufacture of those pernicious poisons, beer and whisky.

Fig. 27.

EAR OF RYE.

Unbolted rye-meal is somewhat more laxative in cases of obstinate constipation than even wheat-meal. In Germany, rye-bread is called *Schwartzbrot*, or *black bread*. The hardy peasantry of Sweden make rye-cakes, which are baked only twice a year and become almost as hard as a board, a principal article of food.

This grain is liable in some seasons to be affected with a morbid excrescence called *spurred-rye*, or *ergot*, which is medicinally or toxicologically a narcotic poison. Several epidemics have prevailed in Europe in consequence of eating rye-bread made of this diseased grain; and no little havoc has been

Indian Corn—Corn Meal—Hominy—Samp—Green Corn.

made with children and mothers in America, in consequence of the introduction of this abnormal production into the allopathic materia medica.

Indian Corn, or *Maize* (*Rea Mays*), was found native when this country was first discovered, and it now constitutes the principal bread corn of a large portion of the United States, Mexico, and a great part of Africa. The varieties chiefly cultivated in America are, the *yellow* in the Northern, and the *white* in the Southern and Western States. The latter is much the largest, the stalk growing from seven to fourteen feet in height.

Fig. 28. EAR OF CORN.

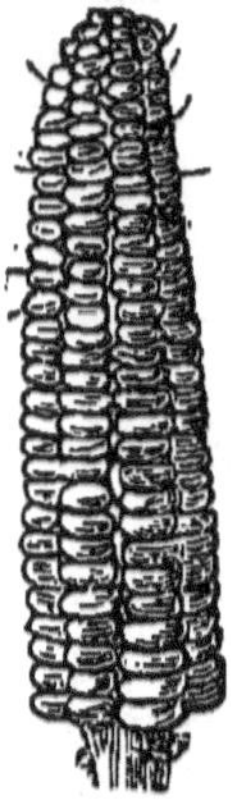

Physiologists are divided in opinion about the nutritive value of corn as compared with other grains, but expérience seems to have settled the question long ago; for the American and West Indian laborers, and the athletic peasantry of the Tyrol, who subsist mainly upon it, think no other bread as strengthening. Corn-meal contains but little gluten, and therefore will not make good fermented bread unless mixed with the meal or flour of rye or wheat.

Most of the Indian meal in our market is ground too fine at the mills. Such meal, made into cake or bread, is soft and clammy, whereas that made of coarse-ground meal is light, dry, and much more savory. *Hominy* is a preparation coarser than meal, and *samp* is made by breaking the kernels into still coarser particles.

Green Corn is a favorite and not unwholesome article of food. For the purposes of roasting or boiling in the ear, the *sugar* or *sweet* corn is the best. Probably no single article of diet can supply nutriment with so little labor or cost as Indian corn. Unfortunately, most of it cooked in this country is poisoned with that pernicious article, saleratus, which is employed in cooking it. In the Southern and Western States corn-bread is sadly deteriorated by the plentiful admixture of lard or other grease.

ALIMENTS, OR FOODS PROPER. 55

Buckwheat, or Beechwheat—Skin Diseases—Millet, or Hirse.

Buckwheat (*Pollygonum fagopyrum*) fig. 29), sometimes called *beechwheat* from the resemblance of its seed to the nuts of the beech-tree, has no natural affinity with the cereal grains or grasses, but is similar in alimentary properties, and is sometimes employed in bread-making. It is less nutritive than wheat, contains more sugar, but less gluten and starch. It is usually cooked in the forms of pottage, puddings, or griddle cakes. Various skin diseases have been attributed to its employment as food; and they are really *attributable* to the melted butter, and sugar, pork, greasy sausages, etc., with which buckwheat cakes are usually eaten.

Fig. 29.

BUCKWHEAT PLANT.

Millet, or *Hirse* (*Panicum sorghum*) (fig. 30), forms the chief sustenance of the inhabitants of the arid regions of Arabia, Syria, Nubia, and some parts of India. It is culti-

Fig. 30.

ITALIAN MILLET.

vated for the purposes of bread-making in some of the northern countries of Europe, and to a small extent in this country. It will not, however, grow luxuriantly except in a warm clim-

Peas—Beans—Lentils—Pea-Meal—Parched Peas—Split Peas—Lima Beans.

ate. The seeds are extremely small, and round like mustard, and are often used as a substitute for rice and sago in making mushes, puddings, etc. They contain a large proportion of sugar, which circumstance has caused the brewers to appropriate them largely to the manufacture of intoxicating drink.

LEGUMES.—*Peas, Beans,* and *Lentils* are similar in proximate constituents to the cereal grains. The varieties of pulse called *kidney bean* and *garden bean* were formerly employed by the English peasantry in bread making. *Pea-meal* is sometimes used for adulterating flour. *Parched peas* have been employed in the cultivation of ground coffee—one of the few frauds in alimentary articles which benefit more than they injure the party defrauded. *Split peas* are one of the best articles for making vegetable soup. *Green peas* and the young tender pods of garden beans are excellent relishes in their season. The best green peas in this market are the *marrow fat* variety, raised plentifully on Long Island.

Einhoff gives the following composition of leguminous seeds, as the result of chemical analysis:

	Peas (Pisum sativum).	Garden Bean (Vicia Faba).	Kidney Bean (Phaseolus vulgaris).	Lentils (Ervum Lens).
Starch	32.45	34.17	35.94	32.81
Amylaceous fiber	21.88	15.89	11.07	18.75
Legumine (*Casein*)	14.56	10.86	20.51	37.32
Gum	6.37	4.61	19.37	5.99
Albumen	1.72	0.81	1.85	1.15
Sweet Extractive matter	2.11	3.54	3.41	3.12
Membrane	—	10.05	7.50	—
Water	14.06	15.68	(dried)	—
Salts	6.56	3.46	0.55	0.57
Loss	0.29	0.98	—	0.29
	100.00	100.00	100.00	100.00

Lima Beans are one of the richest of the legumes. These and marrow-fat peas are dried in the green state, and sold in our markets during the winter months. By soaking in cold water over night they make an excellent green vegetable, on being boiled, for the dinner meal.

Chestnut—Horse-Chestnut—Butternut—Almonds—Walnut.

Nuts are divided into the *farinaceous,* of which the chestnut is the chief example, and *oleaginous* including the butter-nut, walnut, almond, and, indeed, nearly all the remainder of the nut tribe.

CUPULIFERÆ.—The *Chestnut* (*Castanea vesca*) was much used as food by the ancients; and is now made into bread in some countries. Boiled chestnuts and milk form a common dish among the peasantry of the south of France. The tree is one of the largest of the forest, and often lives over 1,000 years. Roasted or boiled the fruit is very light and digestible. The seeds of the *horse-chestnut tree* are similar in composition, but less pleasantly flavored.

OLEAGINOUS SEEDS.—The *Butternut* is one of the most oily of the nut seeds. The tree is very common in the American forests.

Almonds, both sweet and bitter, are the fruit of the *Amygdalus communis.* The *Sweet Almond* is mostly employed as a desert, and in flavoring cakes and puddings.

Bitter Almonds are always poisonous. They yield both volatile oil and prussic acid when distilled with water, but contain neither in the natural state; another evidence that elements unknown among the constituents of organic substance may be formed in the different stages of their decomposition. Prussic acid is also formed in the mouth when the almonds are chewed. As a flavoring article, these poisonous seeds are extensively employed by cooks and confectioners.

The *Walnut* (*InglausRegia*) is a native of the East. The sap of the tree is sweet, and sugar has been made from it. The seeds abound in oil, and in some countries are grated into tarts and puddings. Walnut oil has been employed as a substitute for olive oil in cooking, and also in the manufacture of soap. An extract from the green leaves makes a permanent brown dye, which is said to be used by the gipsies to give a dark color to the children they steal,

Hazel, Cocoa, Pea, Brazil Nuts—Filberts—Pistachio and Madeira-Nuts.

The *Hazel nut* is the wild, and the *Filbert* the cultivated state of the same tree (*Corylus avellana*). They contain but little oil. The differen, varieties of filberts in our markets are the *Spanish nut, cob-nut, red filbert*, and *white filbert*.

The *Cashew nut* (*Anacordium Occidentale*) is a production of tropical climates. The nut (fig. 30), somewhat resembles the walnut, and has an agreeable and mildly acid taste. The kernel is contained in two shells, between which is a thick rust-colored liquor, highly inflammable, and so caustic as to blister the skin. This liquor is used as an indelible ink for marking linen. The kernel itself abounds in a delicious milky juice when fresh; and is said to be preferable to the walnut. The juice also makes a good indelible black ink.

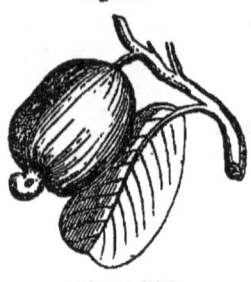
Fig. 31.
CASHEW NUT.

The *Cocoa-nut*, which some authors insist in pronouncing *cacao-nuts*, is the fruit of one of the palms (*Cocos Nucifero*). It grows wild abundantly in eastern Asia and the islands of the Indian seas, and has spread from thence throughout the tropical regions. The trees blossom every four or five weeks, and flowers and fruit are often seen together on the same tree. The fruit (fig. 31) is a white hollow kernel, filled with milk when fresh, and contained in a very hard shell. It is eaten raw, or rasped and made into cakes or fritters. The fresh milk of the cocoa-nut is an excellent fluid for moistening the meal or grits in the preparation of *uncooked* bread or cakes, and the grated kernel is an agreeable and nutritious article to flavor them with.

Fig. 32.
COCOA-NUT.

Peanuts, Brazil-nuts, and *Madeira-nuts* are well known in our markets, being for sale at most of the groceries and fruit stores. The *Pistachio-nut* grows in Sicily and Syria on a kind of pine tree. Its taste very much resembles that of sweet almonds.

The *acorn* of the oak tree (*Quercus*) was an important article of food in the early ages; hence the frequent allusions to it by the classical writers. Its flavor is somewhat rough and disagreeable to the palates of " society as now constituted."

§ 2. FLESHY FRUITS.—These may be thus arranged:

Drupaceous, or Stone Fruits. Drupes.	Peach, Nectarine, Apricot, Plum, Cherry, Olive, Date.	Pepones, Gourds, Curcubitaceous Fruits.	Cucumber, Mush-melon, Water-melon, Pumpkin, Squash.
		Syconus.	— Fig.
Apple, or Pomaceous Fruits.	Apple, Pear, Quince, Aku, Medlar.	Sorosis.	Mulberry, Pine-apple.
		Æterio.	Strawberry, Raspberry, Blackberry, Blueberry, Brambleberry,
Baccate, or Berried Fruits.	Currant, Gooseberry, Whortleberry, Barberry, Buffalo Berry, Cranberry, Elderberry, Grape.		
Orange, or Aurantiaceous Fruits.	Orange, Lemon, Lime, Citron, Shaddock, Pomegranate	Foreign Fruits not Classified.	Breadfruit, Durion, Guava, Manna, Litchi, Jujube, Juvia, Papau, Avocador Pear, Anchovy Pear, Mango, Banana, Plaintain, Mangostan
Solanaceous Fruits.	Tomato, Egg Plant.		

Peaches and Peach Orchards—Freestones—Clingstones—Shortening-in.

DRUPES.—The *Peach* (*Amygdals persica*) is a native of Persia. The tree is of rapid growth but short-lived. It often bears fruit the third year, and in some instances the second year, from the seed. The most extensive peach orchards in this country are found in New Jersey, Delaware, and Maryland, from which the New York and Eastern markets are principally supplied. In New England it is an uncertain fruit, although some fine specimens have been raised as far north as the State of Maine. The best peaches have a firm flesh, thin skin, deep bright color toward the sun, with a yellowish-green opposite. They are divided into *freestones* and *clingstones*. The former, in which the flesh easily separates from the stone, are regarded as generally the best flavored.

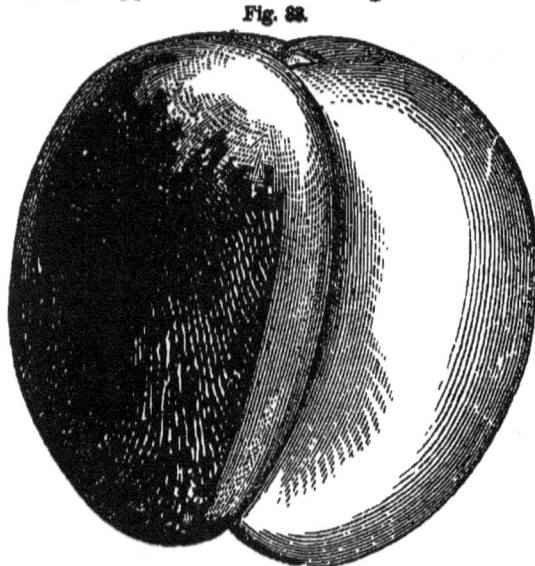

Fig. 33.

THE PEACH.

Fig. 34.

SHORTENING IN.

The method of pruning peach trees, called *shortening-in* (fig. 34), procures not only a beautiful tree, but early fruit and abundant foliage.

The young leaves of the peach are often used in cookery as a flavoring ingredient.

The varieties of the fruit are almost innumerable; two or three hundred have been enumerated in the catalogues of horticultural societies.

ALIMENTS, OR FOODS PROPER. 61

Nectarine—Varieties of Plums—Prunes—The Apricot.

The *Nectarine* is a variety of the peach, hardly differing in appearance except in being smooth-skinned instead of downy. Both fruits are sometimes seen growing on the same tree, and each fruit is often produced from the seeds of the other.

The *Plum* (*Prunus domestica*) is a native of Asia, America, and the south of Europe. A great variety of domestic plum fruits have been cultivated from them. The *Green-gage* (fig. 35) is considered as the standard of excellence. The *Magnum Bonum* is the largest kind, and much employed for preserving. The *Damson* was brought into Italy 114 years B. C. from Damascus.

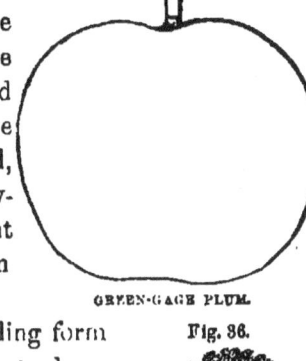

Fig. 35.

GREEN-GAGE PLUM.

Fig. 36.

THE DOMESTIC PLUM.

The plum tree is of a low-spreading form (fig. 36), rapid growth, and moderate duration. It requires but little pruning, save cutting away useless and decaying limbs. The most profitable crop will be produced by planting 360 to the acre, or ⅔ of a rod apart.

Dried plums are called *prunes*. Table prunes are prepared from the larger and sweeter varieties. The smaller and more acid, when dried, are called *medicinal prunes*.

The *red* or *yellow plum* is indigenous in this country, from Canada to Mexico. A variety called the *Chickasaw plum* is a native of the country west of the Mississippi, and is extensively cultivated in Arkansas and the south-western States.

The *Apricot* (*Prunus armeniaca*) is a species of plum, and, like all of the plum tribe, orignated from the *wild sloe*, a common hedge shrub. It seems to be intermediate between the peach and plum, the fruit resembling the peach externally,

Varieties of the Cherry—Advantages of its Cultivation—The Olive.

while the stone is like that of the plum. In this country it flourishes best in the Middle States. About a dozen varieties are raised in the United States. Apricots are abundant, in the wild state, in China and Japan, and in the hills adjacent to the Ganges.

The *Cherry* (*Cerasus duracina*) is a native of most temperate countries. More than two hundred varieties of trees are enumerated, from the small *choke-cherry* shrub, to the vast *black-cherry* forest tree. The *common cherry tree* (*Cerasus vulgaris*), fig. 37. is of a moderate size and spreading form. Some varieties of the tree are very ornamental. Almost all kinds of cherry shrubs and trees bear a pleasant and wholesome fruit. The most valuable varieties are easily propagated by budding and grafting. In our markets, the cultivated berries are found from the last of May to about the middle of July; and are usually retailed at six to twelve cents a pound. Fig. 38 is an outline of one of the best varieties of the fruit, called *Ohio Beauty*. My friend, Mr. E. Cable, of Cleveland, Ohio, who has given great attention to the cultivation of this and many other fruits, assures me the cherry can be made one of the most profitable, as it is one of the most delicious, of our native fruits.

Fig. 37.
COMMON CHERRY.

Fig. 38.

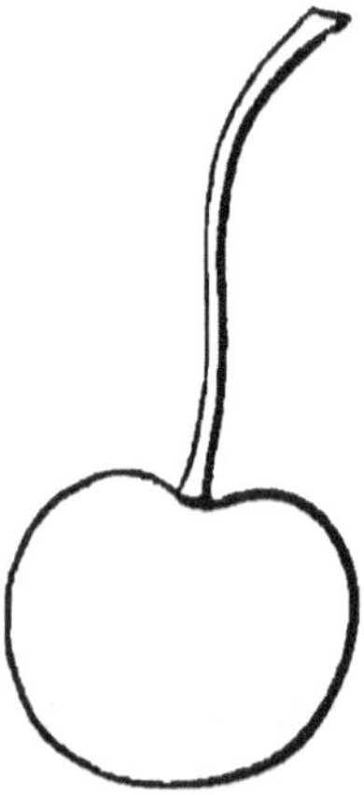

OHIO BEAUTY.

The *Olive* (*Olivia europæa*) was "sacred to Minerva." The tree is indigenous in Syria, Greece, and the north of Africa; and its name has many interesting historical associations. Wild olives, it is said, still exist on the "Mount of Olives," near Jerusalem. The cultivated olive (fig. 39) grows most abundantly in Spain and the south of France, but the fruit does not ripen well farther north. The

Aliments, or Foods Proper. 63

Salad or Sweet Oil—Preserved Olives—The Date—The Apple.

fruit is rather bitterish. The pulp is replete with a bland oil, called also *salad* or *sweet oil*, for the production of which the olive is extensively cultivated. In Britain, Italy, Spain, Portugal, and the Grecian islands, it is much employed as a culinary article in place of butter, and it is certainly a more wholesome article, either as a seasoning or food. *Preserved* or *pickled olives* are greatly admired by many persons as a "digester," but, like all other pickled commodities, are fruitful sources of indigestion.

Fig. 39.

OLIVE BRANCH AND FRUIT.

The *Date* (*Phœnix dactylifera*) forms a principal article of food for the inhabitants of many parts of Egypt, Arabia, and Persia. The fruit is extremely sweet, and very nutritious. The Arabs reduce dried dates to a kind of meal of which date-bread is made, and on which alone they subsist during long journeys. A single date tree, which is a species of palm, will bear from one to three hundred pounds of fruit in a single season. The young shoots are edible, resembling asparagus. The best dates are large, softish, but little wrinkled, of a reddish-yellow color outside, with a whitish membrane between the flesh and stone.

Pomaceous Fruits.—The *Apple* (*Pyrus malus*) is one of our most hardy, and probably the most valuable of all our fruits. The tree is usually of a low-spreading form (fig. 40), though sometimes growing to a very large size. It has been known to bear fruit when over 200 years old. All the varieties of our luxurious apple fruit originated from the

Fig. 40.

THE APPLE TREE.

Varieties of the Apple—Abuse of the Apple Crop—Cultivation.

wild crab-tree of Europe. No fruit is more easily cultivated or preserved, and none flourishes over so large a part of the earth's surface. A great many choice varieties grow readily in all the temperate regions, and some kinds are produced in rather cold latitudes.

In Homer's time the apple was regarded as one of the *precious fruits*. The varieties that may be produced by cultivation are innumerable. A catalogue of the London Horticultural Society, published in 1831, enumerated 1,500 sorts of apples; and Mr. Cole, author of the "American Fruit-Book," says that more than 2,000 varieties have been produced in the State of Maine.

I can imagine no branch of agriculture, "domestic economy," or even "political science," more useful to mankind than that of raising good apples. This kind of farming would tend wonderfully to elevate the human race above its swine-eating propensities. At present a large portion of the apple crop of the world is perverted to hog-feeding and cider-making—neither animal nor liquor, when fed or made, being fit for food or drink.

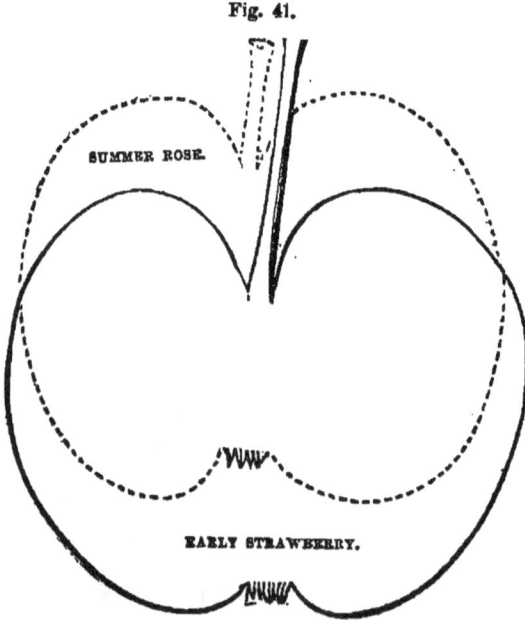
Fig. 41.
SUMMER ROSE.
EARLY STRAWBERRY.

A little attention to pruning, budding, grafting, and transplanting would enable our American farmers

ALIMENTS, OR FOODS PROPER. 65

Summer Rose—Early Strawberry—Fall Pippin—Mother Apple.

and fruiterers to supply our markets, profitably for themselves, with an abundance of sweet, mellow, luscious apples, so rich and savory, indeed, that but little else than a piece of good bread would enable the veriest epicure to make a luxurious meal.

In fig. 41 the dotted lines represent the general shape of the Summer Rose, a fine variety of the garden apple, and the black lines the Early Strawberry, a pleasant early apple which originated near this city.

The *Fall Pippin* is the leading apple during the fall months in this market; and various sorts or qualities of *greenings*, some of which are very fine table apples to be eaten uncooked, are most abundant in winter.

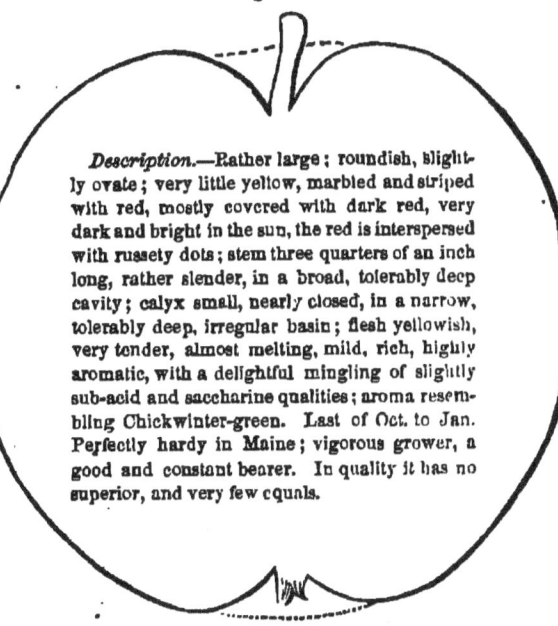

Fig. 42.

Description.—Rather large; roundish, slightly ovate; very little yellow, marbled and striped with red, mostly covered with dark red, very dark and bright in the sun, the red is interspersed with russety dots; stem three quarters of an inch long, rather slender, in a broad, tolerably deep cavity; calyx small, nearly closed, in a narrow, tolerably deep, irregular basin; flesh yellowish, very tender, almost melting, mild, rich, highly aromatic, with a delightful mingling of slightly sub-acid and saccharine qualities; aroma resembling Chickwinter-green. Last of Oct. to Jan. Perfectly hardy in Maine; vigorous grower, a good and constant bearer. In quality it has no superior, and very few equals.

THE MOTHER APPLE.

Fig. 42 is an outline of the Mother apple, which is but a fair sample of what all apples might be by proper cultivation.

The Pear—Extraordinary Trees—Pears grafted on the Quince.

The *Pear* (*Pyrus communis*), is a hardy tree, even more so

Fig. 43.
than the apple, and will grow on almost any soil. It has been known to live several hundred years. The Endicott pear tree, imported by Gov. Endicott in 1629, is still flourishing in Danvers, Mass. Near Vincennes, Ill., is a tree ten feet in circumference, which in 1834 yielded 184 bushels. Its propei cultivation appears to be very imperfectly understood, hence its duration is very uncertain

THE PEAR TREE.

In its original state the fruit was austere and almost innutritious; but cultivation has developed its delicious and nutritive properties. Almost all kinds of pears grow well, grafted on the quince. Many varieties have been tried, and some have attained excellence.

Dietetic writers in general, and medical men in particular, seem to regard the whole list of pomaceous fruits, if indeed they do not so regard all fruits, as doubtful, if not dangerous, articles of nourishment. The following conflicting, not to say ridiculous, notions of eminent medical authors are in point.

Pereira says, "Apples and pears are very agreeable fruits, but they are not in general regarded as easy of digestion." Professor Lee says, "Although apples are very generally used in the raw state, yet we have much doubt as to their being easily digested, especially by the dyspeptic." Dr. Forsyth remarks, "Pears are of a more flatulent tendency than plums, peaches, or apricots, especially the hard winter pears, which are eaten at a time when the stomach requires stimulating rather than cooling food." And Dr. Bell observes, "The apple is inimical to the dyspeptic, the rheumatic, the gouty, and those troubled with renal and cutaneous diseases." *Per contra*, Dr. Beaumont's experiments prove that apples, even when raw, are readily digestible.

ALIMENTS, OR FOODS PROPER. 67

Varieties of the Pear—Manner of Selecting—The Quince.

Among the best early or summer pears are the *Madeleine, Summer Virgalieu* (fig. 44), *Sugar Top, Zoar Seedling, Bloodgood,* and *Rostierer.* Among the best fall pears may be named the *Muscadine, Stevens' Genesee, Brandywine, Washington, Flemish Beauty, Buffum, Swan's Orange,* and the *White Doyenne* or *Virgalouse*—called also the *Virgalieu* of New York, and the *Butter-pear* of Pennsylvania. Among the winter varieties the *Prince's St. Germain, Lewis, Columbia,* and *Easter Bergamot* are much esteemed.

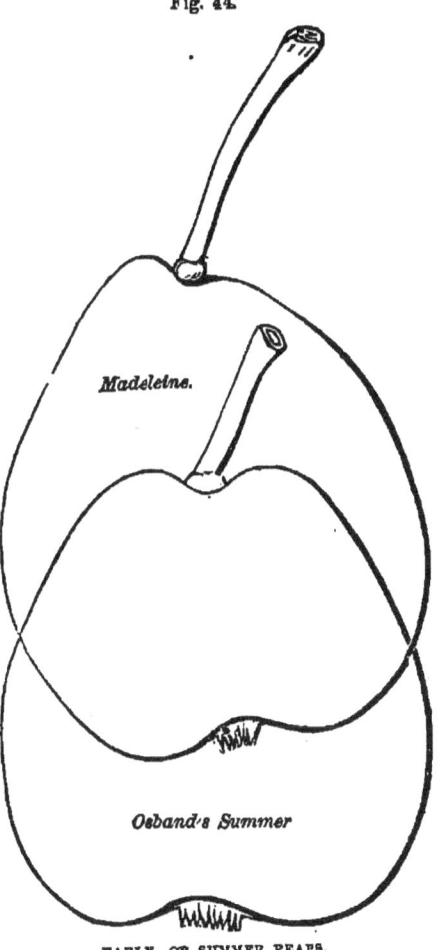

Fig. 44.

Madeleine.

Osband's Summer

EARLY, OR SUMMER PEARS.

Those who select any species of pomaceous fruit in our markets must judge of its quality more by their own senses than its name, as each may be improved or deteriorated by the season, soil, manure, or other circumstances of its cultivation.

The *Quince* (*Pyrus sydonia*, fig. 45) is a small shrub usually growing to eight or ten feet in height. It grows wild on the banks of the Danube, and is a native of Austria. In this country it flourishes only in the Middle and Western States.

The fruit is highly fragrant, but very acid; hence it is principally employed to flavor other fruits. The chief varieties are the *apple-shaped*, *pear-shaped*, *Portugal*, and *musk*. Fig. 46 is an outline of the former.

Fig. 45.

THE QUINCE TREE.

The quince tree will grow well in a variety of soils, as in most cool situations near streams, a clayey loam, dry gravelly ridges, etc. The tree should be "shortened-in."

Fig. 46.

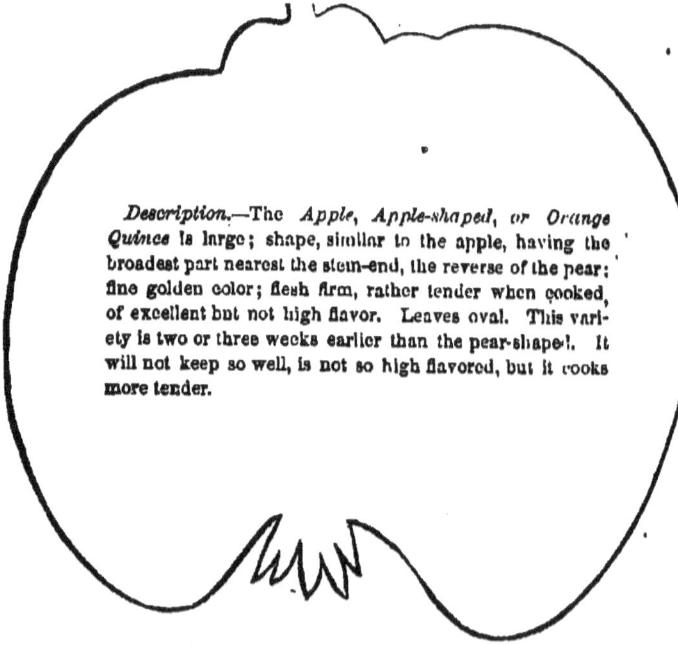

Description.—The *Apple*, *Apple-shaped*, or *Orange Quince* is large; shape, similar to the apple, having the broadest part nearest the stem-end, the reverse of the pear: fine golden color; flesh firm, rather tender when cooked, of excellent but not high flavor. Leaves oval. This variety is two or three weeks earlier than the pear-shaped. It will not keep so well, is not so high flavored, but it cooks more tender.

THE APPLE, APPLE-SHAPED, OR ORANGE QUINCE.

The *Aku*, or *Aker* (*Blighia sapida*), is a native of Guinea, and but little known in this country. The fruit (fig. 47) is a pome about the size of a goose's egg, of a mild acid flavor, and very nutritive. It would probably grow well among the oranges of our Southern States.

The botanical name of this fruit is complimentary to Capt. Bligh, who, in 1793, carried it from its native country to Jamaica, where it has continued to thrive ever since. And this historical circumstance affords a hint by which all our

Fig. 47.

THE AKEE.

agriculturists or fruiticulturists might profit the world immensely. I have no doubt that transplanting and "crossbreeding" among the fruits of the earth would tend to improvement, as the application of the same law of organization does in the animal kingdom. And notwithstanding I admit that, as a general rule, the grains, roots, fruits, and vegetables which can be best cultivated in a particular climate or locality constitute the best food for the people of that climate or locality, still every species of vegetation may be *naturalized* in places where it is not indigenous.

Our farmers are far from being ignorant of the method of improving the breed of domestic animals; and there is nothing more required to improve the quality of all alimentary substances than an adaptation of the same principles to the peculiar circumstances and habitudes of plants and vegetables. And this subject has an incalculable importance in the consideration, that just in proportion as we improve the quality of the vegetable substances on which human beings subsist, just to that extent shall we "improve the breed" of the highest being in the scale of animated nature.

The *Medlar* (*Mesphilus germanica*) is a native of the south of Europe, and in nutritive qualities and value resembles a small apple. The fruit seldom ripens until after it is gathered.

Berried Fruits—Varieties of Currants—The Gooseberry.

BERRIED FRUITS.—The *Currant* (*Ribes rubrum*) is a small hardy shrub, very productive, easily cultivated, and flourishes on almost every kind of soil. The fruit is sharply acid, yet very pleasant, and if stewed may be eaten either green or ripe. There are several small and a number of large varieties of the berry; but the latter are superseding the former in our markets.

One of the best kinds of this fruit is a new variety from England, called *May's Victoria* (fig. 48). The *red Dutch*, the *white Dutch*, the *black Naples*, and *Knight's sweet red* are among the other varieties seen in our markets. The *red* and *white* currants differ but very little, except that the latter is rather less acid. The *Missouri currant* of the Rocky Mountains, and the *red flowering currant* of the western part of America are fine ornamental flowering shrubs.

The *Black Currant* (*Ribes nigrum*) is a distinct species. It grows abundantly in Russia and northern Europe, and, as is the case with all kinds of currants and gooseberries, is often employed in making champagne and other wines.

The *Gooseberry* (*Ribes grossularia*) is a native of cold and

Fig. 48.

MAY'S VICTORIA.

ALIMENTS, OR FOODS PROPER. 71

temperate climates. It may be easily cultivated on almost any soil. New varieties may be raised from the seed, and the most desirable kinds may be propagated by grafting.

Fig. 9.

HOUGHTON'S SEEDLING.

The best varieties are known as *Houghton's Seedling* (fig. 49) *Crown Bob* (fig. 50), *Whitesmith* (fig. 51), *Red Warrington, Roaring Lion, Green Walnut*, etc..

Numerous varieties of this fruit are known, over three hundred having been enumerated in some English catalogues. They are,

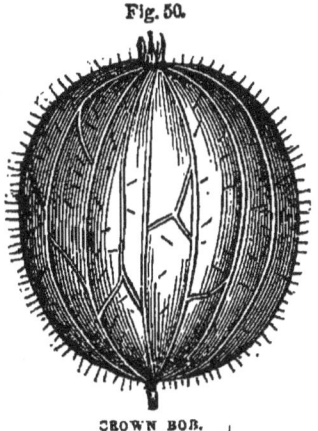

Fig. 50.

CROWN BOB.

Fig. 51.

WHITESMITH.

however, generally distinguished into the *red, yellow, green*, and *white*, according to the color they assume when ripe. The different sorts ripen from June till September.

The *Whortleberry* (*Vaccinium myrtillus*), also called *Bilberry*, the *Black Whortleberry* (*Vaccinium resinosum*), and the *Low Blueberry* (*Vaccinium tenellum*), are varieties of the same shrub. The first named grows in moist lands from two to six feet high, and the last mentioned grows in beds or bunches on dry hills, from six to twelve inches high. The fruit of both kinds is very sweet and pleasant, and easily improved by cultivation. Our market is largely supplied from Long Island, and nearly all the uncultivated fields within a circuit of one or two hundred miles yield this fruit abundantly. The average price of the berries in New York is about three dollars per bushel. The dried berries are excellent for flavoring puddings, cakes, etc.

BARBERRY TREE.

The *Barberry* (*Berberis*) (fig. 52), is a small prickly shrub, four to ten feet high, growing spontaneously on hard gravelly soils, and in cool, moist situations. The flowers are small and very beautiful. The fruit (fig. 53) is very acid and astringent, and has thus far been used chiefly in preserves, pickles, tarts, etc. Proper cultivation would no doubt soon develop a more pleasant quality of fruit.

BARBERRY FRUIT.

The bark and wood are employed in coloring yellow. The beauty of its flower, and its rapid growth and durability, render it useful for making hedges.

The *Buffalo berry*, or *Shepherdia* (fig. 54), is also an ornamental shrub, whose small, round, acid fruit is regarded as excellent for preserves. Like many other sour fruits, it needs the renovating influences of intelligent fruit-culture.

BUFFALO BERRY.

The *Cranberry* (*Oxycoccus macrocarpus*) (fig. 55), grows wild in marshes, meadows, swamps, etc., but by being cultivated on high land it has produced larger and better fruit. The berries are very sour, but are highly valued for tarts, jellies, and sauces. They are also excellent

Aliments, or Foods Proper. 73

Elderberries—Juniper Berries—The Grape; its Uses and Perversions.

if well stewed and sweetened. Good cranberries usually retail in this city from ten to fifteen cents per quart.

Fig. 55
CRANBERRY.

Elderberries are sometimes eaten, though they are not so pleasant as most other berries. Dried elderberries are sometimes sold in our groceries for dried whortleberries, which they resemble considerably, yet are of much less size. The flowers, leaves, and inner bark of the elder tree, and fermented juice of the fruit, have enjoyed a high reputation for medicinal virtues; but in those days Water-cures were not in fashion.

Juniper berries—the berries of the common juniper tree—(*Juniperus communes*) which grows wild on the hills in many countries, are a sweetish-aromatic and somewhat bitterish fruit, and are eaten sometimes in the form of conserves. A volatile oil obtained from the cells of the shell of the nut has been used to flavor Holland gin, "Scheidam Schnapps," and other "medicinal beverages."

The *Grape* (*Vitis vinifera*) ranks beside the apple at the head of the fruit kingdom. It flourishes well from the twenty-first to about the fifteenth degree of north latitude. It was known to most of the natives of antiquity, and several varieties are found in the wild state in this country. Though the fruit of the vine has been perverted to the purposes of wine-making, by which the nations have become drunken, no fruit is capable of affording a greater amount of luxurious and wholesome food. In Syria, bunches of grapes have been known to weigh forty pounds. A single vine at Hampton Court,

England, many years ago, produced, on the average, a ton of grapes annually. A patch of land of a few feet square, with very little trouble or expense, would supply a family with an abundance of this luscious fruit.

The most extensive graperies in this country are near Cincinnati, in the vicinity of Philadelphia, and at Croton Point, near New York.

Fig. 56

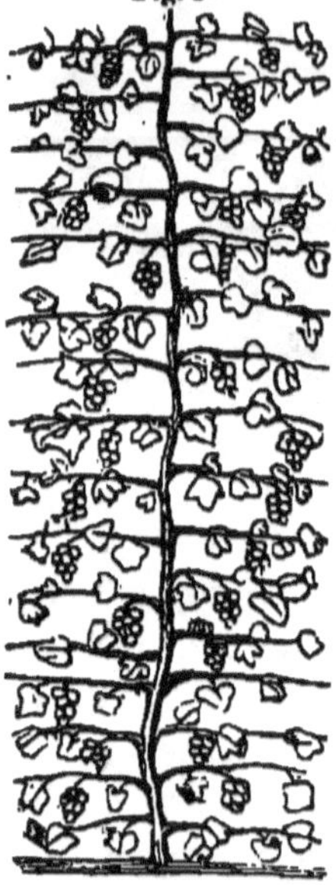

The vines may be trained in a variety of ways to suit the fancy or to accommodate the locality, as the *cane* or *renewal* system, the *fan* system, the *spur* system, etc. Figure 56 is a representation of the latter method.

A variety of foreign grapes have been tried in this country, but do not succeed as well as the native. Of these the *Isabella* and *Catawba* are principally cultivated. The Isabella (fig. 57) is the sweetest, and is generally preferred in this market. The Catawba (fig. 58) is preferred at the West.

Fig. 57.

ISABELLA.

SPUR TRAINING.

The *raisins* of our shops are *dried grapes*. *Muscatels* and *bloons* are sun-dried. The *black currant* of our groceries is the *small* or *Corinthian* raisin.

Fig. 58.

CATAWBA.

AURANTIACEOUS FRUITS.—The *Orange tree* (*Citrus*) is an example of extraordinary productiveness, a single tree having been known to produce twenty-five thousand in a single season. The fruit in our market is distinguished into the *Sweet orange* (*citrus aurantium*), and the *Seville orange* (*citrus vulgaris*). The lat ter are rough and sour, and often called *bitter oranges*. As oranges are the product of warm climates, the dietetical value of the fruit with us depends very much on its degree of maturity when gathered. They will not keep long unless taken from the trees before ripening; but when they possess a mild, rich, moderately acid flavor, they are not objectionable, though far inferior to many of our domestic fruits.

The *Lemon* (*Citrus limonum*) is chiefly valued for its *antiscorbutic* properties, which, indeed, it possesses *in common with all other fresh fruits and vegetables*. It contains more acid than the orange, and is seldom employed except as a mere flavoring ingredient of culinary preparations.

The *Citron* (*Citrus medica*) is another variety of the same tribe of plants. The fruit is seldom used except for making acidulous drink; the rind is often candied with sugar for a sweetmeat.

The *Shaddock* (*Citrus decumana*) (fig. 59) belongs also to the orange family. In China, where it is indigenous, it is said to be a sweet and agreeable fruit; but in other countries, where its cultivation has been neglected, it has become soured and degenerated.

Fig. 59.

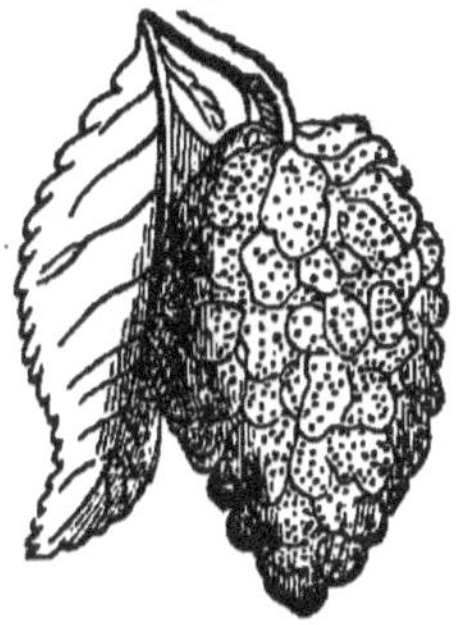

THE SHADDOCK.

Fig. 60.

THE LIME.

The *Lime* (*Citrus acida*) is another variety of the same genus. The fruit (fig. 60) is much smaller than the lemon. It is very acid, and the lime-juice, and most of the citric acid of commerce, are manufactured from it. But as vegetarian stomachs have no demand for strong acids, as mere relishes or seasonings, it must for them be regarded as among the things more curious than useful.

The Pomegranate—Tomato, or Love Apple—Okra, or Gambo—The Cucumber.

Fig. 61.

BRANCH AND FRUIT.

The *Pomegranate* (*Pumica granatum*) (fig. 61) is a native of Europe and Asia. The fruit is about the size of a large peach, very beautiful, pleasantly acid or sweet. In the Bible it is included among the fruits of Palestine, with the vine, fig, olive, and other "pleasant fruits." The tree grows about twenty feet high, and is highly ornamental, being covered with beautiful scarlet and very fragrant blossoms.

Of the *Tomato*, or *Love-apple* (*Solanum lycopersium*), little is said in works on fruit and diet, for the reason that it is usually regarded as a mere condiment or pickling ingredient. Botanically, it is allied to the potato; and under proper cultivation, its fruit, which is pleasantly acid, has become one of our best summer luxuries. When perfectly ripe it is excellent without either cooking or seasoning; when but partially ripe it should be stewed for an hour or more. The earliest tomatoes in our market often sell at fifty cents per quart.

The *Okra*, called at the South *Gambo*, may be mentioned here. It is sometimes seen in our Northern gardens, but is not sufficiently appreciated. It is a very pleasant, mucilaginous aliment, containing a moderate proportion of starch, which, no doubt, would increase by proper cultivation. It is an excellent addition to stewed tomato, and also a good ingredient in tomato soup. This fruit is now raised in large quantities on the farms of the North American Phalanx, Monmouth County, New Jersey. It may be easily cut into slices, dried, and kept the year round.

PEPONES. --The *Cucumber* (*Cucumis satirus*) is a valuable garden fruit, though usually rendered pernicious by the salt, pepper, vinegar, and oil with which it is seasoned. To healthy appetences none of these extraneous seasonings are

Melons—Pumpkins—Squashes—Cultivation of Squashes and Cucumbers.

desirable; be..e to well-trained vegetarian stomachs it is both palatable and wholesome, however it may be with dyspeptics.

The *Melon* (*Cucumis melo*) is the generic term for all the varieties of *musk* and *watermelons*. The *Muskmelon* is a delicious fruit, and very easily digested by most stomachs. Some varieties, as the *nutmeg*, are exceedingly sweet and considerably nutritive. The *cantaloupe* is a famed variety in Italy. A warm sandy soil produces the richest fruits.

Watermelons are somewhat less nutritive, and, to weak stomachs, more liable to occasion griping or colic. Some of the curcubitaceous fruits should not be eaten until fully ripe. The cucumber, however, appears to be innocuous in all stages of its growth.

Of *Pumpkins* we have few varieties; but a good quality of any fruit is better than a great variety. The most common in our markets are the *common red* and the *West Indian*. Both are excellent for sauce or pies. The dried fruit may be kept good the year round. The dried fruit is pulverized by the Shakers, and sold under the name of *pumpkin powder*.

Squashes are found in our markets in much greater variety than pumpkins, and many kinds are equal to the best pumpkins for pies. The *cream*, *marrow*, and *Lima* are among the most delicious kinds for either sauce or pies. Squashes are generally classed as Summer or Winter varieties. The latter sometimes grow to an enormous size. I have seen them of over 200 pounds weight.

In choosing squashes or pumpkins, those of the firmest, heaviest texture are to be preferred.

Squashes and cucumbers may be raised in almost any yard or vacant place, in the following manner: Take a large barrel or hogshead, saw it in two in the middle, and bury each half in the ground, even with the top. Then take a small keg and bore a small hole in the bottom. Place the keg in the center of the barrel, the top even with the ground, and fill in the barrel around the keg with rich earth, suitable for the growth of cucumbers. Plant your seed midway between the edges of the barrel and the keg, and make a kind of arbor a foot or two high for the vines to run on. When the ground becomes dry, pour water in the keg, in the evening—it will pass out of the keg into the barrel, and raise up to the roots of the vines, and keep them moist and green. Cucumbers cultivated this way will grow to a great size, as they are made independent both of drought and wet weather. In wet weather the barrel can be covered, and in dry the ground can be kept moist by pouring water in the keg.

Syconus.—The *Fig tree* (*Ficus carica*) is a native of Asia, and formed a principal article of food among the inhabitants of ancient Syria and Greece. It is remarkably sweet, very nutritious, and, like the cereal grains, will flourish in a wide range of latitude. It will grow well in our Northern States if housed during the cold season. In the Southern States some excellent crops are raised.

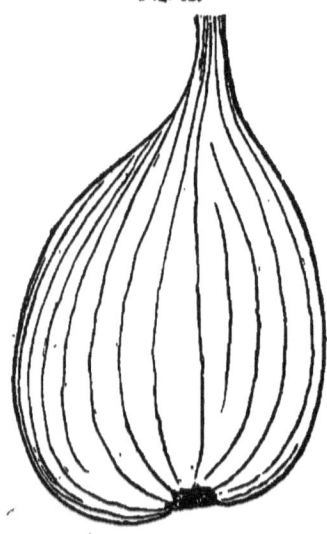

Fig. 62.

BLACK FIG OF THE AZORES.

There are several excellent varieties of the fruit sold in our market. The best are from Turkey, Italy, and Spain. *Smyrna figs* are deservedly of high repute. The *black fig of the Azores* (fig. 62) is a fine and very productive kind. Two crops in a year have been raised under glass in this country. In South Carolina the *Alicant* fig bears early and abundantly.

Figs are generally prepared by dipping the ripe fruit in a scalding hot ley made of the ashes of the fig tree, then dried in ovens or in the sun, and packed close in boxes or chests.

ALIMENTS, OR FOODS PROPER. 79

Varieties of Mulberry—The Pineapple—The Strawberry—Its Market Value.

Sorosis.—The *Mulberry tree* (*Morus*) is a native of Asia, and has been chiefly valued as food for the silkworms. The fruit is pleasantly acid, and was highly esteemed by the Romans. It is easily cultivated, and the fruit, which is among the most delicious and wholesome of berries, is readily propagated by seeds, cuttings, layers, and roots.

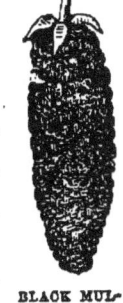

Fig. 63.

BLACK MULBERRY.

. There are three well-known varieties—the *white* (*morus alba*), employed mostly in feeding silkworms; the *black* (*morus nigra*), whose fruit (fig. 63) is large and excellent; and the *red* (*morus rubra*), the fruit of which is small, yet very pleasant.

The *Pineapple* (*Bromelia ananus*)—regarded by many as the most delicious of fruits—is a native of South America, the West Indies, and the hotter parts of Asia and Africa. Like most of the pleasantly-acid fruits, it contains both malic and citric acids in nearly equal proportions. This fruit may be raised in all temperate latitudes by the employment of artificial heat. In the New York market a fair quality of the pineapple is found at almost all seasons of the year.

Etærio.—The *Strawberry* (*Frugaria vesica*) is one of our favorite summer fruits. It is peculiar to the temperate regions of the Eastern and Western hemispheres. Excellent strawberries grow wild on new lands in many parts of the United States; and many varieties are cultivated near our large cities. Probably Cincinnati is the greatest strawberry market in the world. A good crop yields $300 to $500 the acre; and in some seasons more than $1,000 have been realized for the crop of a single acre. Among the best varieties are the *Early Virginia* (fig. 64), *Hovey's Seedling, Nectarine, Duke of*

Fig. 64.

EARLY VIRGINIA.

Kent, Hudson, Swainstone's Seedling, Alpine Bush, Burr's New Pine, Mulberry, etc.

Fig. 65.

HOVEY'S SEEDLING.

Hovey's Seedling (fig. 65) is one of the most productive varieties. One man can pick and hull one hundred quart boxes in a day.

In the wild state the strawberry has perfect flowers, like the apple, pear, etc. But owing to high culture and new seedlings, many varieties now vary from this primeval form. Some are mostly staminate, and will in no case produce large crops; others are pistillate, and alone will yield but little, and that imperfect fruit; but with a perfect, or staminate, kind to fertilize them, they will yield larger crops than can be obtained even from perfect kinds.

Fig. 66.

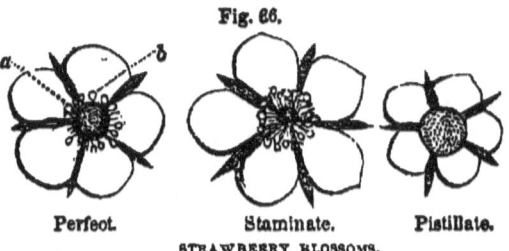

Perfect.   Staminate.   Pistillate.

STRAWBERRY BLOSSOMS.

In the left blossom of fig. 66, the center (*a*) is a little cone, similar to a small green strawberry, and is composed of pistils, and the little stems around it (*b*) represent the stamens, with anthers at top, which contain the fertilizing dust. In the middle blossom the center is small, as the pistils are imperfect, while the stamens are fully developed. In the right blossom the pistils or center organs are full and large, and

Anomalous Condition of the Strawberry—Raspberry—Thimbleberry.

no stamens are perceptible. The flower-leaves, or petals, are smaller than in the other conditions.

The strawberry is not wholly staminate nor pistillate, like those plants that were originally and are invariably only one or the other; but the staminate kinds have rudiments of pistils, and the pistillate kinds have stamens imperfectly developed. Hence partial crops on such. Cultivators are aware that plants produce their fruit on pistillate flowers, and that the pollen of the staminate is necessary to fertilize them.

"To Longworth belongs the honor of first publishing to the world this anomalous condition of the strawberry, and the mode of turning it to good account; and his system is now almost universally adopted. There will be living monuments to his memory while the rains fall, the sun shines, and science, equally genial, beams on the human mind."—*American Fruit-Book*, by S. W. COLE.

The *Raspberry* (*Rubus idæus*) derives its name from the rough spines with which the bush is covered. There are several sub-varieties of the *black* and *red* berries. The American *black raspberry* is sometimes called *thimbleberry*. It is very hardy, easily cultivated, and yields excellent fruit. One of the best kinds of the red is the *Red Antwerp* (fig. 67). Among the black kinds, or rather blue-black, the *Franconia* (fig. 68) is deservedly esteemed.

Fig. 67

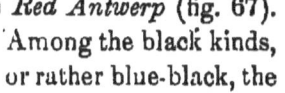

RED ANTWERP.

FRANCONIA.

Fig. 68.

Other choice fruits are the *Ohio Ever-bearing*, *Yellow Antwerp*, *Fastolff*, and *Orange*. The *American red raspberry* is one of the sweetest and most delicate of berries.

The *Blackberry* (*Rubus fruticosus*) grows abundantly on most new lands in this country and is easily cultivated in gardens. We

Blackberries—Dewberry—Bread Fruit—Durion—Guava.

have several varieties of this fruit, among which are the *white blackberry* and the *black blackberry!* No berry in the world is richer in flavor than some kinds of the blackberry when fully ripe. Fig. 69 is a cut of the fruit of the *High Bush* (*Rubus villosus*).

Fig. 69.

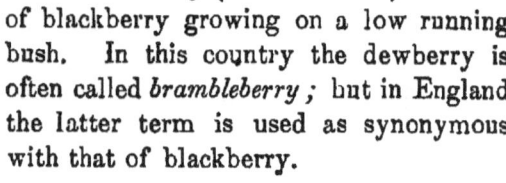

HIGH BUSH.

The *Dewberry* (*Rubus cæsius*) is a kind of blackberry growing on a low running bush. In this country the dewberry is often called *brambleberry;* but in England the latter term is used as synonymous with that of blackberry.

UNCLASSIFIED FRUITS.—The *Bread fruit* (*Artocarpus*) is a native of the northeastern parts of Asia, and the islands of the Pacific. There are two kinds of bread fruit. The first, called *Jaca*, though not very palatable, grows to a large size, often weighing 30 pounds. The bread fruit proper (fig. 70) is eight or nine inches long, yellowish-green, and covered with hexagonal warts. The pulp is partly farinaceous. Its taste is between that of wheat and roasted chestnuts. The tree is extremely productive, two or three of them yielding food enough for one person's sustenance. The fruit has been cultivated in the West Indies, but in this country it will not flourish, except in the hot-house.

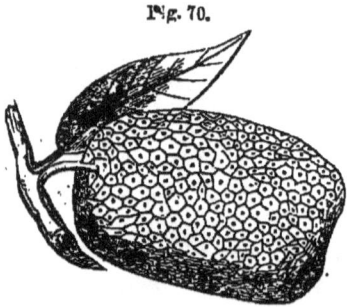

Fig. 70.

THE BREAD FRUIT.

The *Durion* (*Durio zibithinus*) is an Eastern fruit, growing on a lofty tree, in warm latitudes, sometimes of the size of a man's head. Its pulpy part, which is of a creamy subsistence, is very nutritive.

Of the *Guava* (*Tridium*), some varieties are natives of

The Mamma—Litchi—Jujube—Papau—Avocado—Anchovy—Mango.

Asia, and others of America. The *white guava* is abundant in the West Indies. It is a pleasant, pulpy, juicy fruit, about the size of a hen's egg.

The *Mamma* (*Mammen Americana*) is also a native of the West Indies. The tree is large and tall, and the fruit resembles a russet apple in size and shape, and the apricot in flavor.

The *Litchi* (*Dimocarpus litchi*) is a Chinese fruit, about as large as the orange, and of a sweet, agreeable flavor.

The *Jujube* (*Siryphus*) is a favorite fruit of Spain and Italy. In China it is abundant. The French apothecaries make it into a paste or lozenge, which is sold at the shops.

The *Juvia* (*Berthollatia excelsa*) is the fruit which incloses the triangular grains called *Brazil nuts*. I am not aware that it has ever been brought to this country.

The *Papau* (*Carica papaya*) grows on a tree which has no branches, in the East and West Indies. It is about the size of an ordinary melon, and contains an acid milk, which contains a large proportion of fibrin, like that of animal flesh.

The *Avocado pear* (*Sausus persica*), sometimes called the *Alligator*, is a West Indian fruit, about the size of the apple. Its pulp is very delicious, and considered superior to the peach.

The *Anchovy pear* (*Grias cauliflora*) is also a West Indian fruit. In taste it resembles the mango.

The *Mango* (*Mangifera indica*) is one of the most esteemed of the tropical fruits. It has a thin skin and an interior pulp, which is slightly acidulous and gratefully aromatic.

The trees on which this fruit grows rise to forty or fifty feet in height. In India many varieties are cultivated. The fruit will not keep long after ripening, but is then exquisitely fine-flavored and very nutritious.

The *Banana* (*Musa sapientum*) abounds over the torrid zone of America, and is a principal food for millions of the human family. It is said to produce more nutriment from the same space of ground than any other plant of the vegetable king dom. One thousand square feet will produce four thousand pounds of fruit; which is said to be forty-four times greater than potatoes can yield, and one hundred and thirty-three times greater than can be obtained from the same space of wheat.

The fruit is six to ten inches long, and something like the cucumber in form. Excellent bananas are found in the New York market during several months of the year.

THE PLANTAIN.

The *Plantain* (*Musa paradisica*) is similar to the banana, but even more luscious. It is a native of Asia and Africa; but is cultivated in the West Indies. The fruit (fig. 71), which grows in clusters, is about the size of the cucumber. When ripe it turns yellow, and its taste is sweet and mealy, like the richest muskmelon.

MANGOSTAN.

The *Mangostan* (*Garcinia mangostana*) (fig. 72) is about the size and shape of the orange, and one of the most delicious of fruits. Its flavor mingles that of the pineapple and strawberry. The tree is very beautiful, and indigenous in Sumatra, Java, and adjacent islands.

§ 3. ESCULENT ROOTS.

The principal aliments of this division are the turnip, carrot, parsnep, beet, potato, artichoke, yam, radish, and skirret.

THE TURNIP.—Of the *Turnip* (*Brassica rapa*), which in botany is called a *cruciferous* or *siliquose* plant, there are several varieties of edible roots; and, as with all roots which

Navet, or Naven—Varieties of Turnips—The Carrot.

are employed as food, their gustatory properties and nutritive value vary with the soil and mode of cultivation. The French *navet*, or *naven*, though resembling the carrot in shape, is a variety of turnip. The turnip is a favorite vegetable all over Europe and America, and in Russia it is eaten as a fruit.

Fig. 73 is a representation of the plant above the ground. The pods are filled with very small seeds, an ounce counting fourteen to fifteen thousand. The green leaves make excellent spinach.

The *Swedish Turnip* is one of the largest in size, but coarse and insipid. The *Russia*, or *yellow*, and the *common white* are both excellent. Some of the very best in our market are raised at Southold, L. I. In some parts of New Jersey a fine quality is produced. The *ruta baga* is a variety of very large size, but chiefly employed in the feeding of cattle. The *Maltese Golden Turnip* is much raised, and of excellent quality.

FLOWERS AND PODS OF THE TURNIP.

THE CARROT.—Of the *Carrot* (*Daucus carota*) many varieties have been produced by climate and culture. The leaves (fig. 74) are of a light, feathery vellum, and in the time of James the First were used by the ladies to adorn their head-dresses, as a substitute for the plumage of birds. Probably the idea—"Nature, when un-

UMBEL OF THE CARROT.

adorned, adorned the most," was not then in fashion. The carrot is very sweet, containing about ninety-five parts of sugar to one thousand. It is also more nutritive than the turnip. The *orange carrot* is often raised by the farmers for the purpose of coloring butter.

THE PARSNEP.—The *Parsnep* (*Pastinaca sativa*) is, like the carrot and turnip, biennial. There are many kinds of the root cultivated, all of which are apparently modifications of one variety. The root is even sweeter and more nutritious than the carrot, and to most persons much more palatable. It is very liable to be deteriorated by improper or too much manuring, a fact, however, which applies to all of our succulent roots and garden vegetables. The best parsneps are of a brittle texture, very tender, and of a sweet and slightly aromatic flavor, entirely devoid of bitterness.

THE BEET.—Of the *beet-root* two varieties are commonly cultivated—the *red* (*Beta vulgaris*) and the *white* (*Beta cicla*). Of the red variety, one is round like the turnip, and the other is long like the carrot. I have seen specimens of the latter at the Fairs of the American Institute eighteen inches long, and four or five inches in diameter. In France, a sub-variety, which is striated internally, is used in the manufacture of sugar.

The white beet has very small, slender roots, and large succulent leaves; it is employed only as a spinach, for which it is excellent. The *mangel wurzel* is a coarser kind of beet, cultivated for the feeding of cattle and milch cows.

Beet-root is considered more nutritive than any other esculent root, except the potato; and contains about twelve per cent. of saccharine matter.

THE POTATO.—The *Potato* (*Dulcamara tuberosum*) is of more nutritive value than all other foods which grow under

Varieties of Potatoes—Preparations of Potatoes—Potato Disease.

the surface of the earth. Indigenous to South America, it was not generally cultivated in England till the middle of the eighteenth century. It is found abundantly in the wild state in Chili and Peru; and the *ground-nut*, which is found in all the wilderness parts of North America, is supposed by many to be the original from whence all our fine varieties of potatoes are derived by cultivation.

According to chemical analyses, the best potatoes are almost, if not quite, as nutritive, pound for pound, as the best flesh-meat; and certainly twenty or thirty pounds of them can be raised at the expense that will fatten a single pound of beef or pork.

The best early potato in the New York market is the *Mercer;* and for winter use the *Kidney* is to be preferred. Still, much depends on the locality of their growth, as well as on the kind of root cultivated. Of each of these kinds there are several sub-varieties, as the *Early Shane, Early Champion, Monarch, Red Round Kidney, Lady's Finger, Blue Nose, Round White Kidney, Castor, Bread Fruit*, etc. All potatoes are more valuable as they are more mealy or farinaceous, and inferior as they are watery and waxy.

Potato-flour, or the dry starch powder of the root, has been sold in England under the name of *Indian Corn Starch, Bright's Nutritious Farina, English Arrow-Root*, etc.

The *Sweet Potato (Convolvulus batata)* is also a tuberose root, common in warm countries, and very extensively cultivated in the Carolinas, Virginia, Delaware, New Jersey, and some other States. The *potatoes* of Shakspeare, and the *Spanish potatoes* and *batatas* of other authors, are the root we generally designate as the sweet potato.

The potato has lately been found to be wonderfully antiscorbutic; a property which all fresh and wholesome aliments possess in the same degree.

A disease, or degeneration of this tuber, called *potato rot,* has prevailed extensively for several years past, and apprehensions are seriously entertained that the crop will be ultimately destroyed. Various speculations have been published relative to the causes and remedies; but they are in the main extremely fanciful. I am fully of opinion that the vegetable kingdom degenerates very much after the manner of the animal kingdom, and that the principal, if not the exclusive, cause of the trouble with the potato is the planting of poor or imperfect tubers. Nor can I see any rational way of effecting a cure, except by reproducing the potato in its pristine vigor from the balls or seeds. Three years will suffice in this way to renovate the crop completely. I am informed by Mr. D. A. Buckeley, of Stone Hill Farm, Williamstown, Mass., than whom no man raises finer potatoes, that this is the method he has pursued for a long time, with invariable success.

THE ARTICHOKE.—There are two plants of this name—the *Jerusalem* (*Helicansus tuberosus*), and the *Garden* (*Cynara scolymus*); although, botanically, they are in no way allied to each other. The former is a native of Brazil, but has been cultivated in most parts of America and Europe. It resembles the potato more nearly than it does any other tuber, but is not so mealy nor nutritious. The *garden artichoke* is but little used, though no doubt cultivation would do as much for it as it has done for the potato.

THE YAM.—The *Yam* (*Dioscorea sativa*) grows in wild luxuriance in the island of Ceylon and on the coast of Malabar. It is also extensively cultivated in the West Indies and in Africa. The root is farinaceous, like the potato, more nutritious, and is eaten, roasted or boiled, as a substitute for bread. The root is palmated, and divided somewhat like the fingers of the hand. A variety called the *winged yam* is often three feet long and weighs thirty pounds.

THE RADISH.—The *Radish* (*Raphanus sativus*) is used

more as a condiment than food. Some varieties of the root, however, are very bland, and to well-used stomachs not unhealthful. The strong acrid kinds are injurious to any stomach. There are many sub-varieties of the radish, but they are generally divided into the *turnip-shaped* and the *spindle-shaped* roots. The color of each varies from white to every shade of red, and from that to dark purple.

THE SKIRRET.—The *Skirret* (*Siam sasarum*) is a native of China, and but little known in this country. The root is composed of several tap roots about the size of the little finger. It is very white, sweet, and pleasant.

§ 4. BUDS AND YOUNG SHOOTS.

This section comprehends the *bulbous-rooted* plants—the roots being in reality subterranean buds. *Onions, Leeks, Garlic, Chives, Shallots*, and the *Rosambole of Denmark*, are of this class. They are very pungent, owing to an acrid volatile oil, and to weak stomachs exceedingly objectionable. We have, indeed, so many better things to eat, that it were well if all persons would let them alone. None but torpid nerves and half-palsied organs of taste ever desire such acrimonious aliments.

Asparagus, though agreeing botanically, is very different dietetically, being one of the most wholesome and nutritive of the spinaceous plants. The term asparagus, however, comprehends the common garden vegetable of that name (*Asparagus officinalis*), sometimes also called *Sparrow-grass;* the *Sea-kale* (*Crambe maritima*), growing naturally in many places along the sea-shore; the *artichoke* proper (*Cynara scolymus*), also a maritime plant in its wild state; the *Cardoon* (*Cynara cardunculus*), a native of Candia, and similar to the artichoke; the *Rampion* (*Campanula sapunculus*), a native of England, though not much cultivated; the *Prussian Asparagus* (*Ornithogalum pyrenacum*), an inferior kind of asparagus

Cabbages—Savoy—Greens—Cauliflower—Broccoli.

raised in some parts of Europe; and the *Bladder Campion* (*Silene inflata*), which is seldom seen in this country.

The common asparagus, or sparrow-grass, is as delicious as any vegetable of the kind ought to be, and as wholesome as any can be, hence our horticulturists would do well to let this variety supersede all others of the species.

§ 5. Spinaceous Plants.

Under this head I shall include the three orders of Tiedeman, viz.: Leaves, Leaf-stalks, and Flowers; Receptacles and Bracts; and Stems.

The section comprehends the *Cabbage tribe*, including the *Savoy, Greens, Cauliflower, Broccoli*, and also most of those plants whose tops and leaves are employed under the general term of spinach.

Cabbages.—The whole family of cabbages (*Brassicacea*) are the cultivated progeny of a small wild plant—the *sea-colewort* (*Brassica oleracea*). In general they are wholesome and very nutritive. The *loose-headed* cabbages are called *Bosecoles*, or *Kales*, of which there are several varieties; as the *Scotch kale, German kale,* or *curlies, Russian kale,* etc. The *close-headed* are those whose leaves are formed into a round head, as the common *white* and *red cabbages;* or into a long head, as the *Savoy*. The best known varieties of this subdivision are the *drum-head* and the *sugar-loaf*. The *red cabbage* is an excellent test for acids and alkalies. The former turns its blue purple color red, and the latter green.

Close-headed cabbages are called *savoys*. They are of a tender texture, very sweet, and not injured by frost.

Brussels sprouts are a sub-variety of savoys. Small green heads, like cabbages in miniature, shoot out from the junction of the leaves and sprouts, which are very delicate and nutritious.

The *Cauliflower* and *Broccoli* form a head of both the stalks

ALIMENTS, OR FOODS PROPER. 91

Sourkrout—Spinach—Varieties of Spinaceous Plants.

and leaves. They are not so nutritive as the common white and red cabbages, nor so palatable without seasonings.

Sourkrout, or *sauerkraut*, is a preparation of fermented cabbage, and although highly lauded by the medical profession, and by dietetical writers as medicinal and wholesome, it has nothing intrinsic to recommend it.

SPINACH.—Those plants whose leaves and leaf-stalks are nutritive and wholesome, and require no other preparation, than simply boiling in water, are very numerous. In common use are *young cabbages, potato-tops, dandelion-tops, mustard leaves, parsley, cowslips, deer-weed, beet-tops,* etc. Some of the spinaceous plants—mustard, for example—are acrid and pungent, but lose these objectionable properties on being boiled. A bitter or an astringent principle resides in some of them, as the dandelion and the cowslip, which impairs their flavor, though not existing in sufficient degree to effect materially their dietetic qualities.

A variety of plants coming under the present head are employed as *salads*, the principal of which are *Lettuce (Lactucca sativa), Garden Cress (Lapidium sativium), Water Cress (Nasturtium officinale), Rape (Brassica rapus), Burnet (Poterium sanguisorba), Celery,* or *Smallage (Apium graveolens), Lamb Lettuce,* or *Corn Salad (Felix olitoria), Endive (Chicorium endivia), Chickory, Succory,* or *Wild Endive (Chicorium intybus),* etc. Most of them are too strong and acrimonious to be healthful; and those who avoid strong, rank animal foods, and eschew alcohol and tobacco, can hardly desire them. The lettuce tribe are injurious on account of containing the narcotic juice from which opium is made.

Most of the plants employed as spinach belong to the botanical family *Chenopodeæ ;* they have very small greenish flowers, formed into variously-shaped heads, resembling balls, bunches, spikes, etc.

Fig. 75 represents the commonly cultivated varieties of the

Spinacia Oleracea. The garden sub-varieties which we find in the New York markets have very soft and succulent leaves, with small and very tender stems.

The *New Zealand Spinach* (*Tetragonia expansa*) (fig. 76.) is said to be the only native plant of the isles of Australia which has been transplanted to the kitchen-gardens of Europe. It produces an abundance of large tender leaves, which in that climate grow luxuriantly during the hottest weather.

Fig. 75.

SPINACH.

Fig. 76.

NEW ZEALAND SPINACH.

ALIMENTS, OR FOODS PROPER. 93

Sorrel—Dock—Varieties of Rhubarb—Seasoning Herbs.

The leaves of the *Chenopodium* (*Chenopodium quinoa*), to which the New Zealand variety has some resemblance, are esteemed both in this country and Europe. The seeds of the yellow variety are used as a substitute for millet.

The *Sorrel* (*Rumex acetosa*) is sometimes eaten as spinach, though it is too acid to be agreeable to most palates. Stewed and sweetened, it makes very pleasant pies. *Wood sorrel* (*Oxalis acetosella*) yields oxalic acid combined with potash. It is obtained in the dry state by simple evaporation, and is then called *salt of sorrel*. It has also been called the *essential salt of lemons*, and used as a substitute for lemons in making acidulous beverages. This salt is useful in removing spots of ink or iron-molds from linen.

Some varieties of *Dock* (*Rumen*) are sometimes eaten, though rather sour and harsh. The *Patience Dock* (*Rumen patienta*) is a hardy perennial plant, called by the Germans *winter spinach*.

The *Rhubarb* (*Rheum*) is employed both as a spinach and for making tarts and pies. It is strongly though pleasantly acid. The varieties usually cultivated in our gardens are the *Rheum rhaphonicum* and *Rheum hybridum*. This plant also contains some proportion of oxalic acid. A variety called *Rheum undulatum* is said to be of the finest flavor. The *Rheum palmatum* (fig. 75, see page 94) is the plant whose root is used in medicine. The foot-stalks of its radical leaves are much smaller than those of the other kinds; hence it is not cultivated for mere culinary purposes.

SEASONING HERBS.—There are many *sweet* or *savory* herbs used as seasonings or condiments which may be properly mentioned here, though I do not consider them either dietetical or useful. They may be *medicinal;* but in the hydropathic system all such medicine is considerably worse than useless. The principal articles of this class are *Sage, Thyme,* the *Mints, Dill, Fennel, Tansy, Marjorum, Tarrago, Nasturtium,* or *In-*

Medicinal Rhubard—Ferns—Lichens—Seaweeds—Mushrooms.

dian Cress, Chervil, Savory, Rosemary, Lavender, Basil, Balm, Angelica, Anise, Cummin, Caraway, Coriander, Sumphire, etc.

Fig. 77.

RHUBARD—RHEI PALMATUM.

§ 6. FLOWERLESS PLANTS.

The *Ferns, Lichens, Seaweeds,* and *Mushrooms* which are

Iceland Moss—Koran—Reindeer Moss—Irish Moss—Toadstools.

eaten, or eatable, may be conveniently considered under this title. I do not regard the whole tribe as worth the ink spilt in describing them, only as showing the vast variety of eating material there is in the world, and the resources to which one may resort in extremity. Natural appetences never require nor desire such food, and the pampered and abnormal taste can not be satisfied were the earth and sea and air to yield ten thousand times as many animals and vegetables for it to prey and gorge upon.

Those *lichens* which are employed as food contain a starchy matter called *feculoid*, or *lichenin*, usually associated with a bitter principle, which may be removed by soaking in a weak alkaline solution. Of this character are several species of *Gyrophora*, used by the hunters of the Arctic regions and the North American Indians. *Iceland Moss* (*Cetraria islandica*) is extensively used in England, and to some extent in this country. The *Koran*, or *Mamako*, is employed in New Zealand. The *Cetraria nivalis* grows abundantly in the mountainous regions of this country, and the *Reindeer Moss* (*Cenomyce rangiferina*) is a principal food of the deer of our forests.

Several species of *Algæ*, or *Seaweed*, are employed as food. Their chief alimentary quality is mucilage. Of this class are *Pearl Moss* (*Chondrus crispus*), called also *Carrigeen*, or *Irish Moss*, and the *Laver*, sold in the London shops. Some of these substances contain also sugar and starch. The *Ceylon*, or *Jafner Moss*, is a seaweed of India. These articles are much used in making jellies, blanc-mange, etc., for invalids.

Of the *Fungi*, or *Mushrooms*, many varieties are eaten, and some are considered very "delicate." They possess very little nutriment, and are very apt to be poisonous. Those varieties called *toadstools* generally possess noxious qualities. The *Garden Mushrooms* (*Agaricus campestris*, and *Agaricus auruntiacus*) are the principal kinds cultivated for the table.

In fig. 78, *a, a, a,* represent the Var. Campestris, and *b* the Var. Auruntiacus. In some places the same varieties are called *field mushrooms.* All of them are more used as *ragouts* and flavoring agents than for their intrinsic dietetical properties.

Fig. 78.

COMMON, OR GARDEN MUSHROOMS.

Catsup, or *catchup*, is made of the juice of mushrooms mixed with salt and spices.

The Truffle (*Tuber cibarium*) (fig. 79) grows in clusters, several inches below the surface of the ground. Dogs have been trained to hunt for truffles, which they discover by their scent.

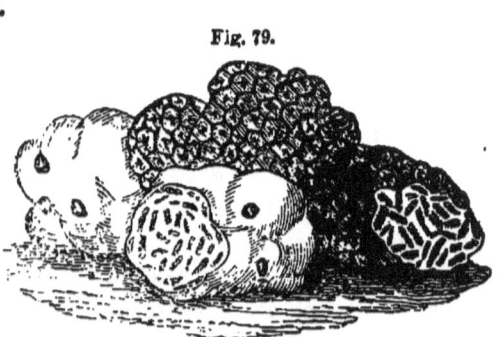

Fig. 79.

BLACK AND WHITE TRUFFLE.

The *Agaricus muscarius* possesses nervine and narcotic properties, and is employed by the Russians, Kamtschatdales, and Korians to induce intoxication. Other domestic varieties

Animal Foods—Mammals—Birds—Reptiles—Fishes.

are known under the names of *boletus, morel, pepper dulse tangle,* etc.

ANIMAL FOODS.—The alimentary principles derived from the animal kingdom are the *proteinaceous, gelatinous, oleaginous,* and the *saccharine* matter of milk; in other words, *fibrin, albumen, casein, gelatin,* and *sugar.* They are yielded by flesh, blood, cartilages, ligaments, cellular and nervous tissue, viscera, milk, and eggs. All the species of animals—beasts, birds, fishes, reptiles, and insects—which human ingenuity has been able to grasp, has been "appropriated" as nourishment, and there is scarcely any part of any animal carcass which has not been more or less employed as human food.

In the most civilized countries the domesticated animals afford the principal flesh-meat; though the practice of eating the oxen which "have plowed for us," the cows which have "given us milk," the lamb which we have petted, and the sheep which "has warmed us with its fleece," seems more becoming the savage than the civilized state of society.

VARIETIES OF ANIMAL FOOD.—The Mammals—*neat cattle, sheep,* and *hogs*—afford the chief supply of this kind of food in this country. To this class also belong the *deer, rabbit, hare, elk, moose, buffalo,* and *bear,* which are employed to some extent in many countries. The Kalmuck Tartars, and some other tribes of the human family, eat their *horses, dogs, cats, rats,* and *mice.*

Of *Birds,* the *common fowl, turkey, goose, duck, partridge, woodcock,* and *pigeon* are principally eaten. A variety of other *game* birds are found at the refectories.

Among the *Reptiles* used as food are the various kinds of *turtles,* and several species of *frogs.* The *flesh of vipers* was once recommended by regular physicians as a restorative diet for invalids!

Our waters afford an innumerable variety of *fishes,* nearly all of which are devoured by the human animal.

Shell-fish—Food derived from Herbivora, Omnivora, and Carnivora.

The *Shell-fish* employed as food are the *lobster, crawfish, crab, prawn, shrimp, oyster, mussel, cockle, whelk, scallop, lim pit, periwinkle,* etc.

QUALITIES OF ANIMAL FOODS.—Unquestionably the very best, or, if any prefer the term, the least injurious, animal food is that derived from herbivorous animals, as *beef, mutton,* etc. Those animals which feed on vegetables exclusively will certainly supply a purer aliment than those which prey on other animals. *Omnivorous* animals, which eat indiscriminately vegetables or other animals, are inferior, as food, to the purely herbivorous, and the *carnivorous*, which eat nothing but other animals, are inferior still. Thus the *hog*, whose filthy carcass is converted into a mass of disease by the fattening process, and whose flesh and adipose accumulations, under the names of *pork, bacon,* and *lard,* are filling all Christendom with scrofula, erysipelas, and foul humors, is even less pernicious to the nutritive functions than is the flesh and blood of the dog, panther, lion, tiger, hyena, vulture, etc.

It is true that most of the cold-blooded animals, as various kinds of fishes, though mainly carnivorous, are not as depraving aliment as is the flesh of warm-blooded or land animals, who eat carnivorously. But this is owing to their cooler temperament. Yet sea-food of all kinds is less nutritive and less wholesome than the flesh of herbivorous or graminivorous animals.

" But the quality of food derived from herbivorous animals may be greatly varied by circumstances. Very young or very old animals are less healthful than young, nearly full-grown, and middle-aged. Animals which have been excessively fattened, or stall-fed, and those which have been hand-worked, are deteriorated as food; and animals that have been 'slop-fed' with liquid preparations, the refuse matters of the kitchen, or the filthy excrements of distilleries, are very un clean and unwholesome "—*Hydropathic Encyclopedia.*

Lean Flesh—Necessity for its Mastication—Epicures.

And when we come to the matter of converting the different parts and structures of animals into the organs and tissues of our own bodies—making them "bone of our bone and flesh of our flesh"—there are many good reasons for choosing. The *lean flesh*, or *muscular fiber*, is the very best aliment any animal can afford; and this is also most wholesome when derived from animals neither much fattened nor emaciated.

"But some allowance must be made for the masticatory ability of human teeth. Flesh-meat requires thorough mastication. Human beings have not the tearing teeth of the tiger and the wolf, nor the cutting motion of the jaw which belongs to the carnivora. Moreover, the teeth, jaws, and gums of most people who live in the ordinary way, are preternaturally sensitive and tender; and in addition to all this, a large portion of people, even young people, in civilized society, wear artificial teeth. They can not, therefore, well masticate tough meat, as is often demonstrated in the cases of choking in the attempt to swallow half-chewed flesh. For this reason the animal had better be in good condition, and only the most tender fibers selected as food.

"Epicures generally have the flesh they procure at market kept until it becomes tender from age; but such tenderness is the condition of incipient putrefaction, and although the article may be very easily disposed of by the teeth, and very quickly *dissolved* in the stomach, it can never be well *digested*, nor can it ever be converted into pure blood and sound tissues. It is advantageous to break up the fibers of tough meat by thoroughly pounding before cooking."—*Hydropathic Encyclopedia.*

In all animal matter the process of decomposition or putrefaction commences the moment that life is extinct; and although the evidences of such putrefaction may not be *offensively* evident to our senses of taste and smell for several hours or days, the fact alone establishes the principle, that the sooner all dead animal matter is eaten after the life-principle has departed the better. The only way it can be kept unchanged for any considerable length of time, is by being frozen immediately after being killed.

The quality of flesh-meat is also affected by the manner in which the animal is slaughtered. All flesh contains more or less blood; and a disproportionate quantity of venous or impure blood. The blood not only contains the natural elements of food, but the waste, dead, and effete matters which, having served their purpose in the organism, are to be expelled from the body, and such accidental impurities as may have obtained admission into the body; hence the more bloody any kind of animal food is, the more unclean and putrescent.

Medico-dietetical writers are continually perpetrating the flattest contradictions, and most singularly absurd blunders on this subject; and I regard the medical profession, taken in the aggregate, as the most ignorant class in community on the whole subject of diet; not that they have not sense and reason like other men; but that they have been miseducated—led away from truth by false theories, and thus are farther from it, more ignorant in all practical senses, than one who has no knowledge save the "light of common sense."

To illustrate: Dr. Dunglison, in a late work (*Human Health*), in speaking of the Roman custom of killing animals by running a red-hot spit through the body, says: "This mode of slaughtering was replete with objections, if regarded in an alimentary point of view. The flesh of animals thus killed is dark colored, owing to the retention of blood in the vessels, and hence it becomes *speedily putrid*." And, again, says the doctor: "When an animal is killed *accidentally*, without bleeding, its flesh is not unwholesome, although it may not be palatable, in consequence of the blood remaining in the vessels." So, if Dr. Dunglison's logic is sound, the wholesome or unwholesome character of the flesh of an animal killed without bleeding depends entirely on the fact whether the killing was by accident or design!

Composition of Flesh—Nutritive Value of Different Parts of Animals.

The Jewish custom of soaking meat half an hour in water, and then letting it lie an hour in salt before cooking, was for the purpose of further cleansing it of its blood ; and the Mosaic regulations concerning the use of flesh generally, were far more philosophical than are the doctrines taught by the medical profession in this nineteenth century on the same subject.

The proximate composition of muscle, or flesh, as given by Brande and Schlossberger, shows that the very best animal food is only about equal to the potato in nutritive value, and hardly one third as nutritious as rice, wheat, and other grains :

100 Parts.	Water.	Albumen or Fibrin.	Gelatin.	Nutritive Matter.
Beef	74	20	6	26
Veal	75	19	6	25
Mutton	71	22	7	29
Pork	76	19	5	24
Chicken	73	20	7	27
Cod	73	14	7	21
Haddock	82	13	5	18
Sole	79	15	6	21

The comparative healthfulness of other parts of animals can be readily determined by the principles already explained. The *oil* or *fat*, next to the blood is the least alimentary substance. The *kidney*, when cooked, always exhales a urinous odor, and, like the *liver*, is an excrementitious viscus, and wholly unfit for food. Next, in the order of unfitness, are the brains, lungs, stomach, intestines, and skin. All of these structures and organs of different animals afford a variety of fashionable and dainty dishes, and all, like "bull-fights" in Spain, have their admirers among both sexes; but we may as well keep the simple truth in view that, just as far as we depart from lean flesh in the selection of aliments from the animal kingdom, just so far does their value depreciate.

" The dietetic character of animal food is also affected by the manner of cooking. It is to be preferred lightly or but moderately cooked, provided a due degree of tenderness of fiber is

secured. In broiled steaks this may be accomplished by pounding; but large, thick, roasting pieces are apt to be tough, if not well cooked. *Broiling*, on all accounts, is the best method of cooking all flesh-meat. *Boiling*, taking care to skim off any floating particles of oil, is better than *roasting;* and this is better *than frying*, which is a method never to be recommended."
—*Hydropathic Encyclopedia.*

The absolute identity, in chemical elements, of pure flesh and pure blood is another argument that muscular flesh or lean meat is the best form of animal food. And as this pure blood and pure flesh are made entirely of vegetable material, this fact affords another evidence—in itself conclusive, unless it can rebutted—that the best aliment for man may be derived directly from the vegetable kingdom. The following are the results of analysis by Playfair and Boeckmann:

Elements.	Ox Blood.	Dry Beef.	Roasted Beef.	Roasted Veal.	Roasted Deer.
Carbon	51.95	51.83	52.590	52.52	52.60
Hydrogen	7.17	7.57	7.886	7.87	7.45
Nitrogen	15.07	15.01	15.214	14.70	15.23
Oxygen	21.89	21.87	24.310	24.91	24.72
Ashes	4.42	4.23			
	100.00	100.00	100.00	100.00	100.00

Next to the flesh of the herbivorous animals, in alimentary value, is the *flesh of birds*. But here, again, is ample room for discrimination. Pereira tells us that the *hawk* and *owl* are not eaten, "partly, perhaps, from prejudice, and partly because those which touch carrion acquire a cadaverous smell"—as though the stench of putrefaction were not of itself a sufficient reason.

The White-fleshed Birds.—*Chicken, turkey, partridge, quail,* etc. are nearly as nutritive and digestible as beef and mutton. Medical writers call their flesh "less stimulating," but the only stimulation of either comes from its impurity, and in this respect *fowl* is generally worse than the best flesh.

ALIMENTS, OR FOODS PROPER. 103

Flesh of Fowls—Fumet—Delicate Morsels—Enlarged Livers—Callipee.

The Dark-fleshed Birds.—Grouse, robin, snipe, woodcock, etc., are more greasy and savory to epicures, but less nutritive and less wholesome. Pereira says of the flesh of these birds: "It is richer in ozmazome, and when sufficiently kept, it acquires a peculiar odor called *fumet*, and an aromatic bitter taste, most sensible in the back. In this condition it is said to be *ripe* or *high*, and is much esteemed as a luxury." Professor Dunglison eulogizes this "fumet," which is as much the stench of putrefaction as is the "cadaverous smell" of carnivorous birds, still more extravagantly. He says: "The solubility of game—grouse, etc., is amazingly increased, as well as the *luxury of the repast* by keeping until it has attained the requisite *fumet*, which indicates that incipient putrefaction is diminishing its cohesion."

The "luxury of putrefying animal flesh" sounds strangely to those whose stomachs and appetences have been for years "cleansed from all flesh." "Carrion crows" might, perhaps, with no violation of the laws of a low order of life, enjoy such a repast.

Geese, ducks, and other aquatic birds, are strong, oily, and hence unwholesome. The *canvas-back*, though considered a great luxury, is very greasy, rancid, and unhealthful.

Fowls are usually fattened for the market by confining them in dark places, and cramming them with barley-meal, mutton suet, molasses, and milk, which usually *ripens* them in a fortnight, but renders the flesh half-putrid and exceedingly obnoxious.

Particular parts of certain birds have long been celebrated as "delicate morsels" by the epicure and the gourmand; as the *brains* of the ostrich and peacock, the *tongues* of the nightingale and flamingo, the *trail* or *intestine* of the woodcock, the *enlarged liver*—fatty degeneration—of the goose.

The flesh of turtles is usually prepared in the forms of steak and soup. The *callipee*, which is considered the most "delicate" part, is the under part of the breast or belly. Sir Hans Sloane remarks: "Persons who feed much on turtle sweat out a yellow serum, especially under the armpits." These reptiles are wholly unfit for human aliment.

Fish aliment is, in a general sense, far inferior to flesh, though, for some reason I never could divine, many dietetic reformers who refuse to eat flesh, and some physicians who prohibit its employment, eat and prescribe fish with unbounded license. But with those who *will* eat fish aliment there is a choice of fishes. As a general rule, the least oily are the most wholesome. Of this kind are the *cod, halibut, trout, whitefish, bass, blackfish, haddock, whiting, sole,* and *turbot.* Among the objectionable and oily kinds are *salmon, eels, herrings, pilchards, sprats, mackerel, shad,* etc.

Of the *crustacean* sea-food, *lobsters, crabs, shrimps,* and *prawns* are the principal. They are exceedingly indigestible, and very productive of skin diseases.

Of the *mollusca, oysters, mussels, clams, scallops, cockles,* and even *snails* are eaten. The oyster is the favorite among them; but although not as indigestible as the crustacea, they are all bad aliments.

Of the *insects* employed as food by some portions of the human family, it is enough to name, as evidences of the deep depravity of human appetite, the *grub-worm, spiders, locusts, grasshoppers, white ants,* and *caterpillars,* all of which have been considered "wholesome" by many people, and pronounced "delicate" by many physicians.

EGGS.—Physiologists are not very well agreed as to the nutritive value of the eggs of oviparous animals. They are moderately nutritious, and when eaten raw or rare boiled are easy of digestion. But their good qualities are rather negative than positive. When poached or fried they are among the worst things that can be taken into the stomach. Hard-boiled eggs are often pickled in vinegar and employed as a condiment, than which nothing can be more unphysiological in the way of aliment. Some writers have contended that eggs, hardened by boiling or frying, *agree* better with laboring people, and those who take active exercise, than in the soft or liquid state. But such persons commit the common blunder of mistaking the momentary feelings of a morbid stomach for the physiological properties of alimentary substances.

MILK.—As the article in the Encyclopedia on the dietetical nature of milk contains precisely what I wish to say now on the same subject, I can do no better than transcribe it:

"The *milk* of the mammals, though an animal secretion, can hardly be called animal food, in strict language. It contains, on the average, nearly ninety per cent. of water, and about ten per cent. of solid matter, consisting of butter, casein, sugar, and various salts. The *cream* of cow's milk, according to Berzelius, consists of butter 4.5, casein or curd 3.5, whey 92.0=100.0. By agitation, as in *churning*, the globules of fatty matter unite, and form *butter;* the residue is called buttermilk; it consists of casein, serum, or whey, and a very small quantity of butter. *Skimmed milk* very soon becomes acid and curdy. The admixture of an acid or rennet (which is the infusion of the fourth, or true stomach of the calf) immediately coagulates it, separating the casein, or curd, from the whey. The addition of acetic acid will cause a still further separation of coagula, which has been called *zieger, bracotte,* etc. After the separation of casein and zieger, the whey left yields *lactic acid, salts*, and some nitrogenous substances, one of which is supposed to be *osmazome*. Osmazome, however, does not appear to be a tangible reality, but a flavor or effluvia developed by the chemical changes which take place in several animal substances during the process of cooking—heating, roasting, boiling, etc. Good milk is a homogeneous but not viscid liquid, not coagulable by heat. When examined by the microscope it appears to consist only of transparent spherical globules. The cream yielded varies from five to twenty per cent., as tested by the *lactometer*, which, by the way, seems to be a very unsatisfactory instrument for the purpose. No secretion is so readily affected by the ingesta, or the general health of the animal producing it, as the milk. The taste, color, and odor of cow's milk are readily modified by the food. Children are in many ways, through the mother's milk, disordered, salivated, narcotized, catharticized, and often poisoned.

"The organic instincts, true to the *first* principle of self-preservation, determine the accidental impurities of the body to this channel as the most ready way of expelling them from the body. Nursing mothers have little idea how much disease, pain, and misery they inflict on their little ones, nor how frequently they commit *infanticide*, by taking irritating aliments and drinks, and injurious drugs into their own stomachs. If I could present this subject to them in all its force, and in all its bearings on their happiness, and on the well-being of the human race, as I hope to attempt in a future publication, I am certain there would be a sudden and very radical revolution in the way of dieting mothers and doctoring children.

The milk produced by cows fed on distillery slops, which, to the disgrace of municipal authorities, *rich* men are permitted to sell to the poor in nearly all our large cities, is not only very innutritious, but absolutely poisonous. In New York, Brooklyn, and Williamsburgh several thousand cows are kept in close and horribly filthy stables, fed on warm slops, and other refuse matters of the distilleries, which rot their teeth, weaken their limbs, and render their whole bodies masses of disease; and their milk is furnished to our citizens as a principal article of diet for their children!

Although milk can not be considered a necessary or strictly natural food for mammals, except during the period of infancy, when the teeth are undeveloped—and no animals of the class mammalia, save man, employ it otherwise—it is nevertheless, when pure, the best form of aliment out of the strict order of natural foods. It contains all the elements requisite for pro-

Butter—Sweet Cream—Fresh Curd—Cheese—An Adage.

. longed nutrition, and except in certain abnormal states of the digestive organs, its moderate employment is attended with no inconvenience.

"Some invalids can not enjoy, and some dyspeptics can not tolerate it; but exceptional cases from morbid conditions are not rules for healthy persons.

"*Butter*, as prepared for the table, is a different article dietetically from its fatty particles as they exist in milk. The former must rank with all animal oils in being difficult of digestion, but slightly nutritive, and liable to generate rancid acids in the stomach. There is, however, a great difference between fresh-made and slightly salted butter, and that which is old and highly salted. Compared with the latter the former is almost innocuous. Melted and cooked butter is, wherever found, a very deleterious aliment. *Sweet cream*, from its solubility in water, and greater miscibility with the saliva, is far preferable to butter. Indeed, I am not aware that experience assigns to it any injurious or even unpleasant effect as an aliment. The fresh curd of milk is perfectly wholesome, and pot cheese, when of milk as soon as it becomes sour, and before it gets bitter, is also a harmless article. Green cheese is not very objectionable, but old, strong cheese is one of the most injurious and indigestible things in existence. It is also one of the most constipating articles to the bowels that can be found. It is a common *fancy* among medical men, and a common *whim* among the people, that old, strong, rank cheese, though itself very indigestible, stimulates the stomach to digest other things; hence almost all the medico-dietetical works quote the old adage:

> "'Cheese is a mity elf,
> Digesting all things but itself.'

"There is more poetry than truth in the doggrel distich. Old cheese occasionally undergoes spontaneous decomposition, during which process acrid and poisonous elements are developed, as is frequently the case with bacon and sausages."

Concentrated or Essence of Milk—Preparation in England.

CONCENTRATED MILK.—By mixing milk with a portion of sugar, it may be evaporated to one fourth its original bulk. Prepared in this way it is sold in this city under the name of *Concentrated Milk*. In England it is called *Essence of Milk*. The "Mechanics' Magazine" gives the details of the process by which it is prepared on a large scale :

"Mr. Moore, an extensive farmer in Staffordshire, has, under a license from the patentee of the new process of concentrating milk, fitted up an apparatus by which he manufactures annually the produce of about thirty cows. The milk, as it is brought from the dairy, is placed on a long, shallow copper pan, heated beneath by steam to a temperature of about 110°; a proportion of sugar is mixed with the milk, which is kept in constant motion by persons who walk slowly round the pan, stirring its contents with a flat piece of wood. This is continued for about four hours, during which the milk is reduced to a fourth of its original bulk, the other three fourths having been carried off by evaporation. In this state of consistency it is put into small tin cases, the covers of which are then soldered on, and the cases and contents are then placed in a frame which is lowered into boiling water; in this they remain a certain time, and after being taken out and duly labeled, the process is complete. The milk thus prepared keeps for a lengthened period. It supplies fresh milk every morning on board ship, and may be sent all over the world in this portable form."

CHAPTER IV.

PRESERVATION OF FOODS.

PRESERVATION OF GRAIN, MEAL, SEED, ETC.—All kinds of grains, nuts, and seeds should be perfectly dried and cleaned, and kept in a cool, well-ventilated place. Dried corn has been kept in good condition for more than eighty years. It is especially important that flour and meal be kept in a clean, sweet room, exposed to no effluvia from vaults, cellars, or sinks, and not injured by smoky fireplaces and stoves. All kinds of flour and meal ought also to be fresh ground; for they will never long preserve, when broken, all the nutritive virtue of the seeds. Grinding the grain exposes its proximate elements to oxidation or fermentation, hence the invariable rule with all farinaceous foods should be to have them ground as near the time of using as possible. It would be a vast advantage to the health of the community if hand-mills were kept in every family.

Wheat-meal will mold or oxidate sooner than fine flour, on account of the mucilage contained in the bran; and Indian meal is very liable to acquire an acid or musty property if long kept. Moths, too, are apt to infect it, especially if stored in a damp place.

Walnuts, filberts, and chestnuts may be preserved a long time by packing them, when perfectly dry, in jars or boxes, with fine clean sand; or they may be buried in the ground, in a pit lined with clean straw.

Lima beans and green peas may be dried in the pure air or in a warm room, when young and tender, and thus kept for winter use. Green corn can be preserved by turning back the husk, all but the last thin layer, and then drying in a warm room or in the sun. It may also be parboiled in a bag, and then dried as above.

PRESERVATION OF VEGETABLES.—During the hot season various kinds of vegetables, as peas, beans, cucumbers, squashes, etc., may be preserved for days in a room attached to an ice-house. The temperature, however, should not be so low as to freeze them. Various kinds of roots, stems, tubers, and leaves may be preserved by simply cutting them in thin slices and drying; but as most of them will keep in the green state long enough in a cool, dry cellar, or buried in the ground below the freezing-point, it is hardly worth the trouble to dry them. Potatoes, turnips, carrots, parsneps, beets, cabbages, etc., will keep nearly the year round in either way. The stalks of rhubarb or the pie plant can be conveniently dried and kept for winter use.

Artichokes, asparagus, carrots, cabbages, turnips, parsneps, potatoes, onions, celery, beets, and, indeed, all other vegetables, may be preserved by being scalded or parboiled, placed in bottles, then into the hot-water bath for an hour, and corked tight.

Drying vegetables to that degree that they may be ground into flour, may be accomplished in the following manner, yet other similar methods will readily suggest themselves to any one who studies the subject. The roots are to be sliced and laid upon metal plates heated by steam.

In fig. 80, a is a shallow vessel for holding the material to be dried; b is a boiler of water heated by a chafing-dish; c, a lamp, the heat from which passes through the boiler in a tube ending in the chimney, d; e, the pipe conveying the steam from the boiler to the bottom of the vessel, a; f is a waste-pipe for the condensed steam; g, a pipe for the waste steam; h, a pipe for adding cold water to the boiler.

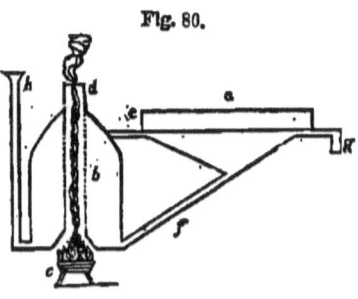

Fig. 80.

VEGETABLE DRYING APPARATUS.

Rules for Gathering Fruit—Preservation of the more Perishable Fruits.

PRESERVATION OF FRUITS.—In gathering fruits for winter use, great care should be taken not to bruise them nor break the skin, as the injured parts soon rot. Apples, pears, etc., intended to be kept as long as possible, should be carefully picked from the trees, not bent nor shook off. They should also be gathered on a clear dry day. The more delicate kinds, as peaches, apricots, and nectarines, should not even be wiped, as this would rub off their bloom or down, and makes them decay more rapidly.

Choice apples and pears may be kept very well, and often the year round, by wiping them gently dry, covering each with dry, soft paper, and laying them on shelves; or on shelves covered with paper without wrapping them. Pears and apples, if gathered a few days before perfectly ripe—not over six or eight—and packed carefully with dry moss, sand, bran, or in baskets lined with stout paper, will keep through the winter.

Pineapples may be kept much longer than usual by twisting out the corners, which, when suffered to remain, absorb and exhaust the juice of the fruit.

There is probably no better way of preserving oranges and lemons than by wrapping them singly in papers, and packing them in jars or in dry sand.

The principal condition on which the preservation of the more perishable fruits depends, is the exclusion of atmospheric air. The more perfectly this is effected, the longer and better will the fruits be kept unchanged. And many fruits may be kept good for months, with a mere trifle of sugar, provided the air is nearly all excluded from the vessels which contain them, when otherwise they could not be kept without being *preserved* in sugar, pound for pound. I have known strawberries, whortleberries, peaches, pears, tomatoes, quinces, blackberries, etc., put up in this way, very nearly as well flavored and fresh in the middle of the winter as when first gathered in their season.

Drying Apparatus—Air-tight Bottles—Keeping Grapes.

Mr. William R. Smith, of the interior of this State, has experimented pretty extensively in this method of preserving fruits, and has supplied our market with good fresh peaches, pears, tomatoes, quinces, etc., in mid-winter.

The North American Phalanx Company are now constructing an admirably planned building for preserving fruits and vegetables in either their ripe or unripe state. The drying apparatus is a series of shallow trays, with open network bottoms, supported above each other on sliding racks, making a double column of drying trays about thirty feet in height, all warmed to any requisite degree by the steam of a boiler in the basement. They are also largely engaged in putting up fruits; and have succeeded in so perfectly excluding the atmospheric air, as to keep tomatoes, berries, peaches, and pears, etc., fresh and undecayed a whole year, and some of them even longer.

They are put up in wide-mouthed quart jars, either of glass or stone. The fruit (except berries) is peeled, quartered, and their pips taken out, and the jars filled. These are then placed in a trough or shallow square tub, into which hot water is allowed to run till it surrounds the jars nearly to the top. The juice is thus heated sufficiently to expel the air, but not so as to boil or cook the fruit. The cork is, lastly, introduced, and covered with paste, cement, sealing-wax, or something impervious to air.

Undried grapes may be preserved a long time by placing them in large jars, filling up the jars with sawdust, and then cementing the lids so as entirely to exclude the air.

The following methods of keeping grapes in good condition long after they have ripened are convenient, and are said to be very successful. "Cut off the grapes, with a joint or two, or more, of wood below each bunch; make a clean cut, and apply sealing-wax, as hot as can be used, to it, and seal the wood closely, so that no air can enter the tissues communicating with the bunch. Then hang the bunches up on cords.

Bottling Gooseberries and Currants—Preservation by Scalding.

with the stalk-ends downward, suspended across a closet in a cool, airy room, taking care that they do not touch each other; cut down as wanted. Or this: cover the table in the fruit-room with fine, dry moss, and on this lay the bunches which have been carefully picked and cleaned of all bad berries, wiping the sound ones with a delicate piece of flannel; leave the bunches on the moss three days, each bunch by itself, which prevents the grapes from being injured by the pressure of their own weight; for want of moss, use cotton. Prepare hoops of proper strength, some three feet in diameter, with strings to suspend them, and attach the grapes to the hoop; take iron wire, just stout enough, when made into an S-shaped hook, to suspend one bunch—now fix one of these hooks to the bottom-end of the bunch, and hang it on the hoop, so as to keep each bunch by itself. When they have hung some eight days, they will be free from moisture, if the weather has not been too damp, and when they are dry, close up the room perfectly tight; examine the grapes every eight days, removing all bad ones."

Green gooseberries and currants, if gathered in very dry weather, may be cut from the stalks carefully, and dropped gently into wide-mouthed bottles. The bottles are then to be corked and rosined or cemented, and buried below the frost, or kept in a very dry, cool cellar. They will keep still better if the bottles are plunged for a few moments in hot water before corking.

Scalding fruit, so as to coagulate the gluten, and thus arrest the fermentation, has been resorted to successfully in preserving some kinds of fruits, especially apricots, gooseberries, currants, raspberries, cherries, and plums. Wide-mouthed stone bottles are filled with the fruit, carefully picked; they are then placed in a kettle filled with cold water nearly to the mouth of the bottles, and the water heated to one hundred and sixty-five degrees. After subjecting the fruit to this degree of heat for half an hour, the bottles are hermetically sealed.

The cranberry, and some of the smaller kinds of apples, will keep for a considerable time by being covered with water.

The juice of the grape, tomato, and probably many other fruits, may be preserved by simply boiling it for a short time, and then afterward secluding it from the atmosphere.

Some fruits of the gourd kind—pumpkins, squashes, etc., can be dried on metal plates heated by steam, sufficiently to be powdered or ground into a fine flour. The Shakers sell the article as pumpkin powder, which is very convenient for making pies expeditiously.

Peach leather and *tomato leather* are prepared by squeezing out the pulp of the very ripe fruit, spreading it out thinly on plates or shingles, and drying in the sun, or by hot air or steam, until quite hard and tough. They may also be dried in a brick oven.

The following method of preserving peaches in tin cans recently appeared in a Mississippi paper, from the pen of a writer who claims to have had considerable experience.

"In the first place, be absolutely certain that the cans are made air-tight. Peal your peaches, cut them in halves, take out the seeds, and fill the cans within a half inch of the top, shaking the peaches down as close as possible. Then take loaf-sugar in the proportion of two pounds to a pint of water, boil and strain. Pour this sirup over the peaches in the cans, and then have the square piece of tin put on, leaving a small vent in the center. Place the cans in a kettle with water enough to come within an inch of the top of the cans. Boil the cans from fifteen to thirty minutes, or longer if necessary keeping the vent open with a knitting-needle, until the air or sirup ceases to flow. Remove the kettle from the fire, and while the cans remain in the hot water close the vent with solder.

"This is decidedly the best plan, as I well know by experience. It takes no more sugar to make the sirup than it will take to sweeten them after you open the cans for use."

Pumpkins and squashes, and the stalks of rhubarb, can be conveniently peeled, cut into slices or strips, and dried in either of the foregoing ways.

The pomaceous fruits—apples, pears, peaches, etc.—peeled, cored, and cut into slices, or, if not too large, simply quartered, preserve their flavor and nutritive properties very well for nearly a year.

The majority of berried fruits retain a good degree of their dietetic qualities the year round, on being dried and kept in boxes or bags in a cool, clean, airy place.

The following valuable remarks on the cultivation of currants and gooseberries, are from a late number of the Vermont Chronicle:

"It is presumed that not one in a hundred understands the simple process of cultivating either currants or gooseberries, although it has been detailed in the horticultural books with which the world abounds. Thousands of persons, with every appliance for success, are still content to live without a plentiful supply of these delicious, healthy, and cheap luxuries, merely because they have not thought of the matter. They have a few stinted bushes set in the grass, with three fourths of the stocks dead, and then wonder why they do not bear in abundance.

"There is not a more beautiful shrub growing than the currant, properly propagated; and the same may be said of the gooseberry. Cultivators who pay any attention to the subject never allow but one stock, or, as the English say, 'make them stand on one leg;' thus forming a beautiful miniature tree.

"To do this you must take sprouts of last year's growth, and cut out all the eyes, or buds in the wood, leaving only two or three at the top; then push them about half the length of the cutting into mellow ground, where they will root, and run up a single stock, forming a beautiful symmetrical head. If you wish it higher, cut the eyes out the second year. I have one six feet high. This places your fruit out of the way of hens, and prevents the gooseberry from mildewing, which often happens on or near the ground, when it is shaded by a superabundance of leaves and sprouts. It changes an unsightly bush, which cumbers and disfigures your garden, into an ornamental dwarf tree. The fruit is larger, ripens better, and will last on the bushes, by growing in perfection, until late in the fall.

"The mass of people suppose that the roots take out from the lower buds. It is not so; they start from between the bark and the wood, at the place where it was cut from the parent root."

The methods of conserving fruits by means of sirup, alcohol, vinegar, and salt, need not be dwelt upon here. The first is, to say the least, very bad, and the last two are outrages upon the human stomach, which no intelligent physiologist or sensible hydropath ought ever to tolerate.

ICE-HOUSES.—These are so intimately connected with the subject of preserving food, that some general plan of constructing them seems appropriate in this place. Fig. 81 is an outline of the method commonly adopted. A well is sunk in the form of an inverted cone, a, b, which is lined with cement or brick-work, of a brick and a half in thickness, and arched over. The ice is put in through the opening g, at top, and taken

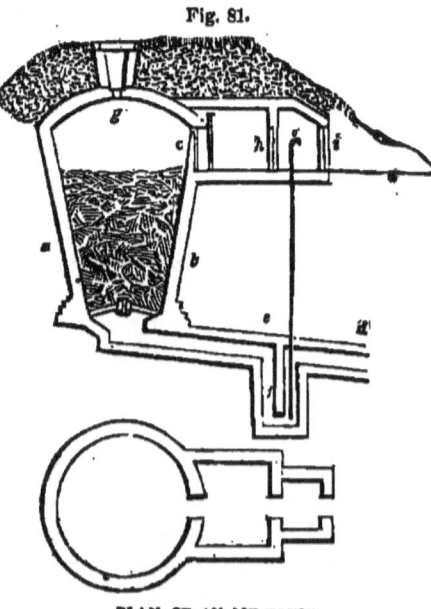

Fig. 81.

PLAN OF AN ICE-HOUSE.

Arrangements about an Ice-House—Economical Contrivance.

out at the side door, *c*; a drain, *d*, *e*, at the bottom carries off the water of the melted ice. The conical form of the well is for the purpose of having the ice keep compact by sliding down as it melts. The walls of the cone should be built with good hard mortar or Roman cement. At the bottom the ice should be supported on a thin wooden grating, or an old cart-wheel, as represented in the cut. Where the situation will not admit of a drain, the bottom of the ice-well may terminate in a small well sunk still deeper, and this emptied by a pump. The passage to the ice-house should be divided by two or more doors, so as to keep a current of external air from reaching the ice.

It is said that ice may be kept for a whole year in the open air by making a pile of it on dry ground (the north side of a hill being preferable), in a conical form, of a considerable size, in winter during a hard frost, and covering it a foot thick with a layer of fagot-wood, then with a layer of straw, and lastly one of thatch. It sheuld be placed on elevated dry ground, and in a shaded place if possible.

CHAPTER V.

THEORY OF NUTRITION.

PREVALENT ERRORS.—Medical writings are full of errors, and the public mind is full of whims concerning the nature, properties, and nutritive virtues of nearly all the substances employed as food. Much of the confusion that prevails on the subject is attributable to a loose and indefinite use of words; and not a little of the error extant is owing to false views of the nature of the nutritive function itself.

For example, the term *stimulus*, or *stimulating*, is often used in different senses, and not unfrequently without any sense at all. Thus, physicians are in the habit of saying to cold, pale, thin, and debilitated patients, for whom some other doctor has recommended a vegetarian diet, that they require a "more stimulating diet," meaning, of course, flesh-meat. And I have heard more than one doctor of the "old school" call "flesh, fish, and fowl" *tonic* or *high* diet, in contradistinction to vegetable food, which they termed *reducing* or *low* diet.

The phrase "high living" is in common parlance applied to the habit of eating so gluttonously of unhealthful dishes as to cause the whole body to become a bloated mass of disease; or else an attenuated wreck of a prematurely worn-out organism—as though it were decidedly vulgar to eat plain, wholesome food and be well. Those who become sick and dyspeptic on concentrated aliments, butter biscuits, and short cakes, plum puddings, and "knic-knacs" innumerable, are said to suffer from the effects of "too good living"—as though healthful living was actually *bad!* Many physiological writers tell us that the reason greasy dishes, gravies, etc., are so obnoxious to the digestive organs is, because they are "too rich" in carbon; as though food which had exactly the right proportion of carbon for wholesome nutriment must necessarily be *poor!* And we not uncommonly meet with a poor, wretched invalid, who has suffered through half a lifetime, more of infirmity and misery than could be related in a month—all attributable to improper dietetic habits—who, on being told that the adoption and rigid persistence in a plain vegetable dietary will in a few years restore him or her to comparative health and usefulness, and very materially prolong the period of existence, replies with solemn, yet almost ludicrous gravity, "I had rather live a little *better*, and not quite so long."

If such expressions do not mislead those who hear them, they do certainly indicate any thing but clearness and precision in the minds of those who employ them ; for no person who entertains definite and correct ideas of the relations of food to health, could ever talk in this nonsensical manner.

DEFINITION OF NUTRITION.—Pure and perfect nutrition implies the assimilation of nutrient material to the structures of the body, without the least excitement, disturbance, or impression of any kind that can properly be called stimulating. All stimulus, therefore, is directly opposed to healthful nutrition, and a source of useless expenditure or waste of vital power.

Different substances taken into the stomach with food, or as food, may excite preternatural actions or commotions—arouse vital resistance—but such effects are no parts of their nutritive operations or qualities. Stimulus has no applicability to food ; it applies only to foreign substances, as drugs, medicines, and other poisons. Brandy applied to a feeble stomach, or the lash applied to a jaded horse, is a good illustration of a stimulant operation. Each induces action without affording material whereby to sustain that action. Rest and *pure aliment* are the only true restoratives in either case; and to neither of these can attach the idea of that preternatural turbulence of the organism which denotes the operation of a stimulus.

The Digestive Function—View of the Abdominal Viscera.

Fig. 82.

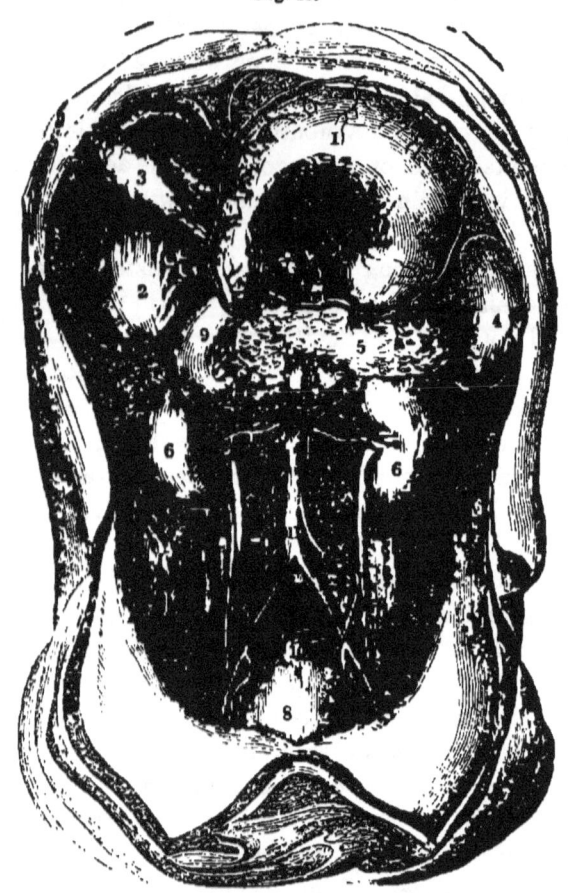

ABDOMINAL VISCERA.

DIGESTION.—Fig. 82 is a general view of the viscera of the abdomen. 1. The stomach raised. 2. Under surface of the liver. 3. The gall bladder. 4. The spleen or melt. 5. The pancreas or sweet-bread. 6. The kidneys. 7. The ureters. 8. the urinary bladder. 9. A portion of the intestine called duodenum. 10. A portion of the lower intestine called rectum. 11. The aorta.

Time of Digestion—Beaumont's Experiments—Digestive Processes.

It is a common error that such articles of food as are soonest dissolved in the stomach are most easily digested. It is well known that tainted meat, or that which has become putrescent by decomposition will "pass along" through the stomach and be resolved into a chymous mass sooner than will fresh meat, or even the best of bread. But it would hardly comport with common sense to call such half-rotted flesh most wholesome or most digestible on that account.

Digestion is a complex function, beginning with mastication and ending with assimilation; and those aliments which best secure the due exercise of all the functions subservient to nutrition, and in the end supply the organism with the best material, are, physiologically, the easiest to be digested.

Much stress has been laid by all late writers on digestion and cookery on the experiments of Dr. Beaumont, who introduced into the stomach of Alexis St. Martan—the stomach having been perforated by a gun-shot wound—nearly a hundred different alimentary substances with a view of ascertaining their "mean time of chymification." I do not regard those experiments as of any scientific importance, beyond that of affording another illustration of principles which can be as well demonstrated without the experiments, viz., that alcoholic stimulants, spices, etc., retard digestion by inflaming the coats of the stomach. As already intimated, it matters not whether a given aliment digests or dissolves in one hour or six, so far as its nutritive value is concerned. This must be determined in some other way.

SUMMARY OF THE DIGESTIVE PROCESSES.—The phenomena of nutrition comprehend the following processes, and in the order named: The food, when solid, is first reduced to fine particles by the teeth and other masticatory organs, at the same time mixed with the solvent fluid secreted by the salivary glands. It then passes into the stomach, where it receives another solvent—the gastric juice, and is subjected to a kind

Changes of the Nutrient Material—Insalivation.

of churning motion by the action of the muscular fibers or coats of the stomach. When it becomes reduced to a homogeneous mass (chyme), it passes into the first intestine—the duodenum. There it receives still another solvent—the pancreatic juice, which completes its solution. Its nutrient portion (chyle) is taken up by the lacteal absorbents, carried through a set of glands (mesenteric) which further elaborate it; it is next passed on to the lungs, where it is vitalized by contact with atmospheric oxygen; thence it passes through the heart and arteries into the fine hair-like structure of vessels (capillaries), where the last process of digestion is performed, and the material of food finally fitted for becoming a part of each organ and structure of the body. Its assimilation with, or adhesion to, the living tissue completes the complex function of nutrition.

But as the philosophy of this subject ought to be understood by every mother and every cook—and every mother ought to be a cook—a few illustrations will be worth the space they will occupy.

INSALIVATION.—No part of the digestive process is more important, and none is, by the great mass of people, so little appreciated, as that of insalivation. In order that every part and particle of our food may be thoroughly mixed with the saliva, nature has provided six distinct glands, three on each side of the jaw, whose office is to secrete the salivary fluid.

The presence of food in the mouth excites the salivary glands to action, and the act of mastication further provokes the flow of saliva. Thus, without some portions of our food being of a solid consistence so as to secure thorough mastication, it can not be properly mixed with the saliva.

It has been noticed that herbivorous animals have a much more copious secretion of saliva than the carnivorous; and it is true, also, that vegetarians of the human species have this secretion more abundant than those who partake of a mixed diet. Spices, condiments, salt, vinegar, etc., tend to check the

Theory of Nutrition. 123

Morbid Salivary Secretion—The Salivary Glands.

secretion by producing an inflammatory condition. Those who defile their mouths with tobacco juice or smoke often have a morbid running or driveling from the mouth, not of true saliva, however, but of a depraved and acrid secretion analogous to a "running at the nose" in the case of "catarrh of the head," and other morbid affections of the mucous membrane.

Fig. 83.

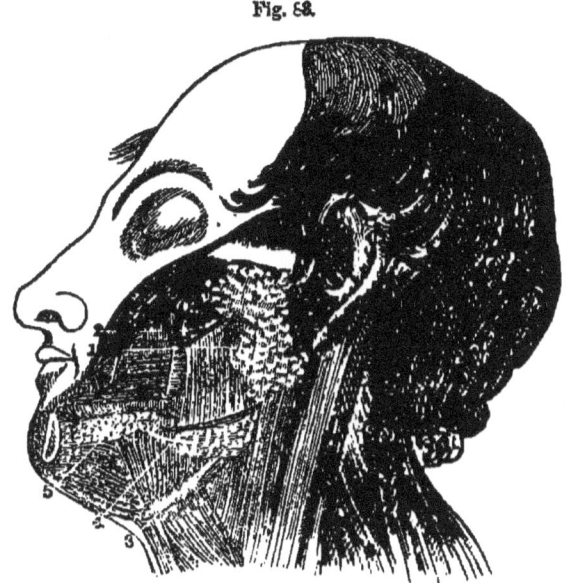

THE SALIVARY GLANDS.

In Fig. 83 are seen all the glands of one side, in their proper situation. 1. The parotid gland. 2. Its duct. 3. The submaxillary gland. 4. Its duct. 5. The sublingual gland.

MASTICATION.—A glance at the anatomical structure of the teeth is alone sufficient to impress the close observer of the teachings of natural history with the importance of "eating slowly and chewing deliberately."

Fig. 84 exhibits a lateral view of all the teeth, *in situ*. The front incisor, or cutting teeth, are sharp on the edges, for the

Fig. 84.

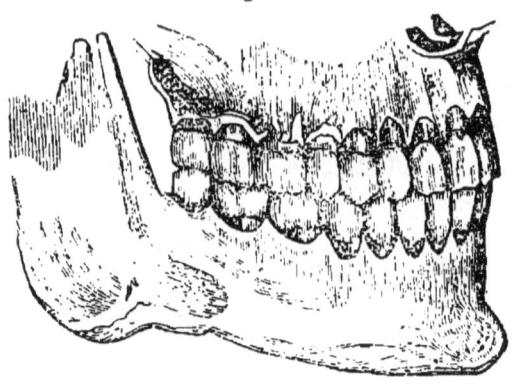

ARRANGEMENT OF THE TEETH.

purpose of cutting or dividing the food into smaller portions; the cuspid, or eye-tooth, which projects a very little beyond the others, grasps more firmly the alimentary substance; the bicuspid come next, having two prominences on their points, to break the alimentary substances into still finer particles; and, lastly, the molars, or grinders, with four or five prominences and depressions each, to reduce and comminute the food to a homogeneal and pulpy mass.

DEGLUTITION.—Fig. 85 is a view of the mouth, showing particularly the soft palate, tonsils, and tongue. 1. Anterior arch of the soft palate. 2. Posterior arch. 3. Tonsils. 4. Uvula. 5. Communication between the mouth and pharynx. 6. The tongue. 7. Anterior or nervous papillæ. 8. and 9. Upper and lower turbinated bones dividing the nostrils into (10) chambers.

The soft palate is composed of muscular fibers inclosed in the mucous membrane of the mouth, and forms a movable partition, suspended, transversely, from the posterior part of the bony arch of the palate. No less than ten distinct muscles enter into the formation of the soft palate, which are so disposed as to render it capable of descending and applying itself

Explanation of the Physiology of Deglutition.

against the tongue, so as completely to close the passage between the mouth and pharynx; and also of ascending obliquely backward toward the posterior head of the pharynx, so as to close up completely the passage between the pharynx and the nose; thus performing the part of a double valve. The conical-shaped uvula hangs pendulous from the center of the soft palate. It assists in completing the valve formed by the soft palate and also in modulating the voice. When destroyed by disease, therefore, both the deglutition of food and the sound of the voice are rendered more or less imperfect.

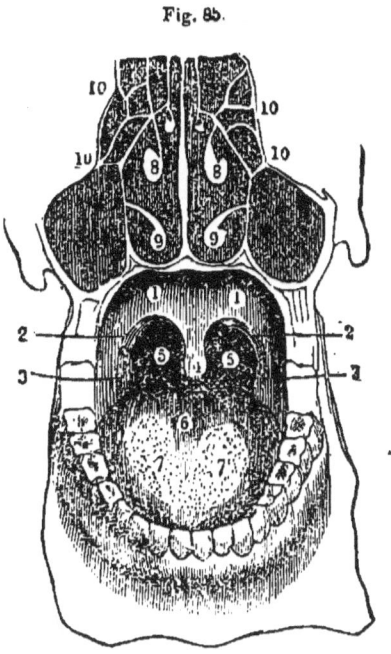

Fig. 8b.

ORGANS OF DEGLUTITION.

Every time the act of deglutition is performed, the openings to the windpipe and to the nose are closed, so that during this operation all access of air to the lungs is stopped, consequently it is necessary that the passage of the food through the pharynx should be rapid. Mastication, a voluntary process, may be performed slowly or rapidly, perfectly or imperfectly, without serious mischief; but life depends on the passage of the food through the pharynx with extreme rapidity and with the nicest precision. It is therefore taken out of the province of volition and entrusted to organs which belong to the organic life, organs which carry on their operations with the steadiness, constancy, and exactness of bodies whose motions are determined by a physical law.

Organs and Parts within and around the Mouth.

Fig. 86.

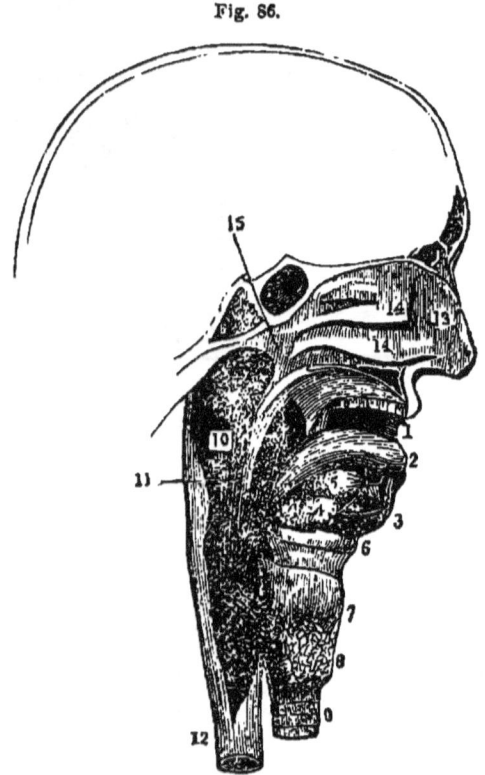

SIDE VIEW OF THE MOUTH.

Fig. 86 is a side view of the mouth, pharynx, nose, etc. 1 Mouth. 2. Tongue. 3. Section of the lower jaw. 4. Submaxillary gland. 5. Sublingual gland. 6. Hyoid bone. 7. Thyroid cartilage. 8. Thyroid gland. 9. Trachea. 10. Interior of the pharynx. 11. Section of the soft palate. 12. The Esophagus. 13. Interior of the nose. 14. The two spongy bones dividing it into three chambers. 15. The posterior communication with the upper part of the pharynx.

The tonsils, which co-operate with the other glandular structures of the mouth in secreting solvent and lucubrating fluids, are inclosed between two layers, produced by the separation of the lateral edges of the soft palate. They are seen in fig. 87, which is a posterior view of the nose, mouth, pharynx, and larynx. 1. Posterior openings of the nose, communicating with the upper part of the pharynx. 2. Posterior surface of the soft palate. 3. Uvula. 4. Back part of the mouth communicating with the pharynx. 5. The tonsils. 6. Back part or root of the tongue. 7. Posterior surface of the epiglottis. 8. The larynx. 9. Opening of the larynx into the pharynx. 10. Cut edges of the pharynx. 11. Esophagus, the continuation of the pharynx. 12. Trachea, the continuation of the larynx. 13. Muscles acting on the pharynx.

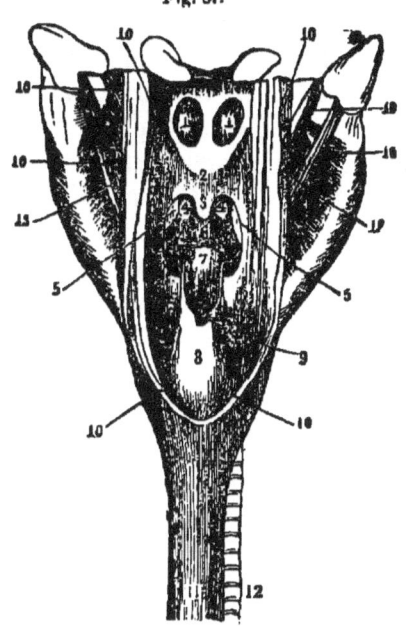

Fig. 87.

THE MOUTH POSTERIORLY.

The tongue is composed of six distinct muscles, the fibers of which are so interwoven as to form an intricate network, and afford a variety and rapidity of motion almost inconceivable; many of which are necessary to bring the food under the operation of the grinding teeth, and to urge it, when properly prepared, into the esophagus, on its way to the stomach. The advantages of pure instincts and unperverted senses in developing the gustatory properties of aliments instead of pepper, salt, and vinegar, are well indicated in the following extract from a late English work (*Philosophy of Health*) by Dr. Southwood Smith:

Sensation and Volition—Mastication—Taste and Smell.

"It is deeply interesting to observe the part performed in these operations by sensation and volition, and the boundary at which their influence terminates and consciousness itself is lost. Mastication, a voluntary operation, carried on by voluntary muscles, at the command of the will, is attended with consciousness, always in the state of health of a pleasurable nature. To communicate this consciousness, the tongue, the palate, the lips, the cheeks, the soft palate, and even the pharynx, are supplied with a prodigious number of sentient nerves. The tongue especially, one of the most active agents in the operation, is supplied with no less than six nerves derived from three different sources. These nerves, spread out upon this organ, give to its upper surface, a complete covering, and some of them terminate in sentient extremities visible to the naked eye. These sentient extremities, with which every point of the upper surface but more especially the apex, is studded, constitute the bodies termed papillæ, the immediate and special seat of the sense of taste. This sense is also diffused, though in a less exquisite degree, over the whole internal surface of the mouth. Close to the sense of taste is placed the seat of the kindred sense of smell. The business of both these senses is with the qualities of the food. Mastication at once brings out the qualities of the food, and puts the food in contact with the organs that are to take cognizance of it. Mastication, a rough operation, capable of being accomplished only by powerful instruments which act with force, is carried on in the very same spot with sensation, an exquisitely delicate operation, having its seat in soft and tender structures, with which the appropriate objects are brought into contact only with the gentlest impulse. The agents of the coarse and the delicate, the forcible and the gentle operations are in close contact, yet they work together, not only without obstruction, but with the most perfect subserviency and co-operation.

"The movements of mastication are produced, and, until they

Pleasure in Eating Essential to Perfect Digestion.

have accomplished the objects of the operation, are repeated by successive acts of volition. To induce these acts, grateful sensations are excited by the contact of the food with the sentient nerves so liberally distributed over almost the whole of the apparatus. To the provision thus made for the production of pleasurable sensation, is superadded the necessity of direct and constant attention to the pleasure included in the gratification of the taste. It is justly observed by Dr. A. Combe, that without some degree of attention to the process of eating, and some distinct perception of its gratefulness, the food can not be duly digested. When the mind is so absorbed as to be wholly unconscious of it, or even indifferent to it, the food is swallowed without mastication; then it lies in the stomach for hours together without being acted upon by the gastric juice, and if this be done often, the stomach becomes so much disordered as to lose its power of digestion, and death is the inevitable result: so that not only is pleasurable sensation annexed to the reception of food, but the direct and continuous consciousness of that pleasurable sensation during the act of eating is made one of the conditions of the due performance of the digestive function."

CHYMIFICATION.—The stomach is a muscular bag, of an irregular oval shape, placed transversely across the upper part of the abdomen, and capable, in the adult, of holding about three pints. The arrangement of its fibres is exhibited in fig. 88. 1. The esophagus, termi-

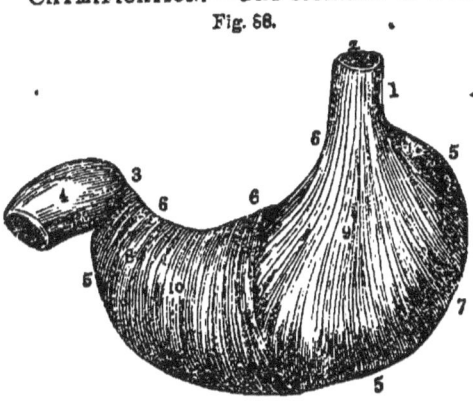

Fig. 88.

MUSCULAR COATS OF THE STOMACH.

ating in the stomach. 2. The cardiac orifice. 3. The pylorus. 4. Commencement of the duodenum. 5. The large curvature of the stomach. 6. The small curvature. 7. Its large extremity. 8. Its small extremity. 9. Its longitudinal muscular fibers. 10. Its circular muscular fibers.

The contraction of the longitudinal fibers diminishes the length, and that of the circular fibers the diameter of the tube; hence the food, acted upon by both sets of muscular fibers is turned, squeezed, and compressed, during digestion, in various directions.

The esophagus opens into the left extremity of the stomach obliquely, by an aperture called the *cardiac orifice;* and at the right extremity the stomach opens into the duodenum by a smaller aperture, called the *pyloric orifice*. Between these orifices are the two curvatures of the stomach, the one above called the smaller, and the lower on the larger curvature. The

Fig. 89.

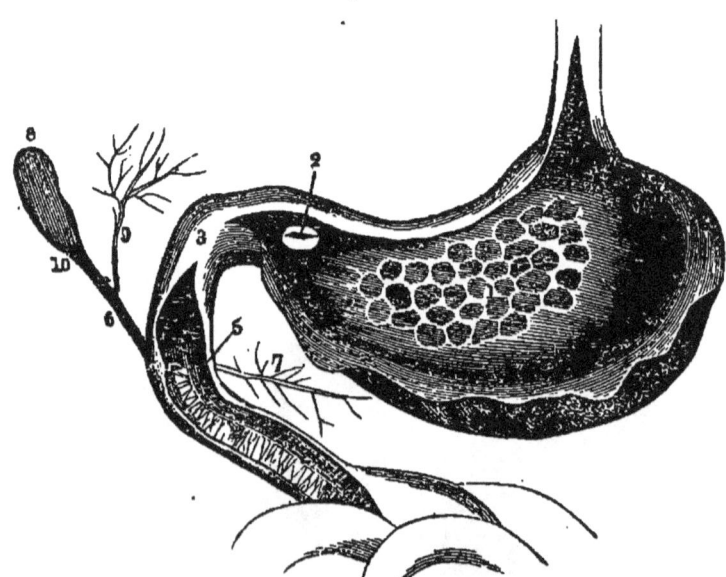

INTERIOR OF THE STOMACH AND DUODENUM.

inner or mucous coat of the stomach is lined with minute bodies called *villi*, which gives its whole surface a velvety appearance. This mucous coat is also plaited into numerous folds, termed *rugæ*, whose object is to enlarge the space for blood-vessels and nerves; and immediately beneath the mucous coat are the follicles that secrete the mucous fluid which lubricates and defends its internal surface.

Fig. 89 shows the internal surface of the stomach and duodenum, and also the entrance of the bile duct from the liver into the alimentary tube. 1. Mucous membrane, forming the rugæ. 2. Pyloric orifice, opening into the duodenum. 3. Duodenum. 4. Interior of the duodenum, showing the valvulæ conniventes. 5. Termination of the bile duct. 6. The common biliary duct from the gall-bladder and liver. 7. Pancreatic duct, terminating at the same point as the bile duct. 8. Gall-bladder, removed from the liver. 9. Hepatic duct, proceeding from the liver. 10. Cystic duct, proceeding from the gall-bladder.

The gastric juice, which is sometimes called the digestive fluid, from its possessing stronger solvent properties than any other of the fluids concerned in digestion, is probably secreted by the minute extremities or arteries which are expanded upon the villi of the mucous coat.

A thick, strong, circular muscle surrounds the pyloric orifice, presenting the appearance of a prominent and even projecting band. This muscular band is the *pylorus*, while the aperture itself is the pyloric orifice. The office of the pylorus is to guard the opening out of the stomach, and prevent the passage of aliment until it has been sufficiently acted upon by the gastric juice and the motions of the stomach.

The importance attached to the nutritive function by the Great Architect of the vital machinery, and its complexity of character, is well indicated in fig. 90, representing the vascular connection between the stomach, liver, spleen, and pancreas. 1. The stomach raised to exhibit its posterior surface.

Vascular Connections of the Stomach—Its Nerves.

Fig. 90.

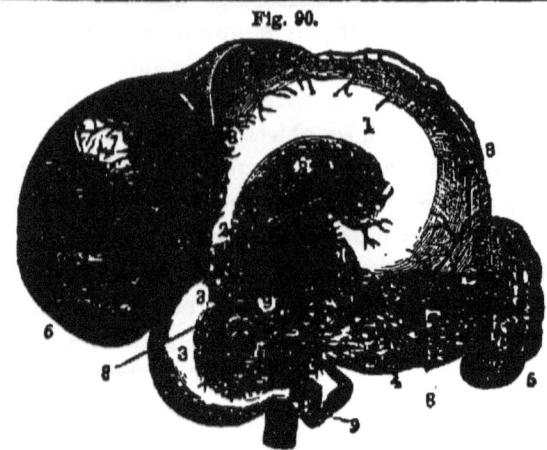

VASCULAR CONNECTIONS OF THE STOMACH.

2. Pylorus. 3. Duodenum. 4. Pancreas. 5. Spleen. 6. Under surface of the liver. 7. Gall-bladder, in connection with the liver. 8. Large vessels proceeding from a common trunk (9), to supply all the above viscera.

The stomach is plentifully supplied with arterial blood, the quantity sent to it being greater than that supplied to any other organ except the brain.

The vessels of the stomach (fig. 91) form two distinct layers, the external of which is distributed to the muscular and peritoneal coats, and the internal to the villi of the mucous coat.

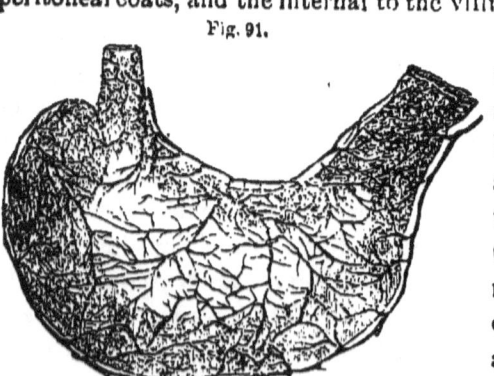

Fig. 91.

BLOOD-VESSELS OF THE STOMACH.

The supply of nerves to the stomach is also abundant, both of the organic and sentient systems. Upon the arteries, the organic nerves are spread out in such numbers as to envelop them completely, forming, as it were, a coat of nervous plexuses. This arrangement is shown in fig. 92. 1. Under surface of the liver, turned up

Fig. 92.

ORGANIC NERVES OF THE STOMACH.

to bring into view tne anterior surface of the stomach. 2. Gall-bla der. 3. Organic nerves enveloping the trunks of the blood-vessels. 4. Pyloric extremity of the stomach and commencement of the duodenum. 5. Contracted portion of the pylorus. 6. Situation of the hour-glass contraction of the stomach. 7. Omentum

Arrangement of Food in the Stomach—Remarkable Change.

In consequence of these organic nerves the stomach is placed, to a great extent, beyond the reach of volition, and enabled, in a state of health, to perform its functions without mental consciousness. Yet their connection with the sentient nerves enables us to experience pleasure when its functions are duly and healthfully performed, and causes us to suffer pain when its office is deranged or disordered. How much distress, and what variety of anguish, a morbid condition of the stomach induces, the victim of dyspepsia only can feel and know.

By the learned and celebrated Mr. Hunter the stomach was termed the "center of sympathies." The appellation is emphatically correct, as relates either to its sound or its morbid conditions.

Says Dr. Southwood Smith:

"The food, on reaching the stomach, does not occupy indifferently any portion of it, but is arranged in a peculiar manner always in one and the same part. If the stomach be observed in a living animal, or be inspected soon after death, it is seen that about a third of its length toward the pylorus is divided from the rest by the contraction of the circular fibers called the hour-glass contraction (fig. 92, C). The stomach is thus divided into a cardiac and a pyloric portion (fig. 92, 6). The food, when first received by the stomach, is always deposited in the cardiac portion, and is there arranged in a definite manner. The food first taken is placed outermost, that is, nearest the surface of the stomach; the portion next taken is placed interior to the first, and so on in succession, until the food last taken occupies the center of the mass. When new food is received before the old is completely digested, the two kinds are kept distinct, the new being always found in the center of the old.

"Soon after the food has been thus arranged, a remarkable change takes place in the mucous membrane of the stomach. The blood-vessels become loaded with blood; its villi enlarge, and its cryptæ, the minute cells between the rugæ, overflow with fluid. This fluid is the gastric juice, which is secreted by the arterial capillaries now turgid with blood. The abundance of the secretion, which progressively increases as the digestion advances, is in proportion to the indigestibility of the food, and the quietude of the body after the repast.

In the food itself no change is manifest for some time; but at length that portion of it which is in immediate contact with the surface of the stomach begins to be slightly softened. This softening slowly but progressively increases until the texture of the food, whatever it may have been, is gradually lost; and ultimately the most solid portions of it are completely dissolved.

"When a portion of food thus acted on is examined, it presents the appearance of having been corroded by a chemical agent. The white of a hard-boiled egg looks exactly as if it had been plunged in vinegar or in a solution of potass. The softened layer, as soon as the softening is sufficiently advanced, is, by the action of the muscular coat of the stomach, detached, carried toward the pylorus, and ultimately transmitted to the duodenum; then another portion of the harder and undigested food is brought into immediate contact with the stomach, becomes softened in its turn, and is in like manner detached; and this process goes on until the whole is dissolved.

"The solvent power exerted by the gastric juice is most apparent when the stomach of an animal is examined three or four hours after food has been freely taken. At this period the portion of the food first in contact with the stomach is wholly dissolved and detached; the portion subsequently brought into contact with the stomach is in the process of solution, while the central part remains very little changed.

"The dissolved and detached portion of the food, from every part of the stomach flows slowly but steadily beyond the hourglass contraction, or toward the pyloric extremity, in which not a particle of recent or undissolved food is ever allowed to remain. The fluid, which thus accumulates in this portion of

Action of the Duodenum—The Stomach during Chymification.

the stomach, is a new product, in which the sensible properties of the food, whatever may have been the variety of substances taken at the meal, are lost. This new product, which is termed chyme, is an homogeneous fluid, pultaceous, grayish, insipid, of a faint sweetish taste, and slightly acid..

"As soon as the chyme, by its gradual accumulation in the pyloric extremity amounts to about two or three ounces, the following phenomena take place.

"First, the intestine called duodenum, the organ immediately continuous with the stomach, contracts. The contraction of the duodenum is propagated to the pyloric end of the stomach. By the contraction of this portion of the stomach, the chyme is carried backward from the pyloric into the cardiac extremity, where it does not remain, but quickly flows back again into the pyloric extremity, which is now expanded to receive it. Soon the pyloric extremity begins again to contract; but now the contraction, the reverse of the former, is in the direction of the duodenum; in consequence of which the chyme is propelled toward the pylorus. The pylorus, obedient to the demand of the chyme, relaxes, opens, and affords to the fluid a free passage into the duodenum. As soon as the whole of the duly prepared chyme has passed out of the stomach, the pylorus closes, and remains closed, until two or three ounces more are accumulated, when the same succession of motions are renewed with the same result; and again cease to be again renewed, as long as the process of chymification goes on.

"When the stomach contains a large quantity of food, these motions are limited to the parts of the organ nearest the pylorus; as it becomes empty, they extend farther along the stomach, until the great extremity itself is involved in them. These motions are always strongest toward the end of chymification.

"The stomach during chymification is a closed chamber; its cardiac orifice is shut by the valved entrance of the esopha gus, and its pyloric orifice by the contraction of the pylorus.

"The rapidity with which the process of chymification is carried on is different according to the digestibility of the food, the bulk of the morsels swallowed, the quantity received by the stomach, the constitution of the individual, the state of the health, and, above all, the class of the animal, for it is widely different in different classes. In the human stomach, in about five hours after an ordinary meal, the whole of the food is probably converted into chyme."

The office which the bile performs in relation to the digestive function, has long been a controverted point. My own opinion is, that bile is wholly an excrementitious substance, although in the process of expulsion it may act as a chemical solvent of fatty matters, which are taken into the stomach with our food, or as a part of it; and may also serve as an antiseptic to other effete matters which pass off by the bowels. Brodie and Mayo, of England, Tiedeman and Gmelin, of Germany, and Leuret and Lassaigne, of France, have each and all satisfied themselves by experiment that the bile is some way recrementitious, and that its presence is necessary to separate the chyle from the chyme in the first intestines. They cut open the abdomen of animals, tied the common gall-duct, then fed the animals as usual, and on killing them some time after, and examining their bodies, found precisely what might have been expected—no chyle in the intestines or lacteals. But my explanation is somewhat different from theirs. In my judgment, the local inflammation and general fever consequent on the injury were sufficient to interrupt the process of digestion, and prevent the due formation of chyle, just as fevers and inflammations do when arising from a variety of other causes.

Nor can I regard the bile, in any degree, as the natural "stimulus" to the peristaltic action of the bowels; nor can I assent to the common doctrine that a deficency of bile is a cause of constipation; for I have known many diarrheas cease the moment a free secretion of bile was poured into the alimentary canal.

That the bile is wholly excrementitious is further corroborated by the fact that the stomach will not tolerate its presence for a moment. When, in a morbid condition of the digestive organs, or by a retroverted action of the duodenum, it is pushed upward into the stomach, violent distress, nausea, retching, vomiting, general trembling, etc., evince its noxious properties.

There is no secretion in the whole system more generally deficient in civilized society than that of the liver; no topic connected with fashionable ill-health is more talked about than biliousness; and nearly all this trouble, it should be known, comes from bad ways of cooking and eating.

The pancreatic juice, secreted by the pancreas, is analogous to the saliva. It enters the duodenum at the same point as the bile does; and no doubt completes the perfect solution of the alimentary matter.

It should be mentioned, also, that the duodenum secretes a fluid similar to, if not identical with, the gastric juice; and, indeed, some physiologists affirm that the solvent property of the duodenal secretion is equal to that of the gastric juice.

CHYLIFICATION.—The intestinal tube is divided anatomically into the *small* and the *large* intestines. The small intestines, taken together, are about four times the length of the body, and are subdivided into the duodenum, jejunum, and ileum.

The large intestines are subdivided into the cæcum, colon, and rectum. Fig. 93 is a view of the whole alimentary canal. 1. Esophagus. 2. Stomach. 3. Liver raised, showing the under surface. 4. Duodenum. 5. Small intestines, consisting of—6. Jejunum and ileum. 7. Colon. 8. Urinary bladder. 9. Gall-bladder. 10. Abdominal muscles divided and reflected.

THEORY OF NUTRITION. 139

Second, Third, and Fourth Stomachs—Separation of Chyle.

Fig. 98.

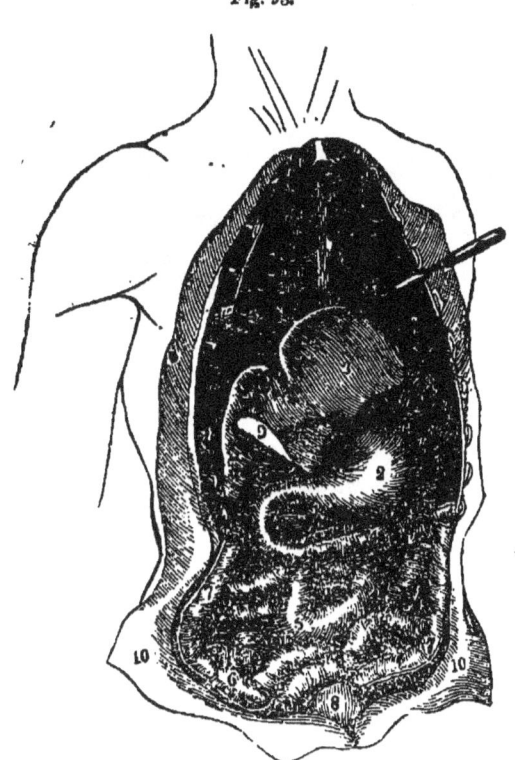

ALIMENTARY CANAL.

In a strict physiological sense the duodenum may be regarded as a second stomach, and the jejunum as a third; and we should scarcely trench on the field of imagination if we called the ileum a fourth; for through the whole length of the small intestines the process of digestion really goes on, a solvent fluid being secreted along their whole inner surface, though most copiously toward the stomach; while lacteal vessels, or chyle-carriers, open their mouths upon every portion of their mucous coat, though most abundantly toward the stomach.

In the duodenum the separation of chyle commences, and

in the jejunum we find an admirable arrangement for retaining the chyle, that time may be allowed for the lacteals to take it up.

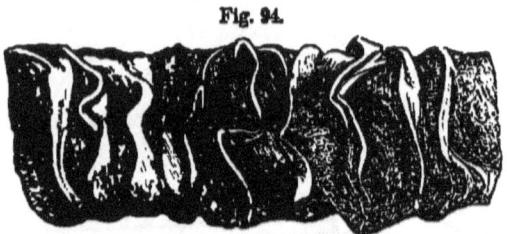

INTERNAL VIEW OF THE JEJUNUM.

Fig. 94 is an internal view of a portion of the jejunum, showing the arrangement of the mucous folds into valvulæ conniventes—valves which retard or moderate the progress of the chylous fluid without arresting its course. The chyle in its downward course along the small intestines gradually disappears, until at the termination of the ileum scarcely any portion of it can be detached.

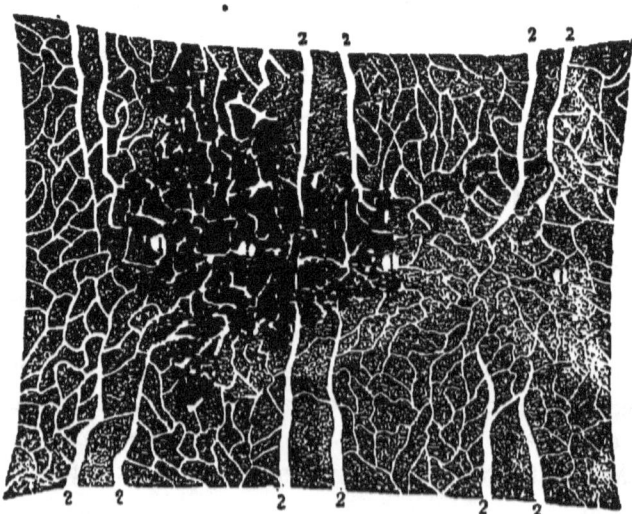

INNER SURFACE OF THE ILEUM.

THEORY OF NUTRITION. 141

Arrangement and Course of the Lacteals.

When the mucous coat of the small intestines is examined several hours after a meal, the lacteal vessels are seen turgid with chyle, and covering its entire surface, as represented in fig. 95. 1. Smaller branches of the lacteals. 2. Larger branches, formed by the union of the smaller.

These vessels, which are so numerous, and of such magnitude as to sometimes almost conceal the ramifications of the blood-vessels, anastomose freely with each other, forming a network, from the meshes of which proceed branches, which, successively uniting, form larger and still larger trunks; and these, perforating the mucous coat, pass for some distance between the mucous and muscular coats, finally perforating both coats, and passing to the outside of the intestine, and, with it, are included between the layers of the mesentery, as

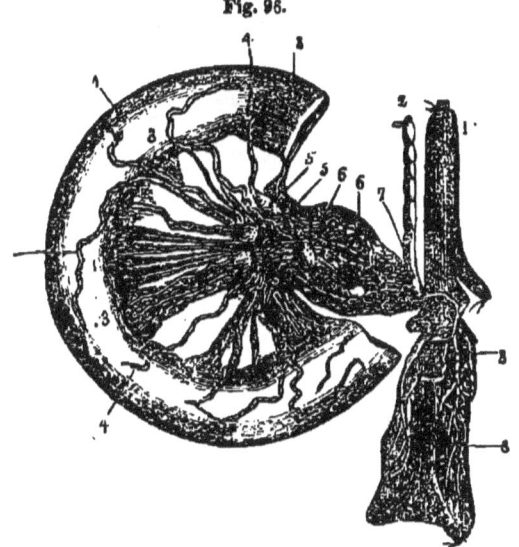

Fig. 96.

COURSE OF THE LACTEALS.

seen in fig. 96. 1. The aorta. 2. Thoracic duct. 3. External surface of a portion of small intestine. 4. Lacteals appearing on the external surface of the intestine after having

142   HYDROPATHIC COOK-BOOK.

Mesenteric Glands—View of the whole Lacteal System.

perforated all of its coats. 5. Mesenteric glands of the first order. 6. Mesenteric glands of the second order. 7. Receptacle for the chyle. 8. Lymphatic vessels terminating in the receptacle of the chyle, or commencement of the thoracic duct.

Within the fold of the mesentery all the different sets of lacteals converge and unite, forming a complicated plexus of vessels, from which the lacteals radiate and advance forward

Fig. 97.

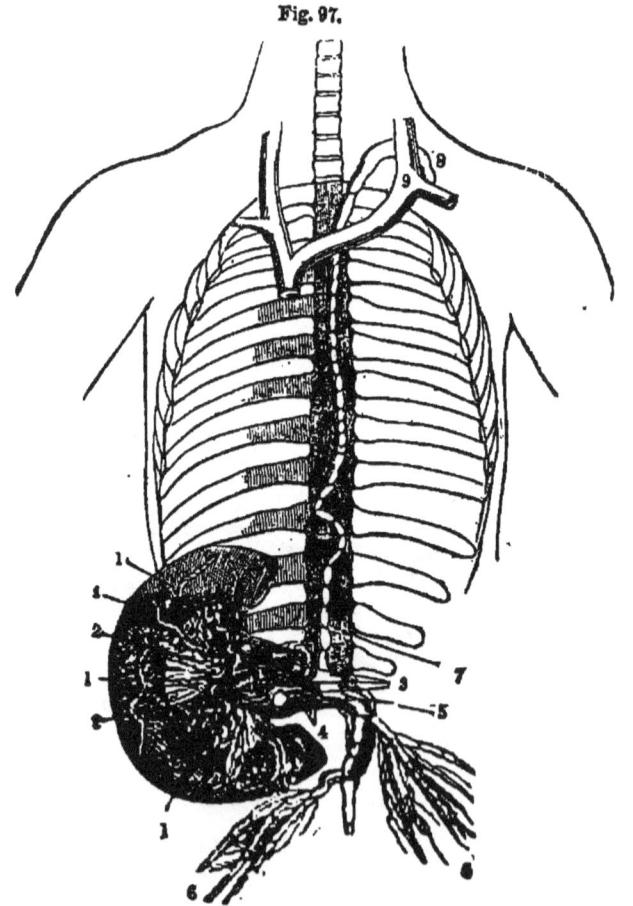

LACTEAL SYSTEM.

The Entire Lacteal System—Receptacle of the Chyle—Defecation.

to the mesenteric glands. These glands are small, rounded, oval, pale-colored bodies, consisting of two sets, arranged in a double row, the set nearest the intestine being the smallest.

Fig. 97 is a view of the entire lacteal system, or the thoracic duct, from its origin to its termination. 1. Lacteal vessels emerging from the mucous surface of the intestines. 2. First order of mesenteric glands. 3. Second order of mesenterio glands. 4. The great trunks of the lacteals emerging from the mesenteric glands and pouring their contents into—5. The receptacle of the chyle. 6. The great trunks of the lymphatic, or general absorbent system, terminating in the receptacle of the chyle. 7. Thoracic duct. 8. Termination of the thoracic duct at—9. The angle formed by the union of the internal jugular vein with the left subclavian vein.

In the first series of glands the lacteals intercommunicate so freely that the glands themselves appear to consist of a congeries of convoluted lacteals. Proceeding onward to the second set, they are there again convoluted in a similar manner; and after passing from thence the lacteals unite into larger and larger branches successively, until they finally form two or three trunks which terminate in the small oval sac called *receptaculum chyli*—in it also terminate the absorbent vessels called *lymphatics*, which bring back to the circulation waste and superfluous matters taken up from every tissue and organ of the body. The chyle and lymph are, therefore, both poured into the venous blood just as it is about entering the right side of the heart, to be immediately transmitted to the lungs for arterialization and purification.

DEFECATION.—In the large intestines is performed the process of *fæcation*—the secretion from the blood of effete matter, and the expulsion of the waste or innutritious portion of the aliment.

The abdominal portion of the digestive organs, with the divisions of the large intestines, are seen in fig. 98. 1. Eso-

Fecal Accumulations—Constipating Food—Large Intestines.

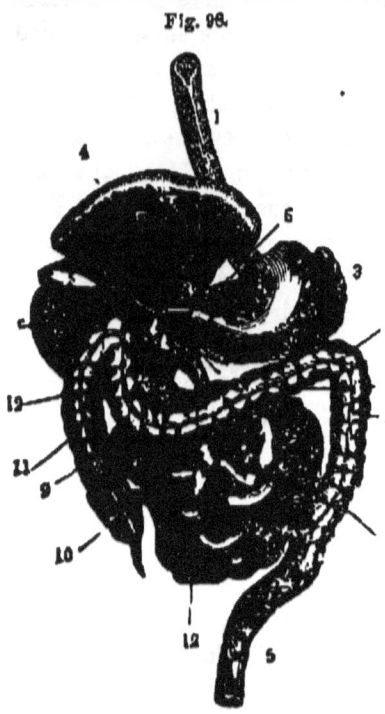

Fig. 96.

DIGESTIVE APPARATUS.

phagus. 2. Stomach. 3. Spleen. 4. Liver. 5. Gall bladder, with its ducts. 6. Pancreas, with its duct. 7. Duodenum. 8. Small intestines. 9. Large intestines, dividing into—10. Cæcum. 11. Ascending colon. 12. Arch of the colon. 13. Descending colon. 14. Sigmoid flexure of the colon, here very imperfectly represented. 15. Rectum.

The question has been lately discussed in the medical world, whether the feces are a secretion from the blood, or the indigestible portions of the food taken into the stomach. In my opinion they are both; the proportions of each varying as the food is more or less nutritive or concentrated.

Fecal accumulations in the large bowels, particularly in the cells of the colon, inducing ulcerations, abscesses, piles, fistulas, concretions, worms, cholera, bilious cholic, dysentery, etc., are very common with those who use constipating food, of which superfine flour is the chief article. I have never known any of these complaints, worth mentioning, in persons whose diet has uniformly been unbolted farinaceous preparations, with the free use of fruits and vegetables.

The large intestines are much shorter than the small, the cæcum being only from two to six, the colon about five, and the rectum about eight inches in length; and their mucous membrane is disposed into apartments or cells, by which the descent of the excrementitious matter is moderated and regulated.

Advice to Mothers—Errors of Medical Teachers—Strange Food.

The final dejection of the non-nutrient ingesta and feculent secretions is, like the prehension, mastication, and deglutition of food, attended with consciousness, and placed under control of the will; an arrangement indispensable to our comfort and convenience, as well as well-being.

PRACTICAL REFLECTIONS.—The intelligent mother who has made herself acquainted with the wonderful structures and elaborate functions by which alimentary matter is converted into the substance of our bodies, will be a thousand times more careful in selecting and preparing the food of her child than she will in choosing the materials and fashion of its clothing. The nature and character of the man or woman has a close relation to what the child was fed upon.

It is strange to me—passing strange—how medical philosophers, familiarly acquainted with the minutest anatomical structures, and profoundly learned in all their physiological relations to each other and to the external world, can talk *oracularly*, as they assume to do, of salt, vinegar, spices, tea, coffee, and even alcohol and tobacco, as necessary or useful condiments and stimulants. There is not "a shadow of a shade" of reason for their employment dietetically; and yet it is the prevailing doctrine of medical books that some of them at least are absolutely indispensable.

In the catalogue of articles comprising the "Industry of All Nations," now on exhibition at the Crystal Palace, under the head of "Substances Employed as Food," we find *chewing tobacco*, various brands of *cigars*, different kinds of *wines, spirituous liquors*, etc. I have no knowledge that a medico-dietetical professor classified the articles in that catalogue under their respective heads, but the real author, whether he is or is not a real doctor of dietetics, has made no greater blunder than ninety-nine hundredths of the medical profession are making every day in the year.

Many persons contend that animal food is more easily assimilated than vegetable, because those specimens of the human being who eat very freely of all sorts of animal foods often become very corpulent; and others argue that, because hogs and other animals can be fattened to an enormous bulk on a liberal supply of the flesh of other animals, that this is more nutritive than vegetable food. But the error arises from a misunderstanding of the true theory of nutrition.

Nutrition, let me say again, is the replenishment of the tissues, not the accumulation of fat or adipose matter in the cellular membrane. The latter is a disease, and a fattened animal, be it a hog or an alderman, is a diseased animal. A well-developed man or beast, of one hundred and fifty pounds weight, would not have an ounce more of real strength, of acting, moving, walking fiber—of bone, nerve, muscle, or sinew—if he or it should be fattened to the bulk of five hundred or a thousand pounds. Fat men, fat women, fat children, and fat pigs, are not examples of excessive nutrition so much as of deficient excretion. And the "Mammoth Pig" now lying on his bed of straw in the vicinity of the Crystal Palace, and groaning stertorously under the load of more than half a ton of dead, effete, adipose excrement, is far from being a specimen of either good looks or good health. Examples of human beings suffering in a similar condition are not rare, and the spectacle they exhibit teaches precisely the same lesson.

Various articles which are not only not alimentary in the least, but actually poisonous, as bitter herbs, aloes, cod-liver oil, arsenic, antimony, etc., are famous for fattening man and animals; and the explanation of this phenomenon has an important bearing, not only on the philosophy of diet, but on that of medication also.

When any of the drugs above indicated are taken into the stomach in what are called medicinal doses, that is, in quantities not so large as to cauterize, nor violently inflame, nor paralyze the organ, the vital instincts at once perceive or feel the injurious impression; they recognize the presence of an enemy,

Modus Operandi of Fattening Agents and Processes.

and the energies of the whole system are concentrated on the part attacked. In this way the digestive function may be for a time morbidly excited or preternaturally energized, at the expense, however, of all the other bodily functions. At the same time the depurating or excretory organs, being deprived of their due supply of nervous power or vital force, allow the excrementitious matters to accumulate; and thus, for a longer or shorter period, the person or creature may grow fatter, and at the same time deteriorate in general health.

If any further testimony is needed to establish the view of I have presented of nutrition, it may be derived from the well-known fact, that lean or thin persons are always more easily cured, either by natural or artificial methods, of the same fevers, inflammations, and of similar chronic diseases, than "fleshy" or fat people, and that thin persons will hold out longer when subjected to extreme cold, and endure longer when deprived of all food, than corpulent persons, as has been repeatedly observed in cases of shipwreck. In fact, excessive alimentation, or rather abnormal accumulation of adipose matter in the cellular tissue is a common and prolific source of infirmities and diseases.

CHAPTER VI.

BREAD AND BREAD-MAKING.

DIFFERENT KINDS OF BREAD.—Bread has been proverbially called the "staff of life;" and *good bread* has been truly regarded as the "perfection of cookery." That person or family who habitually eats good bread, ought never to complain much of indigestion; in fact, poor bread is one of the principal causes of the dyspepsia which prevails almost everywhere among the agricultural population of this country. Those who appreciate good health, and understand the relation of health to happiness, will bear with me if I dwell somewhat lengthily on this branch of our subject.

All breads may be divided into *domestic* bread and *baker's* bread. The principal difference is in the greater degree of fermentation to which the latter is subjected, and the alkaline matters which are generally employed by bakers to neutralize the acid created by excessive fermentation. Either kinds of bread may be *fermented*—rendered light by means of yeast; or *raised*—made light by means of acids and alkalies; or *unleavened*—baked without leaven or risings of any kind. Yeast is, however, in general use in breadmaking, very few bakers or private families making any other kind. It behooves, therefore, all bread-makers who employ a *ferment*, to understand the nature of fermentation.

THEORY OF FERMENTATION.—It may sound strangely to those who are accustomed to read and talk about good, sweet yeast, and beautifully light bread, to hear that fermentation itself is a *rotting process*, a decomposition, and hence destructive of certain proximate elements of the substance subjected to its influence. We may as well understand, therefore, at once, that no kind of bread can be fermented without being to some extent injured; and all breadmakers who employ yeast ought to know how to manage it so as to deteriorate the article as little as possible.

Fermentation is a process involving a series of chemical changes, by which the organic or proximate elements of vegetable substances

Different Stages of Fermentation—A common Error.

are reduced to their ultimate or chemical elements. Different stages of the process have received different appellations, as *panary, vinous, acetous,* and *putrefactive* fermentation.

Panary fermentation is the decomposition of the sugar or saccharine matter of the grain, and the recombination of its elements so as to produce alcohol and carbonic acid gas. *Vinous* fermentation is essentially the same thing, this term being applied to the decomposition of the saccharine matter of fruits. The alcohol produced in bread-making is mostly dissipated by the heat of the oven, the remainder evaporating within a few hours after it is taken from the oven; and the carbonic acid gas, being retained by the tenacious gluten, raises or puffs up the dough.

If the dough is not thoroughly kneaded, good bread can never be made. Why? If the yeast is not intimately and equally mixed with every particle of the meal or flour, the fermentation—the rotting, if you please—will be unequal, and some portions of the bread will be heavy and compact, while others will be light and spongy, and marked with open cavities.

But when yeast is well mixed, the dough must be allowed to raise sufficiently, or it will be raw and clammy; and yet if the fermentation is allowed to proceed too far, the starch and mucilage, as well as the sugar, are, to some extent, destroyed, and *acetous acid* or *vinegar* is formed, rendering the bread sour and disagreeable. This is the *acetous stage of fermentation.* •

But if the process of decomposition goes on still farther, the gluten is more or less destroyed, literally rotted, and *putrefactive fermentation* exists, rendering the bread exceedingly dry, harsh, and unpalatable, especially after it is twelve or twenty-four hours old.

These circumstances serve to show us that the proper management of yeast-bread requires not only careful attention, but also good judgment. A good bread-maker and bad housewife—I say nothing of *vice versa*—are, as might *à priori* be expected, seldom or never seen in the same person.

It is a common error to regard bread as not over-fermented, because it is not sensibly sour to the taste. Fermentation may be carried so far as to destroy the sweetness and richness of the loaf, and yet arrested by the heat of the oven just before any appreciable acid is developed. And it is precisely here that the great majority of domestic bread-makers fail. Bread is too generally pronounced good if it do not feel sticky and heavy on the one hand, nor taste sour on the other. But bread which is "very good" must, in addition to these negative qualities, possess the positive recommendation of being absolutely delicious to the senses of taste and smell.

GENERAL RULES FOR BREAD-MAKING.—1. Although a fair article of fermented bread can be baked in a common cook-stove or range, yet a brick oven is preferable. 2. The best ovens are constructed of an arch of brick, over which is a covering of ashes, and over this a covering of charcoal, with a finishing layer of bricks over all. This arrangement of non-conductors retains the heat so long, that cakes, pies, apples, custards, etc., can be baked after the bread. 3. The fire should always be made nearly on the back side of the oven. 4. A new oven should be heated at least half of the day previous to baking in it, and the lid kept closed after the fire is out until heated for baking. 5. The oven must be heated until all the bricks look red, and are free from all black spots; but not hot enough to burn flour *quickly* when sprinkled on the bottom. 6. Whenever bread looks porous and full of holes, it is ready for the oven. It will then exhale a brisk, pungent, lively, but not in the least degree acid, odor. 7. When bread becomes light enough before the oven is ready, it should be kneaded a little, and then kept in a cool place. 8. When removed from the oven it should be taken out of the pans or basins, and placed endwise in a cool, well-ventilated place. 9. When the dough has been properly kneaded, it should be covered with a napkin or light woolen blanket, and kept at about summer temperature, 60° Fahr., until sufficiently light. 10. In very warm weather, the sponge should not stand over night, but be mixed in the morning early, and baked in the afternoon. 11. The process of fermentation is arrested at a temperature below 30° Fahr., proceeds slowly at 50°, moderately at 60°, rapidly at 70°, and very rapidly at 80°.

UNLEAVENED BREAD.—The best bread that ever was or ever will be made is unquestionably that of coarse-ground, unbolted

Ancient Ways of making Bread—Fermented Breads—Deterioration of Meal.

meal, mixed with pure water, and baked in any convenient way. The earliest bread-makers pounded the grain on a smooth stone, or in a mortar, mixed it with water into a dough, and then baked it in hot ashes, or before the fire. Various savage tribes in this and other countries have long made, and now make in a similar manner, an excellent and delicious corn-bread. The inhabitants of new countries, where flouring mills are not to be found, often, from necessity, make good and wholesome bread in this way: An excellent and well-flavored article may be made from a mixture of wheaten and rye flour and Indian meal, in proportions to suit taste or convenience, beat up with water or milk into a moderately stiff dough, and baked for several hours is an old-fashioned iron baking-kettle. The New England women formerly made this bread in the evening, and covering the kettle with coals and hot ashes, allowed it to remain over night.

For making unleavened bread, the grain should be carefully cleaned—washed, if necessary—and care should be taken to select that which is full and plump. When ground at an ordinary flouring-mill, the stones should be sharp, so as to cut the grain into very fine particles. If ground by dull stones, the bran will be mashed off in flakes or scales. The meal or flour should be fresh ground, and never kept a long time, as it deteriorates surely, though slowly, every day after being ground.

FERMENTED BREADS.—Bread raised by fermentation may be made of the flour or meal of various grains, or of various admixtures of them. But wheat, from its larger proportion of gluten, is superior to all other grains for this kind of bread. Rye contains considerable gluten, and hence a very fair fermented bread can be made of it. Corn contains so little gluten that, though excellent for unleavened bread, it will not make good raised bread alone. Wheat and Indian, or wheat, rye and Indian, in various combinations, can, however, be made into very good fermented bread.

Whether fermented bread be made of unbolted meal, or of fine or superfine flour, it requires essentially the same management. Unbolted flour, however, requires, on account of the swelling property of the bran, a somewhat thinner or softer sponge, and it should be baked about one half longer than bread made of better flour.

RAISED BREAD.—Although bread is *raised* also by fermentation, the term "raised bread" technically applies to that which is rendered light or puffed up by means of acids and alkalies instead of yeast. Whether raised or fermented bread is the best or worst, depends very much on the manner in which the bread-making process is managed. It is a choice of evils.

In making unfermented raised bread, the bicarbonate or sesquicarbonate of soda and hydrochloric or muriatic acid are employed, in proportion of forty grains of the alkali to fifty drops of the acid. Various other alkalies have been more or less employed, but the above are probably the least objectionable. The alkali is dissolved and diffused through the mass of dough, and then the acid is diluted and worked in as rapidly as possible. The raising or puffing-up material is the same as when ferment or yeast is employed; for the hydrochloric acid combines with the soda of the bicarbonate, forming common salt—hydrochlorate of soda—and leaves the carbonic acid gas free to puff up the dough.

The evil, then, with raised bread, is the presence of common salt; and that of fermented bread is the destruction of the sugar, one of the proximate elements of the grain. Which is the worst? Since the publication of the Hydropathic Encyclopedia I have given much attention to this question, but do not find any cause to alter or modify the opinion therein expressed. I will therefore quote:

"Raised bread, or bread made light by acids and alkalies, is used to some extent in this country and in England. It has been thought by some that this method of bread-making was an improvement on the fermenting process; but in numerous experiments, I could never succeed as well with acids and alkalies as with yeast; nor do I conceive the plan to be as healthful, provided both processes are managed in the best possible way. It is true that a part of the sugar is destroyed by fermentation, and it is true that if the acid and alkali usually employed exactly neutralize each other, there is no extraneous ingredient formed and retained in the bread except common salt, while all the natural properties of the grain are left unchanged

Common Salt—Digestibility of Breads—Causes explained.

"Those who esteem common salt an alimentary article, will reasonably presume that this bread is better than fermented; and those who add a large quantity of salt to their fermented bread, as indeed most commercial and public bakers do, will have an additional argument in favor of the raised as compared with the fermented bread. Besides, the raised bread has the actual advantages that it may be put into the oven as soon as mixed, and eaten when recently from the oven, without detriment, which is not the case with the fermented, although most persons do eat this also fresh from the oven, and take the consequences.

"But I do not regard salt as an aliment; in fact, I consider breads of all kinds essentially deteriorated, not only in flavor and consistence, but in physiological properties, by the admixture of salt in any quantity. It is the very last place where salt should be used, if employed at all. All the cereal grains, wheat especially, contain considerable quantities, comparatively, of earthy phosphates, principally phosphate of lime, which is appropriate for the sustenance of the bony structure; but any additional and unnecessary admixture of saline or earthy matter in those aliments which are already specially furnished with saline and earthy materials, must be the *very worst* use we can make of them. If salt must be taken, let it be with those articles of food which contain the *least* instead of the greatest proportions of saline and earthy matters, as grapes, apples, cucumbers, milk, and flesh-meats."

DIGESTIBILITY OF BREADS.—It is a remarkable fact, that unfermented bread if well made, will "sit on the stomach," even with invalids, more easily than the best fermented bread, though the latter may be much lighter and more friable. It is well known—although the fact is commonly disregarded in practice—that leavened bread fresh from the oven is very difficult of digestion, and exceedingly obnoxious to the digestive organs. The reason of this has not been generally understood.

It is, in my judgment, owing to three causes. 1. The presence of the small quantity of *alcohol* which has not been wholly dissipated by the heat of the oven. 2. The presence of a considerable quantity of *carbonic acid gas*, which gradually escapes as the bread becomes stale. 3. The *antiseptic* effect which alcohol has imparted

7*

Antiseptics—Vinegar—Alcohol—Spirits—Salt—Acids and Alkalies.

to the constituent elements of the bread. Alcohol, though powerfully destructive to living matter, is preservative of dead matter. The explanation is, that all living matter, while vital, is undergoing continual transformations; and to be preserved alive, must be kept in a condition or state of perpetual change. But the preservation of dead matter implies that it be kept in a fixed and unchangeable chemical state, its elements being prevented from decompositions or recombinations. It is on this principle that all antiseptics operate. Thus vinegar, alcohol, spirits, common salt, solutions of arsenic, corrosive sublimate, etc., which preserve fruits, seeds, and animal and vegetable substances so long unchanged, totally unfit them for food, while they are of themselves absolute poisons.

All bread, whether raised, fermented, or unleavened, to be digested without undue "wear and tear" of the digestive apparatus, must be light, dry, friable, and so porous as readily to absorb water.

Bread is also comparatively indigestible if underbaked or overbaked. It is a common error that bread can hardly be overdone in baking. The truth is, that its dietetic nature and its digestibility begin to deteriorate the moment it is fairly cooked. We should, therefore, be just as cautious to take it from the oven as soon as baked sufficiently, as we are to have it remain until well done. Those who have never paid attention to this matter, are little aware how much the flavor and wholesomeness of bread is improved by baking it just enough, yet not a moment too long.

When the crusts of loaf-bread are thick and hard, it is customary to wrap the loaf, fresh from the oven, in several folds of wet cloth, to soften it. But this practice is objectionable for the reason that it prevents the free escape of the alcohol and carbonic acid gas, produced by fermentation, thus rendering the bread also more difficult of digestion.

The existence of all saline and alkaline matters which have been added to the flour by the cook—common, or table salt not excepted—renders it to some extent less digestible. The antiseptic property of salt accounts for its injurious effects, and the use of alkalies is one of the most prolific sources of weak stomachs, ulcerated bowels, sore throats, cankered mouths, etc.

BREAD AND BREAD-MAKING. 155

Adulterations of Flour—Bread-making Processes—Setting the Sponge.

QUALITY OF FLOUR AND MEAL.—Unless the grain is well cleaned before it is ground, we can not have the most delicious bread. There is, too, a great difference between fresh-ground and stale flour, the former making incomparably richer, sweeter bread. Those who "eat to live," or to enjoy, had better, therefore, look well to the *kind* of grain, to its being thoroughly *cleaned* from dust, cockle, smut, sand, chaff, etc., and to its being *ground* but a short time before using.

Frauds and adulterations are more generally perpetrated in articles of food, drink, and medicine, probably, than in relation to all other articles of commerce put together. The wheat-meal or Graham flour in market, is not unfrequently an admixture of "shorts" or "middlings," with old, stale, soured, or damaged fine flour; and fine flour is sometimes—more especially in European markets—adulterated with *whiting, ground stones, bone dust*, and *plaster of Paris*. Whiting can be detected by dipping the ends of the thumb and fore-finger in sweet-oil, and rubbing the flour between them, when, if this ingredient be present, it becomes sticky like putty, and remains white; whereas pure flour when so rubbed becomes very dark colored, but not sticky. Stone-dust, or plaster of Paris, may be detected by a drop or two of lemon-juice or vinegar; if either be present effervescence will take place. This test will also detect *chalk, magnesia*, or any other alkali.

BREAD-MAKING.—The following proportions and processes applicable, with slight modifications, to all kinds of bread, may as well be grouped together here, to avoid frequent repetitions.

1. One quart of "wetting," whether of milk or water, is sufficient for about five quarts of flour or meal.

2. Ten quarts of flour or meal are about the quantity for an ordinary family baking, and will make four loaves of about three and a half pounds each.

3. The temperature of the water when mixed with the flour or meal should be about blood-warm.

4. When yeast is used, it should be perfectly mixed or diluted with milk-warm water, and well stirred before it is put into the flour.

5. "*Setting the Sponge*" is a useful precaution against bad yeast,

as, if it does not rise well, the batter may be removed without wasting much of the flour. It is done as follows: Make a deep round hole in the middle of the flour or meal, pour in the yeast; then, with a spoon, stir into the liquid as much flour as will make it a thin batter; and finally sprinkle this over with dry flour or meal until it is entirely covered. The pan or trough is then to be covered with a warm cloth and set in a warm place—by the fire in the winter, and where the sun shines, when practicable, in summer. When the yeast is fresh and sweet, equally good bread may be made without *setting the sponge;* but most bread-makers think the sponge facilitates the subsequent kneading.

6. When the *sponge* is made, it should stand until the batter has swelled and risen so as to form cracks in the covering of the flour; and then the mass should be immediately formed into dough, by mixing in gradually as much warm water as may be necessary. It must then be thoroughly kneaded—molded over and over with the clenched hands—till it becomes so smooth, light, and stiff, that not a particle will adhere to the hands. The dough is next to be made into a lump in the middle of the vessel, dusted over with flour to prevent adhesion, covered with a warm cloth, and kept near the fire about one hour, or until it has become sufficiently light. Lastly, it is to be made into separate lumps, molded on pasteboard, formed into loaves, and placed immediately in the oven.

THE THREE ESSENTIALS.—All bread-makers agree that three things must be exactly right, or good bread can not be made—*the quality of the yeast*—it must be sweet and lively; *the extent or degree of fermentation*—just enough and none too much; and *the heat of the oven*—the bread must be well cooked, but not at all burned. A failure in either particular will result in a poor article of bread. It is impossible, however, to give more precise rules, for after all is said that can be, something must be left to the careful observation and judgment of the cook. Practice here will make perfect; and no bread-maker who duly estimates the importance of good bread, will be long in getting the exact tact in the management of all these particulars.

But another essential, not less important than either of the preceding, may be mentioned, viz., *the quantity of the yeast.* Many a loaf of bread is spoiled or seriously damaged by using too much. The strength of yeast may vary considerably, and its fermenting property deteriorate with age; but of the best fresh hop-yeast, about one large tablespoonful is the proper quantity for an ordinary baker's loaf. If the yeast is old, a larger quantity will be required, but the bread will not be as good. This *fourth essential*, however, like the others, can be perfected only by experience.

FERMENT, LEAVEN, OR YEAST.—I find that the majority of cookbooks recommend distillery or brewer's yeast for domestic bread-making, because it is stronger. It is precisely for this reason that I object to it. I have never seen a good loaf where it was used, nor do I think such an article will ever be seen. When brewer's yeast is employed, the fermentation is so rapid, that after the loaf appears to be light enough, before the process is arrested in the ordinary method of management, some of the constituents of the flour or meal—all of the sugar, probably, and a part of the starch and gluten—will be chemically destroyed, rendering the bread of a strong, harsh, and bitterish taste. To senses of smell and taste as susceptible as all senses ought to be, such bread will also impart an impression of putrescency or rottenness, analogous to that which is always disagreeably perceptible from the fermenting vats and slop-tubs of a distillery.

Fresh hop-yeast is probably the very best ferment we can employ in the making of leavened bread; but as a good article of leaven, comparatively, can be produced in various ways, and as it may suit the convenience of all to have a variety of recipes, the following formularies are therefore given, with which the second part of this work may as well commence.

1. ORIGINAL FERMENT OR YEAST.

Original ferment may be procured, or yeast made without using other yeast, by subjecting any kind of flour or meal to fermentation. Wheaten flour or meal is generally employed; mix the flour or meal with water or milk into a batter or thin dough, and let it stand exposed to the temperature of about summer heat—66° to 70°. Fahr.—until it "rises" or ferments. It will then communicate the fermenting property to any other material capable of undergoing a similar process. The addition of molasses or mashed potatoes will accelerate the process. Most persons add salt also, and many think it indispensable; but it is wholly unnecessary so far as the formation of ferment is concerned. When the ferment or yeast has been once produced, a supply can be subsequently obtained much more easily, by the addition of a small quantity to the fermenting material.

2. Hop-yeast.

Hop-yeast may be most conveniently made in the following manner: Boil a double handful of hops in a gallon of pure soft water for fifteen or twenty minutes; strain off the liquor while scalding hot; stir in wheat-meal or flour till a thick batter is formed; let it stand till it becomes about blood-warm; add a pint of good, lively, fresh yeast, and stir it well; then let it stand in a place where it will keep at the temperature of about 70° Fahr., till it becomes perfectly light. This yeast will keep from one to two weeks, if corked tight in a clean earthen jug, and kept in a cool cellar.

3. Potato-yeast.

Yeast made of potatoes is a favorite with some domestic bread-makers, and it is certain that very good bread can be made with it. It will not keep as long as the hop-yeast, but has the advantages of rising quicker, while it will not impart the sharp, harsh taste to bread that hop-yeast does when not well managed. Mash half a dozen peeled and boiled potatoes; mix in a handful of wheaten flour or meal, and, after putting it through a colander, add hot water until it becomes a batter. When blood-warm, stir in a teacupful of baker's yeast, or hop-yeast, which is the same thing. When sufficiently raised, cork it tight and keep in a cool place. It is not quite as strong as the hop-yeast, and may be used more freely.

4. Milk Risings.

Milk-yeast, or "risings," as this kind of ferment is sometimes called, is made by mixing two tablespoonfuls of flour or meal with a quart of new milk, and keeping the preparation at about or a little below blood-heat for an hour or two. It requires nearly twice

Bread and Bread-making. 159

Yeast Cakes—Hard Flour Yeast—Ferment without Yeast.

as much of this as of the ordinary hop-yeast for a loaf of bread. It makes an agreeable bread for those who are fond of milk, but in warm weather it soon spoils. It should, therefore, be eaten the next day after it is made.

5. Yeast Cakes.

These may be kept for weeks or months, and are made by stirring good, light, fresh yeast into Indian meal, until a fine dough is formed; this is then made into thin cakes and perfectly dried. They require to be dried very soon after being mixed, or the bread raised with them will have a musty, acrid flavor. It is best to dry them by exposure to a current of warm, dry air, or what is commonly called a drying wind. Sunlight or fire seems to impair their properties. Some persons add a little rye-meal, to make the dough more adhesive. This *hard yeast* requires to be kept in a cool, dry atmosphere. One of the cakes, an inch thick, two inches wide, and three inches long, is sufficient for four quarts of flour or meal. They may be soaked in milk or water till completely dissolved, and then used like the fluid yeast.

6. Yeast-rubs.

Hard flour-yeast, or *rubs*, is preferred by some to the yeast-cakes. In making them, the yeast is mixed with wheat-meal or flour, so as to be formed into hard lumps; these are then dried in a warm place, without being exposed to the sun. The finer particles should be used first, and the larger lumps put into a bag and hung in a dry, cool place. Probably the superiority of these " rubs" over the "cakes" is owing to their drying more rapidly, and thus sooner checking the progress of fermentation. Half a pint of them is sufficient for three quarts of flour. It is usual to let them soak from noon till night, on the day preceding that for wetting up the bread.

7. Ferment without Yeast.

The following method for making yeast whenever wanted, is very convenient for those who do not keep yeast on hand. Boil half an ounce of hops and the slices of one good rich apple in a quart of water twenty minutes; strain off the liquid; add to it four spoonfuls of treacle or molasses, and then stir in three quarters of a pound of flour, or sufficient to make the consistency of a thin batter; cover lightly, and set the preparation in a moderately warm place, till fermentation takes place, which will be in a few hours. It may then be mixed with the flour, and the bread made in the usual way. About double the quantity is required as of the common hop-yeast (No. 2).

8. Flour-Yeast.

Another convenient method for obtaining fresh yeast, very similar to that of No. 1, is the following, which is copied essentially from the "Vegetarian Cookery." Boil half a pound of flour and two ounces of brown sugar in one gallon of water for an hour; when milk-warm, put in stone bottles and cork close. It will be ready for use in twenty-four hours. Half a pint of this will be sufficient for ten pounds of bread.

9. Yeast of Dried Peas.

A new and very convenient method of making leaven is the following. Take a large teacupful of split and dried peas; put them in a pint of boiling water; cover them closely to exclude the air; place them by the side of the fire for twenty-four hours, when it should have a fine froth on the top. A tablespoonful of the liquid will raise one pound of flour.

10. Unleavened Bread.

Mix unbolted wheat-meal (Graham flour), or three parts of wheat-meal and one of Indian-meal (coarse ground), with water sufficient to form a middling stiff dough. Some prefer hot water to "scald" the meal. Roll or mold the dough into a thin cake, not more than half or three quarters of an inch in thickness, and bake immediately in a stove or before the fire. This bread-cake will be rather soft, but very sweet and perfectly wholesome. It may also be molded into loaves of rather small size, and baked in the oven or in the old-fashioned baking kettles, or cooked under hot ashes, after the manner of roasting potatoes.

This kind of bread may be made in the same way, of different proportions of rye and Indian, or of wheat, rye, and Indian.

Fine flour with equal parts of Indian or of rye and Indian, makes a fair article of unleavened bread.

11. FERMENTED BREAD.

Good leavened bread may be made with either fine or coarse wheaten flour or meal, or of either of these with various admixtures of rye or Indian, or both; also with either or all of the above, and various proportions of apples, pears, pumpkins, potatoes, potato flour, etc. A wooden bowl or well-glazed earthen pan, large enough to hold double the quantity of flour to be used, is the most convenient kneading vessel. To ten quarts of flour or meal add about three gills of hop-yeast, or a pint of potato-yeast; the fermentation must be carefully watched, and when sufficiently raised, if the oven is not then ready, it must be molded into loaves and kept cool until put in the oven.

12. RAISED BREAD.

Soda, magnesia, saleratus, pearlash, and even ammonia and lime, have been used as alkalies, and vinegar, sour milk, lemon juice, tartaric acid, cream of tartar, and muriatic or hydrochloric acid have been employed as acids, in the manufacture of raised bread without fermentation. So far as healthfulness is concerned, there is little to choose between bicarbonate of soda with sour milk, or this alkali with hydrochloric acid. The next best selection is tartaric acid and the bicarbonate of soda; and next in order, cream of tartar and the bicarbonate of soda. Cream of tartar is, however, very liable to adulteration by the druggists or manufacturers. Saleratus and pearlash are very pernicious articles.

When sour milk and soda are used, the quantity of the soda must be somewhat proportioned to the milk; the more acid or sour the milk, the more of the alkali will be necessary. The point in practice is to have one exactly neutralize the other, so that the bread will neither taste "ashy" or caustic, nor sharp and tart. As a general rule, one teaspoonful—sixty grains or a drachm—of bicarbonate of soda, known also as supercarbonate and sesquicarbonate of soda, is sufficient for a pint of sour milk. When the bicarbonate of soda and muriatic acid are employed, forty grains of the former will neutralize fifty drops of the latter. If tartaric acid be employed, one teaspoonful will be sufficient for one and a quarter teaspoonfuls of the alkali.

But whatsoever materials are employed, they must be managed in the same way. The alkali must be dissolved and thoroughly diffused through the whole mass of flour and when wetted to the condition of a rather stiff sponge, the acid, previously diluted, must be added, and then more flour added, and the acid stirred through the whole with all possible expedition. The more rapidly the acid is diffused through the mass in this way, the lighter will be the loaf, as the carbonic acid gas evolved by the combination of an acid with the base of the carbonate, is every moment escaping after the acid and alkali are brought into contact.

It is important, too, that bread made in this way be put in the oven the moment it is mixed. If allowed to stand only a short time before being placed in the oven, as has often happened with those who, not being theoretical chemists, have undertaken to manage acids and alkalies, it may come out heavy, compact, and "soggy."

It requires baking about an hour, the same length of time as the fermented fine flour bread.

13. WHEAT-MEAL BREAD—GRAHAM BREAD.

In every cook-book I have examined, and in all the medico-dietetical works I have consulted, I find saleratus or pearlash, and salt always in the recipe for making what those books call *brown, dyspepsia,* or *Graham bread*. Those two drugs ought always to be left out. Molasses or brown sugar is also a fixture in the ordinary receipt books, and as a small quantity—a tablespoonful to a common loaf—is not harmful, the saccharine element may be left to taste. Make the sponge of unbolted wheat-meal in the ordinary way, with either hop or potato yeast, but mix it rather thin. Be sure and mold the loaves as soon as it becomes light, as the unbolted flour runs into the acetous fermentation much more rapidly than the bolted or superfine flour, and bake an hour and a quarter or an hour and a half, according to the size of the loaf.

Potato, Rye and Indian, Apple, Pumpkin, and Rice Bread.

14. POTATO BREAD.

Boil and peel a dozen mealy potatoes; rub them through a sieve; mix them thoroughly with twice the quantity of flour or meal; add sufficient water to make a dough of the ordinary consistence; ferment in the usual way with hop, potato, or pea yeast, and bake in a rather hot oven.

15. RYE AND INDIAN BREAD.

Rye and corn may be mixed in any proportions, to suit the taste or fancy. The practical rule to observe in making it is, that when the proportion of rye is the largest, the dough must be stiff and molded into loaves; but when the proportion of corn is the largest, the dough should be made soft, and baked in deep earthen or tin vessels. The greater the proportion of Indian or corn meal, also, the longer the bread requires baking. If it is half or two thirds Indian, it will need to be baked from two to three hours.

The best way to mix the dough is to pour boiling water over the Indian, and stir it till the whole is thoroughly wet; and when about milk-warm, add the rye-meal or flour, with the yeast, and as much more warm, *but not hot* water, as may be necessary.

16. APPLE BREAD.

Boil to a pulp one dozen well flavored, sweet, or moderately tart apples; mix the fruit with twice its quantity of wheaten flour or meal; ferment and bake in the usual manner. This bread is very light, porous, and palatable.

17. PUMPKIN BREAD.

Stew and strain the pumpkin, stiffen it with a little Indian-meal, and then add as much more wheaten flour, with the necessary quantity of potato-yeast; bake two hours. This is an excellent and wholesome bread.

18. RICE BREAD.

To one pint of rice boiled soft and two quarts of wheat-meal add a handful of Indian; mix with milk to make it mold like wheat-bread, and ferment with yeast.

19. Moist Rice Bread.

Mix a pint and a half of ground rice with three quarts of cold milk and water, which will reduce it to a thin gruel; boil three minutes; then stir in wheat-meal till it becomes too stiff to stir with a spoon; when blood-warm add two gills of yeast; when light, bake about one hour.

20. Sweet Brown Bread.

Take one quart of rye-flour; two quarts of coarse Indian-meal; one pint of wheat-meal—all of which must be very fresh; half a teacupful of molasses or brown sugar; one gill of potato-yeast. Mingle the ingredients into as stiff a dough as can be stirred with a spoon, using warm water for wetting. Let it rise several hours, or over night; then put it in a large deep pan, and bake five or six hours. This would be a much more wholesome " wedding cake" than we are accustomed to have proffered us, on certain interesting occasions.

21. Currant Bread.

Take three pounds of flour; one pound of raisins; two pounds of currants; one pint and a half of new milk; and one gill of yeast. Warm the milk, and mix it with the flour and yeast; cover with a cloth, and set it by the fire. When risen sufficiently, add the fruits and mold it; then put it into a baking tin or deep dish rubbed with sweet-oil or dusted with flour; after it has risen for half an hour longer, bake in a moderately hot oven.

22. Scalded Bread.

Stir as much boiling water as will make a stiff paste into one third the quantity of unbolted flour intended to be used; add the yeast, and "set the sponge" with a little lukewarm water. When it has risen quite light, and the scalded flour has become cold, add the remaining flour, and knead well together; let it rise again; put it in a tin, and bake in a quick oven till half done; then remove it to the upper part of the oven, where it should remain several hours—the oven being now moderately cool. It should be kept in a cool, dry place a day or two before it is cut.

CHAPTER VII.

CAKES AND BISCUITS.

23. WHEAT-MEAL CRACKERS.

Mix fresh-ground wheat-meal with pure soft water into a stiff dough. Roll out and cut the mass into thin crackers, not quite as thick as the Boston cracker of the shops, but larger in circumference, and bake in a brick oven. Be very cautious and not overcook or burn them.

24. UNLEAVENED BREAD CAKES.

Wet wheat-meal with pure water into a rather thin dough; or, if preferred, scald the meal by stirring with boiling water; roll it as thin as for crackers; cut into pieces about two inches square, and bake in a range, oven, stove, or before the fire.

25. WHEAT-MEAL WAFERS.

Mix the unbolted flour as above (No. 24), and form the dough into small round cakes, not more than one sixth of an inch in thickness. Bake as above. (Nos. 23, 24, and 25 are all excellent for weak, sour stomach, constipation, worms, bilious affections, etc.)

26. INDIAN-MEAL CAKE—JOHNNY CAKE.

Take coarse-ground but fresh Indian-meal; scald it by stirring in boiling water until a stiff dough is formed; then mold it into a cake three fourths of an inch in thickness, and bake on a board before the fire, or in a stove or range. This is excellent for children, with or without a little milk or molasses.

27. RAISED INDIAN CAKE.

Take one quart of sour milk or buttermilk; two teaspoonfuls of bicarbonate of soda; four ounces of brown sugar, or a gill of molasses; coarse Indian-meal a sufficient quantity. Stir the milk, boiling hot, with the meal until a stiff batter is formed; add the sugar or molasses; then the soda, previously dissolved; after which, mix in meal enough to form a dough, as rapidly as possible, and bake in shallow pans

28. RICH CORN CAKE.

Take one quart coarse white Indian-meal; three pints of scalded milk *cooled;* a teaspoonful of bicarbonate of soda; half a teacup of sugar; and half a dozen eggs well beaten. Mix all together, and bake in pans one hour. This is a good substitute for the baker's "sponge-cake," provided folks *will* have such things.

29. CORN CREAM CAKE.

Take a pint of thick, sour, but not very old cream; one quart of milk or buttermilk; yellow-corn meal sufficient to thicken to the consistency of pound cake; and bicarbonate of soda enough to sweeten the cream; add the soda to the cream; stir in the meal; put it in floured pans, an inch thick, and bake in a quick oven.

N. B. A *quick oven* is so hot that one can count moderately only twenty, while holding the hand in it; and a *slow oven* allows one to count thirty.

30. MOLASSES CAKES.

Take equal parts of Graham flour and fine flour, wet up the flour with warm milk and water; sweeten with sirup or New Orleans molasses; raise with hop, potato, or pea yeast; form into thin cakes, and bake in a stove or oven. They should not be eaten till several hours after coming from the oven.

31. WHEAT-MEAL SWEET CAKE.

Take of unbolted wheaten flour one quart; sweet cream two gills; sour milk two gills; bicarbonate of soda one teaspoonful; and best brown sugar one teacupful. Mix a part of the flour with the cream, milk, and sugar; then add the soda, dissolved in a little water, and stir in rapidly the remainder of the flour. Bake in shallow pans in a quick oven.

CAKES AND BISCUITS.

Indian Slappers—Various Griddle Cakes—Oatmeal Cake.

32. INDIAN SLAPPERS.

Take one quart of Indian-meal; two quarts of milk; and four eggs. Beat the eggs; mix them with the milk; stir in the meal, and bake on a griddle like buckwheat cakes.

33. WHEAT-MEAL GRIDDLE CAKES.

Wet up unbolted or Graham flour, with water or sweet milk, into a batter, and add a little molasses. It may then be raised with yeast, or with tartaric acid and supercarbonate of soda, and baked on a soap-stone griddle without grease.

34. BUCKWHEAT GRIDDLE CAKES.

Make one quart of flour into a thin batter with lukewarm water; add a handful of Indian-meal, and half a teacupful of yeast. Keep it in a warm place over night, and bake in the morning.

35. RICE GRIDDLE CAKES.

Soak over night one quart of *cold*, boiled head rice, in four or five gills of milk or water; the next morning add one quart of milk, and stir in nearly as much flour, and two eggs well beaten. Bake on a soap-stone griddle. Fine bread crumbs or rusked bread, mixed with the rice, improve this cake.

36. WHEAT AND INDIAN GRIDDLE CAKES.

These are made, in all respects, like No. 33, except that the meal is composed of equal parts of wheat and Indian. Those who have to use iron griddles, can prevent the batter from adhering by dusting them with flour; olive oil is much better than butter for the same purpose.

37. OATMEAL CAKE.

Mix fine oatmeal into a stiff dough with milk-warm water; roll it to the thinness almost of a wafer; bake on a griddle or iron plate placed over a slow fire for three or four minutes; then place it on edge before the fire to harden. This will be good for months, if kept in a dry place. Like the wheat-meal or hard crackers, it is an excellent article to exercise too sedentary teeth upon.

38. Potato Cake.

Boil good, mealy potatoes, and when well dried mash them up with a little olive oil or sweet cream, and a proper quantity of yeast, and as much meal or flour as will make the whole into the consistency of dough; roll it into cakes, and when sufficiently light, bake in a moderate oven.

39. Flour and Potato Rolls.

Take one pound of potatoes, one pound and a half of flour, two ounces of sweet cream, three gills of milk, and a small quantity of yeast. Boil and dry the potatoes; mix them with the cream, and half a pint of milk; then rub them through a wire sieve into the flour. Mix the remainder of the warm milk with the yeast and add the mixture to the flour. Let the dough rise before the fire; then make into rolls of any convenient size, and bake in a quick oven.

40. Indian Pancakes—Slapjacks.

To one pint of coarse sifted Indian-meal add a small teacupful of fine wheaten flour; stir them into a quart of new milk, with three or four beaten eggs. Bake on a griddle. These cakes should not be eaten with melted butter; but instead of this, fruit sauce or a little milk may be used as a seasoning.

41. Sour Milk Biscuit.

Take two quarts of sour milk or butter-milk, and three teaspoonsful of bicarbonate of soda, dissolved in hot water. Mix the milk with sufficient flour (fine or coarse as preferred), to make a dough nearly stiff enough to roll; then add the soda and as much more flour as necessary; mold and bake quickly.

42. Shortened Biscuit.

Take wheaten flour (either Graham or fine as preferred), sweet cream, olive oil, or newly-churned butter without salt, and warm milk and water—equal parts. Mix into a thin batter; add hop or potato-yeast, and thicken with flour or meal. When light enough, bake in a slow oven.

Drop Cakes—Muffins—Crumpets—Milk Biscuit.

43. RYE DROP CAKE.

Take one pint of sweet milk, two eggs, and a tablespoonful of sugar. Stir in rye-flour till about the consistency of pancakes, and bake in floured or oiled cups or saucers, half an hour.

44. WHEAT-MEAL DROP CAKE.

Take one pint of milk, two spoonsful of cream, two eggs, and one spoonful of molasses or brown sugar. Mix with these materials wheat-meal enough to make a thick batter. Drop on oiled or floured tins, and bake twenty minutes.

45. CORN-MEAL MUFFINS.

Take one quart of coarse ground and sifted Indian-meal, two spoonsful of sweet cream, one quart of milk, one spoonful of molasses, and half a teacupful of hop or potato-yeast. Make into a thin dough; let it rise four or five hours; bake one hour in muffin rings, or in shallow pans.

Wheat-meal will make excellent muffins managed in the same way.

46. HYDROPATHIC CRUMPETS.

Mix a quart of warm milk, a teaspoonful of sugar, and a gill of potato-yeast, with flour or meal enough to make a rather thin batter. When light, add a teacupful of sweet cream; then let it rise about twenty minutes, and bake it as muffins, or in cups.

47. COCOANUT DROPS.

Take equal parts of grated cocoanut and sifted sugar, and the whites of eggs; beat to a stiff froth, enough to wet the whole to a stiff batter. Bake in drops the size of a penny, on a griddle or oiled plates

48. MILK BISCUIT.

Take one pound of flour or meal, three gills of milk, and a large tablespoonful of yeast. Mix well the dough into small balls, and when risen sufficiently, bake in a quick oven.

49. WATER-CURE WAFFLES.

Mix one quart of fresh wheat-meal with a sufficient quantity of *cold* milk to make a thick batter; then add four beaten eggs, half a teacupful of sweet cream, or one ounce of fresh olive oil, a little sugar, and bake in a quick oven.

50. UNCOOKED BREAD CAKE.

For this, and the two following recipes, I am indebted to Miss E. M. French, of New London, who has experimented considerably in preparing food without cooking. The idea is sufficiently radical; but I doubt not the time will come when methods for preparing various articles of food with very little cooking, if not without any, will be much more highly appreciated than can be expected at present.

Mix with half a pound of figs sufficient ground wheat—coarse Graham flour—to form a dough like well-kneaded bread. The figs should be softened a little with hot water, which will also cleanse them, when they will readily yield to the kneading process. No water is required except what is necessary to soften the figs. The cake or bread may be rolled or cut in the form of biscuit. It should be made fresh whenever wanted for eating.

51. UNBAKED BREAD CAKE.

In this kind of bread or cake the ingredients are cooked before mixing, but not subsequently.

To one quart of ground parched corn add a teacupful of boiled rice; mix the ingredients well, and form a loaf by placing them in a pan wet with cold water. It may, perhaps, be improved by adding uncooked rice flour to form the loaf, when it need not be placed in the pan, but may be rolled or cut in the form of biscuit.

52. UNCOOKED FRUIT CAKE.

To one quart of ground wheat add one large grated cocoanut with its milk. Drop half a pound of raisins into cold water, and remove their stones, and mix them in the cake. A quarter of citron, grated, will add a fine flavor, and make it very rich. In order to keep the cake a few days, crushed sugar, dissolved in a solution of gum Arabic—one ounce to a half teacupful of water, and the juice of a lemon, will make a beautiful frosting. Keep it in a cool place. In summer sugar may be grated over the loaf, which is formed by pressing the dough into the dish with the hand.

53. POTATO SCONES.

Mash boiled potatoes till quite smooth, and knead with flour to the consistency of a light dough; roll it about half an inch thick; cut the scones in any form desired; prick them with a fork, and bake on a griddle.

54. DRY TOAST

For very acid, bilious, and irritable stomachs, dry bread, if *well* toasted, is often the best food that can be taken. The practical point is to have it well and evenly browned, without being in the least degree scorched or burned. The bread should always be toasted just before it is wanted. Bread which is a little soured or over-fermented is improved, though not cured, by toasting..

55. MILK TOAST.

Scald sweet milk, and thicken it with a very little flour or wheatmeal. Carefully toast both sides of either brown or white bread (stale bread is best), cracker, or biscuit, till its color becomes yellowish-brown; then put them in the dish for the table, just covered with the thickened milk gravy.

56. CREAM TOAST.

Toast half a dozen thin slices of stale bread nicely and equally on both sides; turn over them, while hot, half a pint of sweet cream, also hot, and diluted with as much scalded milk.

57. WHEAT-MEAL FRUIT BISCUITS.

Mix Graham flour with just enough of scalded figs—previously washed—to make an adherent dough by much kneading; roll or cut into biscuits half an inch thick, and two or three inches square; bake in a quick oven.

NOTE.—The English unfermented "forthright" bread is made in the same way, with the exception that the meal is wet with water instead of fruit, made into rolls of an inch in thickness, cut deeply across, and baked in a moderately hot oven.

58. Frost Cakes.

Take one pound of potato flour, half a pound of best brown sugar, a teacupful of cream, two eggs, and the rind of a citron, grated. Mix the flour with the cream; then add the eggs, well beaten, the sugar and the lemon; whisk them all together fifteen or twenty minutes, and bake in cheese-cake tins in a moderate oven.

59. Improved Jumballs.

Take one pound of flour, eight ounces of sweet oil, ten ounces of good white sugar, and two eggs. Mix the flour, oil, sugar, and the eggs, well beaten, into a stiff paste; roll it thin; cut it in shreds, and twist them into rings, knots, or any form that fancy may suggest; lay them on baking tins; wet them over with molasses, and bake in a moderately hot oven.

60. Fruit Cake.

Take one pound and a half of flour or meal, one quarter of a pound of sultana or blown raisins, one half pound of black currants, four ounces of sugar, one gill of sweet cream, four eggs, one teaspoonful of bicarbonate of soda, and half a pint of sour milk or sour buttermilk. Mix the soda and cream well with the flour or meal; add the sugar, raisins, currants, and eggs, well beaten; then work all into a dough with the milk as rapidly as possible, and bake in an oiled or floured tin mold an hour and a quarter.

61. Wedding Cake.

Take one pound of well-boiled wheaten grits, half a pound of flour, one cocoanut grated, one quarter of a pound of black currants, one quarter of a pound of powdered sugar, one pint of olive oil or of sweet cream, and eight eggs. Mix the grits well with the cocoanut and fruits; add gradually the eggs, well beaten, and the flour, sugar, and oil or cream. Knead the whole thoroughly to a stiff dough, adding cocoa-milk if too dry, and more flour if too moist, and bake in a rather quick oven.

CHAPTER VIII.

MUSHES AND PORRIDGES.

THE reader will observe that salt is not mentioned as an ingredient of any recipe in this book. But as almost all persons are accustomed to the use of this seasoning, I can only say to them, if they can not bring their appetite at once into subjection to unsalted aliment, they had better use a moderate quantity, and gradually diminish it.

In all the cook books I am acquainted with, salt is put down as a fixture of every dish; and mushes, especially Indian and rice, are usually considered as unendurably flat and insipid, unless abundantly salted. A little experience with unsalted food, and a little self-denial, will, however, enable all persons to relish not only mushes, but all other farinaceous preparations, with no other seaonings than sugar or milk.

62. CRACKED WHEAT MUSH.

As the grits swell very much in boiling, they should be stirred gradually in boiling water until a thin mush is formed. The boiling should then be continued very moderately for one or two hours.

If the grits are ground very coarse, they will require boiling five or six hours. A large coffee mill will serve the purpose very well of grinding for a family.

An ordinary iron pot will answer to boil the grits in, if they are constantly stirred, or if the vessel stand on legs, so that the blaze of the fire is not in immediate contact with it. The double boiler, however (found at most hardware stores), is the most convenient to prevent burning or scorching. It is a tin or iron vessel surrounded by hot water, and contained within another vessel which comes in contact with th fire.

Hominy—Samp—Rye-meal—Indian-meal and Oatmeal Mush.

63. Hominy.

This is generally, in this market, prepared from the Southern or white corn, which is cut into coarser or finer particles of nearly uniform size. It is cooked like the wheaten grits, and usually requires to be boiled one hour. The fine-grained hominy can be well cooked in half an hour, by boiling a few minutes and then steaming it, without stirring, over as hot a fire as can be borne without scorching. All hominy requires soaking before cooking. Two quarts of water are required for one of hominy.

64. Samp.

This is merely a very coarse hominy—the grains of corn being cut or broken into very coarse particles. It should be washed several times, and the water poured through a sieve to separate the hulls; and it requires boiling five or six hours.

65. Rye-meal Mush.

This is made precisely like the mush of cracked wheat, or wheaten grits. It is particularly adapted to those who have long suffered from habitual constipation. To persons unaccustomed to the grain, the effect on the bowels is decidedly laxative. The meal must be fresh ground, and made of well-cleaned and plump grain.

66. Indian-meal Mush.

White and yellow corn meal are made into the well-known mush called *hasty pudding*. Either kind is equally agreeable to most persons. It should be stirred very gradually into boiling water, so as to prevent *lumping;* it will cook very well in fifteen minutes, but half an hour's gentle boiling improves its flavor.

67. Oatmeal Mush.

This, in Scotland, is called *stirabout*. It is a favorite with many persons, and makes a pleasant change of dishes. It is cooked precisely like Indian mush.

Farinaceous Mushes—Corn Starch Blanc-mange—Molded Farinacea.

68. WHEAT-MEAL MUSH.

This is an excellent article for infants and young children—much better than the *farina*, which is so extensively employed. It will do for a change in the cases of adults; but is not equal to the coarser preparations of the grain. It is cooked like Indian mush

69. FARINA MUSH.

This is too nutritive, or, rather, concentrated an aliment for an every-day dish, but will do occasionally for variety's sake. It is made into mush in the same way as Graham flour or Indian meal.

70. RICE MUSH.

Put one pint of plump *head rice*, previously picked over and washed, into three quarts of boiling water; continue the boiling fifteen to twenty minutes, but avoid stirring it so as to break up or mash the kernels; turn off the water; set it uncovered over a moderate fire, and steam fifteen minutes. Rice is "poor stuff" without salt, say the cooks, and cook-books. If you find it so, reader, try a little sirup or sugar.

71. RICE AND MILK MUSH.

Boil a pint of clean head rice fifteen or twenty minutes; pour off the water; add a little milk—mixing it gently so as not to break the kernels—and boil a few minutes longer.

72. CORN STARCH BLANC-MANGE.

Dissolve half a pound of corn starch in a pint of *cold* milk; hen put it into three pints of boiling milk; and boil very moderately five or six minutes.

73. MOLDED FARINACEA.

Nearly all the boiled farinaceous foods may be molded to please the fancy, in teacups, glasses, or earthen molds. Wheaten grits, rice, farina, corn starch, etc., may be put into the molds, or dishes, previously wet in cold water, as soon as cooked, and when cooled turned out on china or glass plates. The addition of a little whortleberry, raspberry, blackberry, or strawberry juice, will afford an innocent coloring material for those who have time and inclination to indulge in such amusements.

74. MILK PORRIDGE.

Place a pint and a half of new milk and half a pint of water over the fire; when just ready to boil, stir in a tablespoonful of flour, wheat-meal, oat-meal, or corn-meal, previously mixed with a little water; after boiling a minute, pour it on bread cut into small pieces.

75. WHEAT-MEAL PORRIDGE.

Stir gradually into a quart of boiling water half a pound of wheat-meal, and boil ten or fifteen minutes. It may be flavored with a little milk, molasses, or sugar.

76. OATMEAL PORRIDGE.

Rub three quarters of a pound of oatmeal into a little cold water, till the mixture is smooth and even; add it to three pints of boiling water; allow the whole to boil gently about twenty minutes. Serve with milk, sirup, or sugar.

77. HOMINY PORRIDGE.

Steep one pound of hominy, prepared as in 63, in water ten hours, and then dried in a stove or oven; pour off the fluid which has not been absorbed; add three pints of milk, and set the whole in a moderate oven two hours, till all the milk is absorbed; pour into saucers, and serve with milk and sugar.

78. SAGO PORRIDGE.

Soak four tablespoonfuls of sago a few minutes in one quart of *cold* water; then boil it gently one hour, and pour it into soup plates.

79. RICE AND SAGO PORRIDGE.

Take equal quantities of rice flour or ground rice and sago, and proceed as in 77.

80. BEAN PORRIDGE.

Mix three tablespoonfuls of bean or lentil flour with one pint of water boil ten minutes, stirring it continually.

CHAPTER IX.

PIES AND PUDDINGS.

As usually made, pastry is one of the worst abominations of modern cookery; I can hardly conceive of any thing more indigestible than the crust of a baker's pie. Still, a great variety of pies can be made, which are as delicious as any one ought to eat, and which are but a slight departure from the use of bread, fruit, and sugar, on physiological principles.

81. Pie Crust.

The crust for pies and tarts may be made comparatively wholesome in a variety of ways. Any kind of flour or meal, or various admixtures of them, may be wet with water and shortened with sweet cream; or the flour or meal may be wet with milk and shortened with olive oil. The succeeding recipes will be a sufficient guide.

82. Wheat-meal Pie Crust.

Dilute sweet cream with a little water; work the meal into it until a stiff dough is formed, and roll it out to the desired thickness.

83. Wheat and Potato Crust.

Mix equal parts of fine wheaten flour and potato flour, or of good mealy potatoes, boiled, peeled, and mashed, with sweet milk; and shorten with olive oil.

84. Meal and Flour Crust.

Take equal parts of Graham and fine flour, and wet into a dough with diluted sweet cream.

85. Raised Pie Crust.

Mix with half a pint of sour milk either fine or coarse flour, or equal parts of both, to make a thick batter; then add half a teaspoonful of bicarbonate of soda, previously dissolved, and stir in flour enough to form the dough or paste, as rapidly as possible. This is not as wholesome as the preceding kinds.

86. Wheat and Rye Crust.

Take half a pint of wheaten flour, half as much rye-meal, one gill of sweet cream, and water enough to form a stiff paste. It may be improved, perhaps, by the addition of one good mealy potato.

87. Bread Pie Crust.

Pour boiling milk on light stale bread or biscuit; let it remain closely covered till cold; then add a little sweet cream or salad oil, and as much flour as will make a paste of the proper consistence.

88. Pumpkin Pie with Eggs.

All kinds of pumpkins, domestic or foreign, make very good pies. But the best in this market are the West Indian. Pare the pumpkin; take out the seeds carefully without scraping the solid part of the fruit; stew until it becomes soft, and strain through a sieve or colander. Beat up one egg for each pint of milk; stir the beaten egg and milk with the stewed fruit until it becomes as thick as can be stirred rapidly and easily; sweeten with molasses or brown sugar, and bake without an upper crust, an hour, in either deep or shallow plates, in a hot oven.

Note.—When a single or under crust only is used, it should be made thicker than when two are used, and also rimmed or raised on the edge.

89. Pumpkin Pie with Cream.

Prepare the fruit as in 88, and instead of eggs use one gill of sweet cream to each quart of milk.

PIES AND PUDDINGS.

Squash Pie—Apple Pies—Carrot Pies—Potato Pie.

90. GRATED PUMPKIN PIE.

Take out the seeds as in 88; grate the fruit close down to the outside skin; sweeten the pulp; mix with milk and cream, flavor with grated lemon, citron, or cocoa, and bake on a single crust.

91. SQUASH PIE.

This is made precisely like the pumpkin pie, and is essentially the same thing. The best squashes for pie-making are the cream, butter, and several varieties of winter. The more firm in texture and sweeter in flavor, the better.

92. GREEN APPLE PIE.

Peel and core moderately tart and ripe apples—pippins, russets, and greenings are excellent; cut them into very thin slices; fill the under crust; then sprinkle over them brown sugar, or pour over molasses to sweeten sufficiently; lay over the upper crust, and bake them in a moderate oven about forty minutes.

93. DRIED APPLE PIE.

Select clean and rich-flavored fruit, and that which is not very sour; stew until soft; sweeten with brown sugar or molasses; place the apples half an inch thick between the crusts, and bake about half an hour.

94. CARROT PIES.

These are not so delicious as pumpkin pies, though some persons are very fond of them. They are made in the same way as the pumpkin pies. The roots should be boiled very tender, then skinned and sifted.

95. POTATO PIE.

Carolina potatoes are generally preferred, though mealy Irish ones do very well. Boil them till quite soft; peel, mash, and strain them; then to half a pound of potatoes put a quart of milk, half a gill of sweet cream, two beaten eggs and bake on a single crust

96. PEACH PIE.

Take juicy and mellow peaches; peel, stone, and slice them; then put them in a deep pie plate lined with the under crust, sprinkle through them a sufficient quantity of sugar, equally distributed; put in about a tablespoonful of water; dust a little flour over the top; cover with a rather thick crust, and bake nearly an hour.

97. DRIED PEACH PIE.

Procure the mildest-flavored and softest dried fruit; stew and sweeten, and make the pie a little thicker than dried apple pie; bake about three quarters of an hour.

98. RHUBARB PIE.

Take the tender stalks of the plant; strip off the skin; stew till soft, and sweeten; press the upper crust closely around the edge of the plate, and prick the crust with a fork, so that it will not burst and let out the juice while baking. It should bake about an hour, in a slow oven.

99. CUSTARD PIE.

Take one quart of rich, sweet milk; beat six eggs with two tablespoonsfuls of sugar, and stir the whole together. Put the crust on the plates, and let it harden a few minutes in the oven or near the fire; then pour in the custard, and bake about twenty minutes.

100. CRANBERRY TART.

Wash the berries in a pan of water, rejecting all the bad ones; simmer them until they become soft and burst open; sweeten with half a pound of sugar to a pound of the fruit; place it again over the fire till it comes to the boiling point; then place it on a thick under crust, and bake in a moderate oven.

101. WHORTLEBERRY PIE.

This is one of the most delicious and wholesome of pies. Wash and pick over the ripe berries; place them an inch thick on the

Berry Pies—Strawberry Tart—Dried Fruit Pies.

under crust; strew a little sugar over them; put on the upper crust, and bake half an hour.

102. BLACKBERRY PIE.

This is nearly or quite as good as the preceding, and made in the same way. The berries should be ripe, or nearly so, and as fresh as possible.

103. RASPBERRY PIE.

Either the black or red berry is excellent for pies. The latter is very sweet and requires but a trifle of sugar.

104. STRAWBERRY PIE.

This is made in the same way as the other berry pies. This fruit is rather acid, and requires considerable sugar to make it pleasant.

105. STRAWBERRY TART.

Stew the fruit until soft; sweeten with brown sugar, about six ounces to a pound of the fruit, and bake moderately on a single crust.

106. GREEN CURRANT PIE.

Currants will make good and wholesome pies at nearly all stages of their growth. They only require to be stewed, and sweetened according to their degree of acidity, and baked between two crusts in the ordinary manner. The addition of a little dried or green apple gives a fine flavor.

107. GOOSEBERRY PIE.

This is made in the same way as the preceding, but requires a larger proportion of sugar. The berries should be nearly or quite full grown. A little apple may be used if preferred.

108. DRIED FRUIT PIES.

These may be made of various dried berries—currants, raspberries, whortleberries, etc., or of any of these mixed with dried apples, peaches, pears, or plums. They are merely to be mixed in

Puddings of Rice—Sago, Pearl Barley, Bread, and Cracked Wheat.

proportions to suit taste or convenience, sweetened, and baked in double crusts, in the usual way.

109. RICE PUDDING.

Wash and pick over half a pint of good *head rice*; mix it with two quarts of cold sweet milk; sweeten with a teacupful of sugar; bake it in a moderate oven three hours.

110. SAGO AND APPLE PUDDINGS.

Take six ounces of sago, previously washed and picked, five large rich apples, peeled, quartered, and cored, and one teacupful of sugar. Pour boiling water on the sago; let it stand till cold; then mix in the apples and sugar, and bake about an hour.

111. PEARL BARLEY PUDDING.

Pick and wash half a pound of pearl barley; soak it in fresh water over night; pour off the water; add one quart of new milk and a teacupful of sugar; and bake one hour in a slow oven.

112. BARLEY AND APPLE PUDDING.

Pick and wash half a pound of pearl barley; soak it in water twelve hours; then put it into a pan with three pints of water; let it boil two hours; pour it into an oiled pie-dish; put in half a pound of apples, sliced; add two ounces of sugar, and bake one hour in a moderate oven.

113. BREAD PUDDING.

Pour a quart of boiling milk on as much light bread (either brown or white), biscuit, or cracker, broken or cut into small pieces, as will absorb it; cover it, and let it remain till quite cool; then sweeten, and bake an hour and a half.

114. CRACKED WHEAT PUDDING.

Boil wheaten grits till quite soft; then dilute the mush with milk to the proper consistency—it should be rather thin; sweeten and bake one hour.

Hominy, Indian-meal, Tapioca, Snow, Christmas, and Macaroni Puddings.

115. HOMINY PUDDING.

Mix cold boiled hominy with milk till sufficiently diluted; sweeten, and bake in a hot oven an hour and a half or two hours.

116. INDIAN-MEAL PUDDING.

Take half a pound of Indian-meal, one quart of milk, one quarter of a pound of sugar, and two eggs. Boil the milk; mix it with the meal, and add the sugar; when nearly cold put in the eggs, well beaten, and make a thin batter; bake it in a quick oven three hours.

117. TAPIOCA PUDDING.

Pour a pint of warm milk on half the quantity of tapioca; let it soak till dissolved; then add another pint of milk, sweeten, and bake about one hour in a moderate oven.

118. SNOW PUDDING.

It is a singular fact that puddings may be made light with *snow* instead of eggs—a circumstance of some importance in the winter season, when eggs are dear and snow is cheap. Two large tablespoonfuls are equivalent to one egg. The explanation is found in the fact that snow involves within its flakes a large amount of atmospheric air, which is set free as the snow melts. This knowledge may be applied to any kind of pudding, as the two succeeding recipes will show.

119. CHRISTMAS PUDDING.

Mix together a pound and a quarter of wheaten flour or meal, half a pint of sweet cream, a pound of stoned raisins, four ounces of currants, four ounces of potatoes, mashed, five ounces of brown sugar, and a gill of milk. When thoroughly worked together, add eight large spoonfuls of clean snow; diffuse it through the mass as quickly as possible; tie the pudding tightly in a bag previously wet in cold water, and boil four hours.

120. MACARONI SNOW PUDDING.

Take three ounces of macaroni, one pint of new milk, one gill of cream, four of brown sugar or molasses, and eight tablespoonfuls of snow. Simmer the macaroni in the milk till well mixed; add the sugar and cream; then stir in the snow quickly, and bake immediately till lightly browned.

121. Rice and Apple Pudding.

Boil half a pound of rice in half a pint of milk till it is soft; then fill the pudding-dish half full of apples, which have been pared and cored; sweeten with brown sugar or molasses; put the rice over the fruit as a crust, and bake one hour.

122. Sweet Apple Pudding.

Put a dozen good, ripe, sweet apples, which have been pared, cored, and cut into slices, into a quart of milk, with a pint of Indian-meal; bake three hours. If the apples are not very sweet, a little molasses may be used.

123. Snow-ball Pudding.

Pare and core large, mellow apples, and inclose them in cloths spread over with boiled rice, and boil one hour. Dip them in cold water before turning them out. They may be eaten with sirup, sugar, or sweetened milk.

124. Apple Custard.

Pare and core half a dozen good, ripe, mealy, and moderately tart apples; boil them in a small quantity of water till rather soft; put them into the pudding-dish, and sugar them over; then add eight eggs, which have been beaten up with three tablespoonfuls of sugar, and mixed with three pints of milk; bake half an hour.

125. Cottage Pudding.

Mix two pounds of pared, boiled, and mashed potatoes with one pint of milk, three beaten eggs, and two ounces of sugar; bake three quarters of an hour.

126. Farina Pudding.

Mix ten ounces of farina with half a pint of cold milk; put one quart of milk over the fire, and, while it is boiling, stir in the farina gradually, and let it simmer fifteen or twenty minutes. It may be served with milk, fruit, jelly, or sugar.

PIES AND PUDDINGS.

Puddings of Figs, Cocoa, Apple, Berries, Eggs, Potatoes, and of Green Corn.

127. FIG AND COCOA-NUT PUDDING.

Wash one pound of figs in warm water; soak them till soft; add to them one grated cocoa-nut with its milk, and four ounces of sugar; then knead with them all as much wheat-meal as can be worked into a rather soft dough. (If in the cold season, three or four spoonfuls of snow will make it still lighter.) Tie it in a pudding-bag, not very tight, as it will swell some, and boil two hours.

128. BAKED APPLE PUDDING

Boil one pound and a half of good apples with a gill of water and half a pound of brown sugar, till reduced to a smooth pulp; stir in one gill of sweet cream or of olive oil, a tablespoonful of flour or of fine bread crumbs; flavor with a little lemon juice or grated lemon, and bake forty minutes.

129. BERRY PUDDING.

Make a batter of one quart of flour or meal, three pints of milk, and three eggs. Stew three pints of either blackberries, whortleberries, black currants, raspberries, or morella cherries, and sweeten to suit the taste; stir them into the batter, and bake.

130. CUSTARD PUDDING.

Mix with a pint of sweet cream or of new milk one tablespoonful of flour, three beaten eggs, and two tablespoonfuls of sugar. Bake for half an hour.

131. POTATO APPLE DUMPLINGS.

Boil any quantity of white mealy potatoes; pare them, and mash them with a rolling-pin; then dredge in flour enough to form a dough; roll it out to about the thickness of pie crust, and make up the dumplings by putting an apple, pared, cored, and quartered, to each. Boil them one hour.

132. GREEN CORN PUDDING.

To one quart of grated ears of green corn add a teacupful of cream, one gill of milk, a tablespoonful of flour, and two ounces of sugar; mix all together, and bake an hour and a half.

CHAPTER X.

WHOLE GRAINS AND SEEDS.

Quite a variety of excellent dishes may be made of whole grains and seeds, by simply boiling or roasting; and for those who insist on more complicated cookery, seasoning with a little milk or salt may render them sufficiently palatable.

133. Boiled Wheat.

Take good plump wheat; wash it perfectly clean, and pick out all smut, cockle, blasted grains, etc.; boil it in *pure soft water*, until the grains are softened through, which process will require several hours. It may be eaten with or without cream, sugar, molasses, or milk. Rye and barley may be cooked in the same way.

134. Boiled Rice.

Be careful and select for this purpose the large, plump kernel called *head rice;* boil it in pure soft water and in a covered vessel about twenty minutes, stirring it gently occasionally; then set it off from the fire, and in a place just warm enough for it to simmer; let it remain an hour and a half *without stirring;* the grains may then be taken out full and unbroken.

135. Parched Corn.

The most convenient method of parching corn is, to put the grains in an apparatus made of wire on purpose, called "corn parcher," and hold them over burning coals, shaking or turning them continually.

Most of the parched corn, or "dyspepsia corn," sold at the fruit stands, has a very salty, greasy taste, owing to its having been seasoned with salt and hog's lard, on the erroneous notion that such preparations would cause it to "pop" better, as well as taste more agreeable.

Cooked Chestnuts, Peanuts, Green Peas, Green Beans, Dried Beans and Peas.

136. BOILED CHESTNUTS.

These make a perfectly wholesome and very delicious food. The principal difficulty attending their use is their scarcity. As they are liable to be infected with worms, they should be carefully picked over previous to being boiled. They will cook sufficiently in about an hour. Chestnuts may be roasted in about fifteen minutes.

137. ROASTED PEANUTS.

Peanuts may be cooked in the same manner as parched corn, or baked in a stove or oven. They are healthful food as a part of the regular meal—at all events, to stomachs accustomed to plain living.

138. BOILED GREEN PEAS.

Put the peas into just enough water to cover them, immediately after they are shelled; let them boil about twenty minutes, or until done. When the pods are fresh and green, it will improve the dish to boil them also fifteen or twenty minutes in as little water as will cover them (having washed them previously); turn off the juice, and add it to the peas.

Those who will use salt should add it to the peas after they are cooked, instead of salting the water in which they are boiled

A little milk, with a trifle of sugar, if preferred, makes a good seasoning enough.

139. BOILED GREEN BEANS.

The common garden, kidney, and Lima beans are all excellent dishes, prepared by simply boiling till soft, without destroying the shape of the seed. A little milk or cream may be stirred in, when they are cooked sufficiently, if any seasoning is desired. They usually require boiling an hour and a half.

140. DRIED BEANS AND PEAS.

Dried beans usually require boiling two hours or two hours and a half; and dried peas nearly twice as long. Beans and peas which have been dried in the green state, should be soaked in cold water over night, after which they can be boiled sufficiently in about two hours.

141. Boiled Green Corn.

Trim off the husks and silk; throw it into hot water, and let it boil half or three quarters of an hour, according to the size of the ear. The sweet or sugar corn is the best for this purpose. It should never be boiled in salted water, as this makes it harder and comparatively indigestible.

142. Roasted Green Corn.

Remove the husks and lay the ears over red-hot coals on a gridiron. It is "not bad" roasted by laying the ears directly on burning coals, care being taken to turn them before they are burned injuriously.

143. Succotash.

This is usually made of green corn and garden beans, although string beans are sometimes added. Cut the kernels of corn from the cob; and stew them and the beans, closely covered, in water or milk, for about three quarters of an hour. If a richer dish is wanted, stir in a little cream, and let the whole simmer for ten minutes longer.

Some persons string the beans, and then cut them into small pieces, before mixing and stewing—a plan only to be recommended to those who have abundance of time for "small things."

Lima beans and sugar corn make an excellent succotash; to which a proportion of marrow-fat peas are sometimes added.

CHAPTER XI.

GRUELS AND SOUPS.

GRUELS are merely thin mushes; they are appropriate preparations for many invalids—in the convalescent state after febrile and inflammatory diseases—and are frequently serviceable in cases of constipation, especially when attending acute diseases. Accompanied with dry toast, stale bread, or hard crackers, they help to make a variety for well folks.

Soups are dishes intermediate between gruels and mushes; and, if properly made, are not objectionable as changes, though not to be commended as leading or every-day dishes. Some of the following recipes, I am well aware, will taste "flat" to many palates, when the addition of a little salt would render them very "good eating." I must, therefore, leave this part of the subject to their own discretion.

144. WHEAT-MEAL GRUEL.

Mix two tablespoonfuls of wheat-meal smoothly with a gill of cold water; stir the mixture into a quart of boiling water; boil about fifteen minutes, taking off whatever scum forms on the top. A little sugar may be added if desired.

145. INDIAN-MEAL GRUEL.

Stir gradually into a quart of boiling water two tablespoonfuls of Indian-meal; boil it slowly twenty minutes. This is often prepared for the sick, under the name of "water-gruel." In the current cook-books, salt, sugar, and nutmeg are generally added Nothing of the sort should be used, except sugar.

146. OATMEAL GRUEL.

Mix a tablespoonful of oatmeal with a little cold water; pour on the mixture a quart of hot but not boiling water, stirring it well; let it settle two or three minutes; then pour it into the pan carefully, leaving the coarser part of the meal at the bottom of the vessel; set it on the fire and stir it till it boils; then let it boil about five minutes, and skim.

147. Farina Gruel.

Mix two tablespoonfuls of farina in a gill of water; pour very gradually on the mixture a quart of boiling water, stirring thoroughly, and boil ten minutes.

148. Tapioca Gruel.

Wash a tablespoonful of tapioca, and soak it in a pint and a half of water twenty minutes; then boil gently, stirring frequently, till the tapioca is sufficiently cooked, and sweeten.

149. Sago Gruel.

Wash two tablespoonfuls of sago, and soak it a few minutes in half a pint of cold water; then boil a pint and a half of water, and, while boiling, stir in the farina; boil slowly till well done, and sweeten with sugar or molasses.

150. Currant Gruel.

Add two tablespoonfuls of currants to a quart of wheat-meal or oatmeal ground, and, after boiling a few minutes, add a little sugar.

151. Groat Gruel.

Steep clean groats in water for several hours; boil them in pure soft water till quite tender and thick; then add boiling water sufficient to reduce to the consistency of gruel. Currants and sugar may also be added.

152. Arrow-root Gruel.

Mix an ounce of arrow-root smoothly with a little cold water; then pour on to the mixture a pint of boiling water, stirring it constantly; return it into the pan, and let it boil five minutes. Season with sugar and lemon-juice.

GRUELS AND SOUPS.

Rice Gruel—Soups of Tomato, Rice, Peas, and Barley.

153. RICE GRUEL.

Boil two ounces of good clean rice in a quart of water until the grains are quite soft; then add two tablespoonfuls of sugar, and boil two or three minutes. Currants made a good addition to this gruel.

154. TOMATO SOUP.

Scald and peel good ripe tomatoes; stew them one hour, and strain through a coarse sieve; stir in a very little wheaten flour to give it body, and brown sugar in the proportion of a teaspoonful to a quart of soup; then boil five minutes. This is one of the most agreeable and wholesome of the "fancy dishes." Ochre, or gumbo, is a good addition to this and many other kinds of soup.

155. RICE SOUP.

Boil one gill of rice in a pint of water till soft; then add a pint of milk, a teaspoonful of sugar, and simmer gently five minutes.

156. SPLIT PEAS SOUP.

Wash one pint of split peas; boil them in three quarts of water for three hours, and add a tablespoonful of sugar.

157. GREEN PEAS SOUP.

Take three pints of peas, three common-sized turnips, one carrot, and the shells of the peas. Boil one quart of the largest of the peas, with the shells or the pods, till quite soft; rub through a fine colander; return the pulp into the pan, add the turnips, a carrot, sliced, and a quart of boiling water; when the vegetables are perfectly soft, add the young or smaller peas, previously boiled.

158. SPLIT PEAS AND BARLEY SOUP.

Take three pints of split peas, half a pint of pearl barley, half a pound of stale bread, and one turnep, sliced. Wash the peas and barley, and steep them in fresh water at least twelve hours; place them over the fire; add the bread, turnip, and half a tablespoonful of sugar; boil till all are quite soft; rub them through a fine colander, adding gradually a quart of boiling water; return the soup into the pan, and boil ten minutes.

Barley and Green Bean Soups—Vegetable and Barley Broths—Spinach Soup.

159. BARLEY SOUP.

Take four ounces of barley, two ounces of bread crumbs, and half an ounce of chopped parsley. Wash the barley; and steep it twelve hours in half a pint of water; pour off the water; add the bread crumbs, and three quarts of boiling water; boil slowly in a covered tin pan five hours, and about half an hour before the dish is to be served, add the parsley.

160. GREEN BEAN SOUP.

Take one quart of garden or kidney beans, one ounce of spinach, and one ounce of parsley. Boil the beans; skin and bruise them in a bowl till quite smooth; put them in a pan with two quarts of vegetable broth (No. 161); dredge in a little flour; stir it on the fire till it boils, and put in the spinach and parsley (previously boiled and rubbed through a sieve).

161. VEGETABLE BROTH.

This may be made with various combinations and proportions of vegetables. For example—four turnips, two carrots, one onion, and a spoonful of lentil flour. Half fill a pan with the vegetables, in pieces; nearly fill up the vessel with water; boil till all the vegetables are tender, and strain.

162. BARLEY BROTH.

Take four ounces of pearl barley, two turnips, three ounces of Indian-meal, and three ounces of sweet cream. Steep the pearl barley (after washing) twelve hours; set it on the fire in five quarts of fresh water, adding the turnips; boil gently an hour; add the cream; stir in the meal; thin it, if necessary, with more water, and simmer gently twenty minutes.

163. SPINACH SOUP.

Take two quarts of spinach, half a pound of parsley, two carrots, two turnips, one root of celery, and two ounces of cream. Stew all the ingredients in a pint of water—a few lemon parings may be thrown in to flavor—till quite soft; rub through a coarse sieve; add a quart of hot water, and boil twenty minutes.

Vegetable and Rice Soup—Cucumber and Gumbo Soup.

164. VEGETABLE AND RICE SOUP.

Take one pound of turnips, half a pound of carrots, quarter of a pound of parsneps, half a pound of potatoes, and three tablespoonfuls of rice. Slice the vegetables; put the turnips, carrots, and parsneps into a pan with a quart of boiling water; add the rice (previously picked and washed); boil one hour; add the potatoes, with two quarts of water, and boil till all are well done. If too thin, a little rice flour, mixed with milk, may be stirred in, boiling afterward fifteen minutes.

165. CUCUMBER AND GUMBO SOUP.

Take half a dozen cucumbers of moderate size, six ounces of bread crumbs, four ounces of gumbo, one ounce of parsley, and six ounces of sweet cream. Pare and slice the cucumbers; chop the gumbo and parsley into small pieces, and stew them gently three quarters of an hour, stirring occasionally; then pour in two quarts of boiling water; add the bread crumbs and cream, and let the whole stew two hours. If the soup is then too thin, dredge in a little flour, and boil ten minutes longer.

CHAPTER XII.

ROOTS AND VEGETABLES.

166. Boiled Potatoes.

Wash the potatoes without cutting them; put them in boiling water, with not more of the water than is sufficient to cover them; boil moderately until they are softened so that a fork will readily penetrate them; pour off the water, and let them stand till dry.

Young potatoes of medium size will cook in about twenty-five minutes; old potatoes require double the time. When peeled, they will cook in about half the time.

All who would have potatoes well-cooked must observe the following particulars: Always take them out of the water the moment they are done. Ascertain when they are done by pricking with a fork, and not leave them to crack open. When cooked in any way, they become heavy and "watery" by cooking them after they are once softened through. They should be selected of an equal size, or the smallest should be taken up as fast as cooked. Potatoes should never be boiled very hard, as it is apt to break them; nor should the water stop boiling, as it will tend to make them watery. Old potatoes are improved by soaking in cold wate several hours, or over night, before cooking. They should never re main covered after having been roasted or boiled, to keep them hot

167. Boiled Peeled Potatoes.

Pare, wash, and soak them an hour or two in cold water; boil slowly in just water enough to cover them, keeping the vessel *uncovered*; as soon as a fork will pass through them, pour off the water, and let them steam five minutes. This method of cooking renders the potatoes mealy and dry.

168. BROWNED POTATOES.

Take cold boiled potatoes; cut them in slices about one third of an inch in thickness; lay them on a gridiron or in a stove or oven, till both sides are moderately browned.

169. POTATO FOR SHORTENING.

Wash, wipe, and pare the potatoes; cover them with cold water, and boil moderately until done; pour off the water; then put each potato separately into a clean *warm* cloth; twist the cloth so as to press all the moisture from it. Potatoes cooked in this way are light and mealy for *mashing*, and are an excellent article to mix in pastry, bread, cake, and puddings, to make them tender and "short."

170. MASHED POTATOES.

Pare and wash the potatoes; put them in the vessel and cover them with cold water; put them on the fire, and boil slowly till done; dry, and mash them till smooth and without lumps; then stir in a little rich milk or sweet cream.

171. BROWNED MASHED POTATO.

Prepare the potatoes as in 170; place them in a dish, and shape the top tastefully, making checks with a knife, etc.; then put them in a moderately hot stove, range, or oven, till well browned, yet not burned. The flavor of *very old* potatoes may be improved, or rather disguised, in this way.

172. BREAKFAST POTATO.

Wash, peel, and cut into very thin slices, into as little water as they can boil in, so that it will principally evaporate in the process of cooking. Season with a very little milk or cream.

173. POTATO FLOUR.

Grate potatoes, previously mashed and peeled, into a tub or large earthen pan of cold water; let the pulp remain till it falls to the bottom, and the water begins to clear; pour off the water, and add more—which should be pure and *soft*—stirring the pulp well with the hand, and rub it through a hair sieve, pouring water on it plentifully; when the water clears pour it off carefully, and add more, stirring it well, and repeat the process till the farina is perfectly white and the water clear; then spread the farina on flat dishes before the fire, covering with paper to protect it from dust when dry, reduce it to powder; sift it, and preserve it in corked bottles or canisters.

Potato flour is a useful addition to many kinds of puddings, pies, cakes, and breads, especially for those who are not much experienced in our style of cooking, as it makes them more light and tender.

174. POTATO JELLY.

Pour water while *actually boiling* on the potato flour, and it will soon change into a very pleasant jelly. It may be flavored with a little sugar and fruit sauce.

175. ROASTED POTATOES.

Potatoes are richer and more mealy, if carefully washed, and then buried in hot ashes, than when roasted in any other way. But they may be very well cooked, after washing, by roasting in a Dutch oven, or reflector, before the fire, or in any oven moderately heated. The time required is from an hour and a half to two hours.

176. SWEET POTATOES.

They may be baked with their skins on; or peeled and boiled, and then browned a little in the oven; or simply boiled. They are excellent sliced and browned the next day after having been boiled.

177. BAKED POTATOES.

Select those of rather large and uniform size; put them in the oven, and turn them occasionally till sufficiently done.

178. BOILED TURNIPS.

When turnips are sweet and tender, they are best if boiled whole till soft, and then sent immediately to the table. If they are allowed to boil too long they become bitterish. An hour is the medium time. They are less watery and better flavored when boiled with their skins on, and pared afterward

ROOTS AND VEGETABLES.

Preparations of Parsneps—Onions—Carrots—Artichokes.

179. MASHED TURNIPS.

This is the best method of preparing watery turnips, and a good way of cooking all cookable kinds. Pare, wash, and cut them in slices; put them in a pan with as much cold water as will just cover them; let them boil till soft; pour them into a sieve or colander and press out the water; mash them with fresh milk or sweet cream until entirely free from lumps; then put them into a saucepan over the fire, and stir them about three minutes.

180. BOILED PARSNEPS.

Wash the parsneps very clean; split them in halves or quarters, and boil them till tender. Roots of ordinary size may be boiled in one hour or less.

181. STEWED PARSNEPS.

Wash, pare, and cut them into slices; boil until soft in just water enough to keep them from burning; then stir in sweet milk; dredge in a trifle of flour, and simmer fifteen minutes. This is a favorite dish with many persons.

182. BROWNED PARSNEPS.

Cold, boiled parsneps make an excellent relish with breakfast, if the slices or pieces are browned after the manner of potatoes in No. 168.

183. ONIONS

Onions, leeks, and some other acrid vegetables, if deprived of their pungency by boiling or roasting, may be tolerated as a part of the dietary of well persons; but I would dissuade invalids from using them at all. With many they prove decidedly injurious.

184. CARROTS.

Carrots may be boiled, stewed, or browned in the same manner as parsneps (Nos. 180, 181, 182). They are, however, less palatable to most persons, without abundant seasoning. Carrots require to be boiled longer than parsneps.

185. JERUSALEM ARTICHOKES.

Wash and brush, but do not peel them; boil them after tne rules for boiling potatoes; dry, peel, and wash them, seasoning with milk or cream.

186. BOILED BEET-ROOT.

Wash the roots carefully; avoid scraping, cutting, or breaking the roots, as the juice would escape and the flavor be injured; put them into a pan of boiling water; let them boil one or two hours, according to size; then put them into cold water and rub off the skin with the hand, and cut them in neat slices of uniform size. Good beets are sweet enough intrinsically, and need no extraneous seasoning.

NOTE.—Beet-root must not be probed with a fork, as are potatoes. When done, the thickest part will yield to the pressure of the fingers.

187. BAKED BEETS.

Wash the roots clean, and bake whole till quite tender; put them in cold water; rub off the skin; if large, cut them in round slices; but if small, slice them lengthwise. If any seasoning is insisted on, lemon juice is the most appropriate. When baked slowly and carefully, beet-root is very rich, wholesome, and nutritious. It usually requires baking four or five hours.

188. STEWED BEET.

Take baked or boiled beet-root; pare and cut it into slices; simmer in milk or diluted cream fifteen minutes, and thicken the gravy with a little wheaten flour.

189. ASPARAGUS.

Put the stalks in cold water; cut off all that is very tough; tie them in bundles; put them over the fire and let them boil fifteen to twenty-five minutes, or until tender, without being soft. No one has a right to desire a better vegetable than this, with no other preparation than boiling.

It should be cooked soon after being picked, or kept cool and moist in a cellar till wanted.

Roots and Vegetables.

Cabbages—Cauliflowers—Broccoli—Cucumbers—Greens.

190. Boiled Cabbage.

Take off the outer leaves; cut the head in halves or quarters, and boil quickly in a large quantity of water till done; then drain and press out the water, and chop fine. Cabbages require boiling from half an hour to an hour.

It will improve the flavor if the water is drained off when the cabbages are about half done, and fresh water added.

191. Boiled Savoys.

Savoys are a species of cabbage, and should be cooked in the same manner.

192. Stewed Cabbage.

Parboil in milk and water; drain and shred it; put it into a stewpan with a teacupful of fresh milk or a gill of sweet cream, and cook till quite tender.

193. Cauliflowers.

Cut off the green leaves; cleanse the heads carefully from insects; soak them in cold water an hour, then boil in milk and water.

194. Broccoli.

Peel the stalks, and boil them fifteen minutes; tie the shoots into bunches; add a little milk or cream, and stew gently for ten minutes.

195. Stewed Cucumbers.

Pare and cut them into quarters, taking out the seeds; boil like asparagus; serve up with toasted bread and sweet cream.

196. Greens.

Spinach, beet tops, cabbage sprouts, hop tops, mustard leaves, and turnip leaves are excellent for greens. Cowslips, dandelions, and deer weed are also used. They all require to be carefully washed and cleaned. Spinach should be washed in several waters. All the cooking requisite is, boiling till tender, and draining on a colander. Lemon juice is the appropriate seasoning.

197. STRING BEANS.

When very young, the pods need only to be clipped, cut finely and boiled till tender; when older, cut or break off the ends, strip off the strings that line their edges; cut or break each pod into three or four pieces, and boil. When made tender, a little cream or milk may be simmered with them a few minutes.

198. EGG PLANT.

This plant is so unpalatable without an extensive range of seasonings, that I think it not worth bothering with. The "authorities" in cookery give us *onions, butter, salt, black pepper,* and *red pepper*, to assist in getting it down. But if a dish or aliment can not be relished without pungent and irritants enough to set the mouth on fire and the teeth on edge, this fact is *prima facie* evidence that it had better be let alone. If any one likes them boiled in a large quantity of water, like cabbage, or boiled and then stewed in cream or milk, well and good.

199. VEGETABLE MARROW.

Peel the marrows; cut them in halves; scrape out the seeds; then boil about twenty minutes, or until soft; drain them in a sieve; wash them; add a little milk or cream, and simmer a few minutes.

200. SALSIFY—OYSTER PLANT.

Scrape the vegetable; cut it in strips; parboil it; then chop it up with milk and a little sweet cream, and simmer gently till cooked very tender.

CHAPTER XIII.

PREPARED FRUITS.

Cook Books are singularly meager in directions for preparing fruits for the table. Indeed, they hardly recognize them as food; and only give us tedious processes for converting them into sweetmeats, candies, brandied pickles, jams, jellies, marmalades, etc.

The relations of fruit to health, and the relations of cookery to fruit, are subjects eminently worthy the attention of " model housekeepers."

201. BAKED APPLES.

The best baking apples are moderately tart, or very juicy sweet ones. The former, of ordinary size, will bake in about thirty minutes; the latter in about forty-five minutes. Select, for baking, apples of nearly equal size; wipe them dry and clean; put a very little water in the bottom of the baking vessel, and place them in a hot oven.

202. STEWED GREEN APPLES.

Apples for stewing should be well flavored and juicy. Sweet apples, when stewed, turn more or less dark colored, and hence do not appear as well as tart ones on the table, though some persons prefer them. Pare, core, and quarter; put a little water to them, and boil moderately till quite soft, and add sufficient sugar to suit taste—more or less, according to the acidity of the fruit. Some cooks flavor them with lemon; others with a small portion of peaches or other fruits. Good apples, however, are good enough in and of themselves.

203. BOILED APPLES.

Select round mellow apples of uniform size; pare them; boil in as little water as possible, till soft; put them in a vegetable dish;

and slowly pour over them a sirup, made by dissolving half a pound of sugar in a pint of boiling water.

204. STEWED PIPPINS.

A rich apple sauce is made as follows: Peel, core, and quarter half-a dozen ribstone pippins; put them into a pan with six ounces of brown sugar, the juice of a lemon, its thin rind cut into strips, and very little water; stew over a very slow fire till quite tender.

205. STEWED DRIED APPLES.

Select rich, mellow-flavored fruit, which is clear from dark spots or mold. That which is dried on strings is usually the nicest. Wash and pick the pieces; boil in just water enough to cover them, over a slow fire, till partially softened; then add sugar or molasses, and continue the boiling till done. For a change, they may be occasionally flavored with a proportion of dried peaches or quinces.

206. PEARS.

Pears may be baked, boiled, or stewed in the same manner as apples. Some varieties of small, early, and sweet pears are very delicious, boiled whole without paring, and swetened with sirup. The large pears are usually selected for baking.

207. BOILED PEACHES.

When peaches are not well ripened, or too sour to be eaten without cooking, boiling improves them very much. They should be pared—except when the skins are very smooth, clean, and tender—but not stoned; boiled moderately till sufficiently cooked, and then sweetened.

208. STEWED GREEN PEACHES.

Pare them and take out the stones; add a very little water, and a sufficient quantity of sugar, and boil very slowly till well cooked

209. STEWED DRIED PEACHES.

Most of the dried peaches in our markets are sour and unpleasant. But when we can find them of good quality, they are very excellent stewed and sweetened precisely like dried apples.

Uncooked Peaches—Apricots—Cherries—Marmalade.

210. UNCOOKED PEACHES.

When we have peaches as good and ripe as all peaches ought to be, the best way to prepare them is this: Peel them; cut the fruit off the stones in quarters, or smaller pieces; fill the dish; stir in a little sugar, and sprinkle a little more over the top.

211. APRICOTS.

Ripe apricots may be prepared in the same way as peaches, but they are best with no preparation at all. Unripe apricots may be cut into quarters, sweetened, flavored with lemon, and stewed in a little water. They will cook in a very few minutes. Avoid stirring and breaking the pieces, but shake the pan round occasionally to prevent burning.

212. CHERRIES.

Stewing is the only proper method for cooking this fruit. Remove the stalks from the cherries; pick them over carefully, rejecting all unsound ones; put them into a pan, with a very little water, and sugar in the proportion of about three ounces to a pound of cherries; simmer them slowly over the fire, shaking the pan round occasionally till done. If a richer article is wanted, take the cherries out with a colander spoon, and keep them in a basin till cold; reduce the sweetened water to the consistency of sirup, and put it over the cherries.

213. QUINCES

It has been said that quinces commend themselves more to the sense of smell than of taste; hence are better to "adorn" other preparations than to be prepared themselves. When stewed till quite tender, and sweetened, they are, however, very pleasant, yet rather expensive sauce. In the form of marmalade, it is a better seasoning for bread, cakes, or puddings, than butter.

214. QUINCE MARMALADE.

Pare, core, and quarter the quinces; boil them gently, uncovered, in water, till they begin to soften; then strain them through a hair ieve, and beat, in a mortar or wooden bowl, to a pulp; add to each pound of fruit three quarters of a pound of sugar; boil till it becomes stiff, and pour into small molds or sweetmeat pots.

215. Stewed Cranberries.

Wash and pick the berries; stew them in just as little water as will prevent their burning, till they become soft; then add half a pound of sugar to a pound of the fruit, and simmer a few minutes.

216. Blackberries.

When very ripe and sweet, a little sugar dusted over them is a sufficient preparation for the table. If sour, or not quite ripe, they should be stewed till soft, and moderately sweetened. The same rules apply to all berried fruits for which recipes are not given.

217. Whortleberries.

Many prefer these uncooked and unseasoned. If stewed, however, they require but very little sweetening.

218. Raspberries.

Red raspberries are never fit to be eaten till ripe, and then they require neither sugar nor cooking. Black raspberries, when quite ripe, are also best in a "state of nature." If not entirely ripe, they may be stewed a few minutes, and sweetened with a very little sugar or molasses.

219. Strawberries.

Stewing is always an improvement to this fruit, especially for invalids, unless it is "dead ripe." As we usually find them in our city markets, they are picked before the ripening process has matured them, and hence require considerable sugar.

220. Gooseberries.

Though very acid fruits, especially half-grown, are not to be recommended to invalids, as a general rule; yet I find that many who are "on the sick list" can use stewed gooseberries without discomfort, and nearly all well persons can do the same. They should be cooked till thoroughly softened, and sweetened till palatable.

Currants—Plums—Grapes—Pineapple—Tomatoes.

221. CURRANTS.

Green currants, when half or two thirds grown, are more mild-flavored and pleasant than when fully ripe; nor do I find them often disagreeing with ordinary dyspeptics. They require stewing but a short time, and moderately sweetening. The best currants, when quite ripe, may be eaten uncooked, with a sprinkling of sugar.

222. PLUMS.

These must be managed according to their character and flavor. Many varieties are too sour to be eaten without stewing, and the addition of considerable sugar. Some kinds, however, are sweet and luscious enough to require neither.

223. GRAPES.

When the grapes are so sour as to set one's teeth on edge, they should be stewed and sweetened. But good, ripe, well-cultivated Isabellas and Catawbas are incomparably superior in dietetic character, without "the interference of our art." What a blessing it would be to the human race if all the vineyards in the world were made to supply wholesome food for children, instead of pernicious poison for adults!

224. PINEAPPLE.

The only way of preparing this fruit, which, like some others, has more flavor than taste, is that of paring, slicing, and sprinkling with sugar.

225. TOMATOES.

Scald the tomatoes by pouring boiling water on them; peel off the skins; then stew them for an hour, and add a little slightly toasted bread. This is an excellent sauce for hydropathic tables; and the fruit may be improved in flavor by stewing half an hour or even an hour longer.

CHAPTER XIV.

PREPARATIONS OF ANIMAL FOOD.

The flesh of animals affords but few dishes which can be employed consistently with water-cure treatment or physiological habits; indeed, all flesh-eating is, in the strict sense, *un*physiological, and a compromise with the present appetences, habits, or infirmities of a degenerate state of society, consequent on a wide departure from, and long-continued violation of, organic laws; hence, while we "permit" the moderate use of animal food in many cases, we should be especially cautious to make the best possible selections and preparations.

226. Beef Steak.

This should be cut from the sirloin, well pounded, and broiled; but not overdone in the least. For those who have good teeth, "rare cooked" steak is the most wholesome.

227. Mutton Chops.

These should be selected from young animals, but not young lambs; well trimmed of fatty matters, and broiled in the same way as steak.

228. Stewed Mutton.

Stew the chops in a little water till very tender; then dredge a little flour in the water. For feeble teeth this is preferable to the broiled chops.

229. Boiled Mutton.

The leg is the best part for boiling. The time usually required for cooking it is two hours and a half. For health's sake there is little to choose between this and the steak, or chops.

Preparations of Animal Food.

Preparations of Beef—Venison—White Fish—Poultry.

230. Roast Beef.

The sirloin is, on many accounts, to be selected for roasting. The fatty matter should be carefully removed before roasting, as the heat renders it particularly obnoxious to the digestive organs. As is the case with steak, it is most wholesome rare done, provided the teeth are sufficient for its due mastication.

231. Corned Beef.

The lean pieces are to be chosen for boiling; the " round" is one of the best. It should be but *slightly* corned—not allowed to remain in brine over two or three days, and boiled till the fibers are cut easily.

232. Beef Hash.

This is made by chopping cold corned beef or beefsteak into small pieces, and warming it up with three or four times the quantity of cold boiled potatoes in a little water.

233: Venison.

The flesh of the wild deer is usually called venison. It is at least as healthful as that of any of our domestic animals, and may be cooked in the same ways. Nearly all that we see in this market is old and discolored with incipient putrefaction, and entirely unfit for food.

234. White Fish.

The cod, halibut, trout, white-fish, black-fish, perch, and a few other varieties which are not very oily nor strong, are the best. They may be boiled or broiled. The only admissible gravy is water with a little milk and salt, and thickened with flour.

235. Poultry.

Common fowls should be stewed after the manner of mutton chops, or boiled. Turkeys are better boiled than roasted. Chickens, when tender, may be boiled or stewed. When any kind of fowl is stewed or boiled, the floating particles of oil should be carefully removed by skimming.

236. Eggs.

Put them in water at the boiling point, and let them scald (without boiling) about seven minutes—a little more or less according to size. This method will cook them through, and still leave the albumen soft and digestible. If cooked in boiling water they should remain in the water not more than four or five minutes.

CHAPTER XV

RELISHES AND FANCY DISHES.

HYDROPATHICALLY speaking, our catalogue of "fancies" or "dainties," in the eating line, must be rather limited. Nevertheless, if a sufficient amount of "inventive genius" were brought to bear on the subject, a pretty respectable variety could be "got up" without compromising so much with custom as to sink entirely the idea of dietetic reform. At all events, I will try to gather together a single chapter.

237. CUSTARD WITHOUT EGGS.

Take one quart of sweet, new milk, four tablespoonfuls of flour, two tablespoonfuls of sugar. Boil the milk over a brisk fire, and, when boiling, stir in the flour (having been previously mixed with cold milk to prevent lumping). When thoroughly scalded, bake in a crust, or in cups.

238. RICE CUSTARD.

Boil two ounces of ground rice in a pint and a half of new milk; add four ounces of sugar, an ounce of grated cocoa-nut, four ounces of sweet cream, and bake in a slow oven.

239. RASPBERRY CUSTARD.

Boil one pint of cream; dissolve half a pound of sugar in three gills of raspberry juice; mix this with the boiling cream; stir till the whole is quite thick, and serve in custard glasses.

240 APPLE CREAM.

Pare and boil good, rich, baking apples till soft; rub the pulp through a hair sieve; add the sugar while warm; when cold, stir in a sufficient quantity of sweet cream, and serve cold.

241. Snow Cream.

To one pint of cream add four ounces of sugar, one gill of lemonade, and the whites of two eggs, well beaten; whisk the whole to a froth, and serve in a cream dish.

242. Pineapple Ice Cream.

Mix three gills of pineapple sirup with one pint of cream; add the juice of a large lemon, and four ounces of sugar; pour into a mold; cover it with white paper; lay a piece of brown paper over to prevent any water getting in, and set it in the ice.

243. Strawberry Cream.

Mash the fruit gently; drain it on a sieve, strewing a little sugar on it; when well drained (without being pressed), add sugar and cream to the juice, and, if too thick, a little milk. Whisk it in a bowl, and, as the froth rises, lay it on a sieve; and when no more will rise, put the cream in a dish, and lay the froth upon it.

244. Raspberry Ice Cream.

Mash one pound of raspberries; strain off the juice; mix it with the cream; add sugar as required; whisk it; then pour into glasses, and freeze.

NOTE.—The bucket used for freezing should be large enough to allow four or five inches of ice, broken in small pieces and mixed with salt, to be placed below and around the sides of the mold.

245. Curd Cheese.

Add as much sour milk to a quart of new milk as will turn it to a soft curd. Serve with sugar or preserved fruit. This is sometimes called "Turkish yourt."

246. Pot Cheese.

Scald a pint of sour milk till it curdles; strain off the whey, and form the curd into round cakes half an inch thick. The milk should not be old and bitterish. If very sour, a little sweet milk scalded with it improves the flavor of the curd.

The pot or Dutch cheese sold by our market-women, and at some of the milk stores, is usually spoiled by an excessive quantity of salt.

247. Cherry Jam.

Take four pounds of Kentish cherries, one pound of fine sugar, and half a pint of red currant juice. Stone the fruit, and boil the whole together, rather quickly, till it becomes stiff.

248. Apple Cheese.

Take two pounds of apples, pared and sliced; one pound of sugar; the juice and grated rind of a lemon, and a little water. Put them all into a pan; cover, and set it over the fire till the apples are reduced to a pulp, turning the pan occasionally; let it boil twenty minutes, stirring constantly, and pour it into small molds.

249. Grape Sirup.

To four pounds of picked grapes add a pint of water, set them over a moderately hot fire till the grapes are well boiled, keeping the pan, which should be block-tin or brass, covered; strain through a hair sieve, gently pressing the grapes; when cool, cover it with a plate, and let it remain till the next day; then carefully clear it off, and to each pint allow a pound of loaf-sugar, broken; put the sugar into a pan, adding a pint of water to each four pounds; stir it, while cold, till the sugar is partly dissolved; then put it on a moderately brisk fire with the pan covered, stirring it occasionally till nearly boiling; then watch it carefully; and if it rise very much, draw the pan a little forward; let it boil up quickly several times, then moderately, till there is a thick scum formed at the side of the pan; take it off quite clean; then pour in the juice; cover the pan till nearly boiling; remove the cover, and let the sirup boil a quarter of a hour, carefully taking off any scum that may rise. Pour the sirup into a large stone jar in which has been placed a little grated lemon or a few broken pieces of cinnamon, and let it remain one day; then strain it into bottles; cork, and keep it in a cool place.

The above is really a kind of *unalcoholic* wine, and as such can not be too highly recommended for " medicinal and sacramental

Method of Baking Milk, or of Making Milk Gruel.

purposes," in place of the drugged liquors and intoxicating wines so generally employed.

250. BAKED MILK.

Put the milk into a jar; tie white paper over it; let it remain in a moderately warm oven all night, and it w'll be of the consistency of thin gruel.

CHAPTER XVI.

KITCHEN MISCELLANY.

IN a concluding chapter I propose to group together a few recipes of general information, which, though useful to all, are more frequently applicable to the "sphere" of the cook.

251. NEW KIND OF OVEN.

An improved baking oven has been lately patented by a Mr. Carlisle, of Chesterfield, Me. It is built of brick, in the usual manner; but below the hearth is a vacancy for the fire; and the flue runs spirally around the outside of it, so that it is heated from the outside. It requires no sweeping nor wetting of the hearth, and, of course, is exempt from the cracking which is often occasioned thereby; and, if necessary, it may be kept constantly hot.

252. STEAM COOKING.

The application of steam to the boiling of fruits and vegetables is well understood; but it can be applied also in cooking bread, cakes, biscuit, pastry, etc. My own experience has been limited; but as far as I have experimented, I am favorably impressed with this mode of cooking many farinaceous preparations. The following extract from a communication, from D. B. Hale, of Collinsville, Conn., will show what is doing elsewhere in relation to this subject.

253. STEAMING vs. BAKING BREAD.

DR. TRALL—*Dear Sir:* I wish to get your views on a new process of cooking bread, now coming into use among us, and I presume elsewhere. It is simply this: After the dough is prepared precisely as for baking, and placed in the tins, it is steamed in the following manner: Into a boiling pot put half a pint or a quart of water; lay sticks on the bottom crosswise, to set the tins on; keep the water moderately boiling from twenty minutes to an hour, according to the size of the loaf, when it comes out as light and nice as any bread from the oven, and without any crust."

254. Cucumbers in Tubs.

Take a tight box or a tub; cover the bottom with small stones, pour in water to the height of the stones, or even higher; then fill up the box with rich soil, into which plant the seeds.

255. Potato Cheese.

The following method, practiced in Saxony, makes a more healthful article of cheese than that with which our tables are usually furnished in this country: " Boil large white potatoes until cooked; let them cool; then peel, and mash them in a mortar. To five pounds of potatoes add one pound of sour milk, and a little salt; knead the whole; cover it, and let it remain undisturbed for three or four days, according to the season. At the end of this time, knead it again, and place the cheeses in small baskets where the superfluous moisture will evaporate. Then place them in the shade to dry, and put them in layers in large pots, or any other vessels, wherein they must remain fifteen days."

In my judgment this article is more wholesome when fresh made than after standing fifteen days. I recommend, therefore, the omission of the last clause of the recipe.

256. Roasting Apples, Potatoes, Eggs, etc.

After washing, wrap them in two or three coatings of paper; wet the paper; and press it so that it will make an impervious covering. They may then be covered with hot ashes, and baked in the nicest manner. They will cook in this way sooner than by boiling.

257. Burns and Scalds.

In all ordinary cases of burns and scalds the pain can be instantly relieved, and the inflammation very soon abated, by covering the injured part with flour.

258. Cockroaches

It is said that red wafers, scattered in the places they infest, will destroy them. They may also be caught readily in vessels partly filled with molasses. The roots of black hellebore is also said to destroy them.

259. RATS AND MICE.

When these pests of the kitchen are troublesome, and "puss" is not on duty, they may often be very soon disposed of by the following strategy: Put a barrel with a little meal in it, in a place where they "most do congregate." After having been fed long enough to relieve the "oldest and most experienced rat" of his suspicions, fill the barrel one third or half full with water, and sprinkle the meal two or three inches deep on the top of it. In some cases a dozen or more are thus caught in a night.

260. CRACKED IRON.

When an iron vessel, stove, or stove-pipe is cracked, the opening may be stopped with a cement made of ashes, salt, and water.

261. IRON COOKING UTENSILS.

There is a prevalent error that *iron rust* is not only harmless, but really healthful, arising from the fact that physicians frequently prescribe it as a tonic. It is, nevertheless, a *regular* drug poison. Iron utensils for cooking purposes should, therefore, always be kept perfectly dry when not in use; and whenever rust—which is an oxide of the metal—does form, it should be removed by scouring with soap and sand.

262. COPPER VESSELS.

Vinegar and all other acids corrode copper utensils, forming *verdigris* and other violently poisonous oxides and salts. *Every kind of oil and fat* also acts on copper, forming poisonous *carbonates* of the metal. Persons have been poisoned by eating broths and soups which have been allowed to remain some time in copper boilers. All copper vessels used in cooking, therefore, should be immediately cleaned of every corroding ingredient, and nothing of the kind should ever be kept in them a moment after it is cooked.

In 1753, the senate of Sweden prohibited the employment of copper vessels for culinary purposes.

Tinning the inside of copper utensils, *after they are manufactured,* prevents their oxidation, and the consequent injurious effects. But even here we are liable to be defrauded, for manufacturers have been known, in some cases, to have mixed *lead* with tne tin, to cheapen the material, and make it work more easily.

263. LEADEN VESSELS.

Utensils of lead are seldom or never employed for culinary purposes; yet it was once the custom in some parts of England to keep milk in lead pans. Vats of lead have been used in cider-making countries; brewing coppers have sometimes been lined with lead; and the glazing of some kinds of earthenware, in which pickles are made, is made with oxide of lead. All of these are dangerous, and to be avoided if possible.

264. TIN COOKING UTENSILS.

Tin-ware cooking utensils, as *saucepans, tea-kettles*, etc., are sheets of iron coated over, or plated with tin. The same remark applies to *block tin*. As tin does not rust itself, and prevents tho iron from rusting, and as it resists great heat and changes of temperature, its advantages are obvious. Tin vessels, however, require to be carefully watched, and not used after the tinning has worn off. To prevent the tin from being rubbed off, the vessels should be rubbed, when necessary, with the finest whiting, powdered, mixed with a drop of sweet oil, and afterward dusted with the dry powder, and this cleaned off with shamois leather.

The reason that tin vessels *appear* to rust when kept in a damp place is, because, in some places, the iron is imperfectly covered. They should, therefore, be kept dry.

265. ZINC VESSELS.

This metal is not much used in the domestic economy of cooking, and should not be. A patent was once taken out in this country for an improved milk pan made of zinc. Among its pretended advantages were the effects of "causing the milk to throw up more cream, and to prevent it from turning sour"—results owing to the presence of acetate of zinc, formed by the action of the milk on the metal.

Brass, German Silver, Pewter, and Britannia—Fruit Stains—Iron and Ink.

266. BRASS COOKING UTENSILS.

Brass is a mixture of zinc and copper, and was formerly much used in the manufacture of cooking utensils. Recently it has been nearly superseded by tinned iron. Brass vessels, when employed, however, require all the precautions appertaining to copper.

267. GERMAN SILVER.

This is composed of copper, arsenic, and nickel, and is oxidized by acids. Hence the spoons made of this material should never be used in cooking processes; indeed, they ought not to be used at all.

268. PEWTER DISHES.

These are, also, nearly out of date. This metal is an alloy of tin, lead, and antimony, and easily acted on by acids, and acid fruits. The danger to be apprehended from their use is very nearly in proportion to the lead employed; and as this is the cheaper material, the manufacturer has some inducement to cheat, and the customer a corresponding risk of being poisoned. The safest way is to let them alone.

269. BRITANNIA METAL.

This is a compound of block tin, antimony, copper, and brass. It is not liable to corrosion by acids, and is safe for all the purposes to which it is usually applied—the manufacture of teapots, measures, spoons, etc.

270. FRUIT STAINS.

These can often be removed by wetting the stain with ammonia. Diluted muriatic acid—two parts water to one of the acid—will frequently succeed. Soak the stained part two or three minutes, and rinse in cold water.

271. IRON MOLD AND INK SPOTS.

Wet the spots with milk, and then cover them with common salt—washing the garments afterward. Delicate fabrics, when stained with ink, are often restored by dipping them in melted tallow.

272. Papered Walls.

To clean them without injuring the paper, gently sweep off the dust, and rub them with soft muslin cloth. Stale bread is better still.

273. Painted Wood.

Put a very little sal-soda in the water, and wash the paint with flannel and soft soap; then wash off the soap, and wipe with clean. linen.

274. Starch and Paste.

Poland and flour starch should be first stirred smoothly into cold water; boiling water should then be poured on gradually, with constant stirring, until sufficiently thinned, after which it should be boiled a few minutes. In making common paste the flour should be managed in the same way.

275. Trays, Knives, and Forks.

Never pour hot water on tea trays nor salvers; nor put the handles of knives or forks into hot water. It will destroy the polish, and loosen the handles.

276. Frozen Potatoes.

More starch or flour can be obtained from frozen potatoes than from fresh ones. When potatoes are accidentally frozen, therefore, this hint may be turned to good account.

277. Dresses on Fire.

When one's clothes have caught fire, the only safe method of proceeding is to *smother it*. If the lower garments are on fire, sit upon them; if the upper ones, throw around a blanket, shawl, etc.

278. Water-proof Cement.

Mix equal parts of vinegar and milk; turn off the whey, and mix with it five eggs; beat the whole together; then add sifted quicklime till it acquires the consistency of a thick paste. This cement resists the action of water, and also of fire to a high degree; and is hence very useful in mending cracked ware, broken vessels, etc.

Fire-proof Cement—Ready Rat-trap—Cheap Water-proof Paste.

279. FIRE-PROOF CEMENT.

Make a pailful of whitewash in the usual manner; add two pounds of brown sugar, three pounds of fine salt, and one pound of alum. Mix them thoroughly. This cement may be used on fences, the roofs of houses, around fireplaces, etc., as a protection against fire.

280. READY RAT-TRAP.

Fill a smooth kettle to within five or six inches of the top with water; cover the surface with bran or chaff; place it where the animals are infestuous, and many of them will fall into the water and drown.

281. CHEAP WATER-PROOF PASTE.

Mix oil or lard with fine pieces of India-rubber; simmer over a slow fire until incorporated to the consistency of paste.

Index.

	Page
Acetic acid	42
Acids, organic	42
Acorn	59
Adulterations in flour	50
Aku, or aker	68
Albumen	44
Alimentary principles	24
Alimentary canal	139
Aliments	48
Alligator	68
Almond oil	42
Almonds	57
Analysis of food	22
Anchovy pear	83
Angelica	94
Animal albumen	44
Animal casein	45
Animal fibrin	44
Animal food	97, 206
Animal jelly	45
Anise	94
Apples	63
Apple bread	163
Apple cheese	211
Apple cream	209
Apple custard	184
Apple pie	179
Apples, prepared	201
Apples, preserved	111
Apricots	61
Apricots, prepared	203
Arrow-root gruel	190
Arrow-root starch	39
Artichoke	88
Artichoke, Jerusalem	198
Ascending filter	81
Asparagus	89, 198
Aurantiaceous fruits	74
Avocado pear	83
Bacon	44, 97
Baked apple pudding	185
Balm	94
Bananas	83
Barberry	72
Barley	52
Barley apple pudding	182
Barley broth	192
Barley-meal	22
Barley soup	192
Basil	94
Bass	104
Bean porridge	175
Beans	22, 56
Beans and peas, dried	187
Beef	98, 206, 207
Beets, cooked	198

	Page
Beet-root	56
Beet tops	91
Berried fruits	70
Berry puddings	185
Bilberry	71
Birds	97
Bitter almonds	57
Biscuits	164
Blackberries	81, 204
Blackberry pie	181
Black-fish	104
Black bread	58
Black currant	70
Blanc-mange	46
Bleaching sirups	87
Blood in flesh	100
Blubber	42
Blueberry	72
Blotches, cutaneous	44
Boletus	97
Box filtering apparatus	83
Bracotte	107
Brains, as food	44
Brass cooking utensils	217
Brazil nut	58
Breads	148
Breads, digestibility of	158
Breads, fermented	151, 161
Bread fruit	82
Bread-making	150, 155
Bread pie crust	178
Bread pudding	182
Breads, raised	152, 161
Breads, unleavened	150, 160
Britannia metal	217
Broccoli	90, 198
Broth, vegetable	192
Brown bread, sweet	168
Brussels sprouts	91
Buds	89
Buckwheat	55
Buckwheat cakes	167
Buffalo berry	72
Burnet	91
Burns and scalds	214
Butcher's meat	22
Butter	42, 107
Butter cakes	44
Butternut	57
Cabbage	90, 199
Cakes	164
Calcium	27
Callipee	108
Candies	86
Canna starch	38
Cantaloupe	77

Index

	Page
Caraway	94
Carbon	26
Cardoon	89
Carnivora	94
Carrots	22, 8·, 197
Carrot pie	179
Cashew-nut	58
Cask filters	82
Casein	44
Caseum	45
Cassava bread	88
Caterpillars	104
Cattle	97
Cauliflowers	90, 199
Celery	91
Cement, fire-proof	219
Cement, water-proof	218
Cereal grains	49
Cheese	44, 107
Chemical elements	24, 25
Chenopodium	93
Chestnuts	57, 109, 197
Cherries	162, 203
Cherry jam	211
Chickou	102
Chickory	91
Chives	89
Chlorine	27
Christmas pudding	183
Churning	107
Chylification	139
Chymification	129
Cistern filtering	31
Citric acid	42
Citron	75
Clams	104
Cleansing filters	82
Cob-nut	58
Cockle	104
Cockroaches	214
Cockroaches, story of	xii
Cocoa-nut	58
Cocoa-nut drops	169
Codfish	104
Compound aliments	21
Common salt	27
Concentrated milk	108
Confectionery	80
Cook-book makers	ix
Cooking utensils	215, 217
Cooling water	85
Copper vessels	215
Coriander	94
Cork filters	82
Corn cream cake	166
Corn-meal muffins	169
Corn, parched	186
Corn salad	91
Corn starch	38
Corn starch blanc-mange	175
Cottage pudding	184
Cowslips	91
Cow-tree	48
Crabs	104
Cracked iron	215
Cracked wheat mush	178

	Page
Cracked wheat pudding	182
Cranberries	72, 204
Cranberry tart	180
Cream	107
Cream toast	171
Cress	91
Crumpets	169
Crustaceans	104
Cucumber and gumbo soup	198
Cucumbers	76, 190
Cucumbers in tubs	214
Cummin	94
Curd cheese	210
Currants	70, 205
Currant bread	168
Currant jelly	190
Currant pie	181
Custard pie	180
Custard pudding	185
Custard without eggs	209
Dandelion	91
Dates	63
Deer-weed	91
Defecation	143
Deglutition	124
Dewberry	62
Diet, philosophy of	15
Digestibility of breads	153
Digestion	120
Digestive apparatus	144
Digestive processes	121
Dill	98
Distillery milk	106
Dock	98
Dresses on fire	218
Dried beans and peas	187
Dried fruit pies	181
Dried peas yeast	160
Drupes	60
Dried toast	171
Ducks	108
Durion	52
East Indian arrow-root	40
Eels	44, 104
Eggs	104
Eggs, yolk of	44
Eggs, cooked	208
Egg plant	208
Elements of food	24
Elderberry	78
Endive	91
Enlarged liver	103
Ergot	53
Eruptions	44
Erysipelas	44
Esculent roots	84
Essence of milk	108
Fancy dishes	209
Farina gruel	190
Farina mush	175
Farina pudding	184
Fat	42, 101
Fat pork	44
Fattening	146
Fecal accumulations	144
Fennel	98

INDEX.

	Page		Page
Ferment	157, 159	Guava	82
Fermentation	148	Gum	85
Fermented breads	151, 161	Haddock	104
Ferns	94	Halibut	104
Fibrin	44	Hand mills	51
Figs	76	Hashes	44
Fig and cocoa-nut pudding	186	Hawk	102
Filberts	58, 109	Hazel-nut	58
Filtration, of sugar	37	Herbivorous animals	21, 98
Filtration, of water	29	Herrings	44, 104
Fish	97, 104, 207	High diet	118
Fire-proof cement	219	Hirse	55
Fire, remedies for	214, 218	Hogs	97
Flannel filter	30	Hominy	54, 174
Flesh, lean	09	Hominy porridge	176
Fleshy fruits	59	Hominy pudding	183
Flour, adulterated	154	Hop yeast	158
Flour and potato rolls	168	Honey	87
Flour, quality of	154	Horse chestnut	57
Flour yeast	160	Hydrogen	26
Food	48	Hydropathic crumpets	169
Forks	218	Ice houses	116
Fowl	103	Improved jumballe	170
Frost cakes	172	Indian corn	54
Fruit cake	172	Indian cress	94
Fruit pies, dried	181	Indian-meal cake	164
Fruits, prepared	201	Indian-meal mush	174
Fruits, classified	59	Indian-meal gruel	189
Fruits, preserved	111	Indian-meal pudding	183
Fruit stains	217	Indian pancakes	168
Fungin	41	Indian slippers	167
Fumet	108	Infanticide	106
Gambo	76	Ink spots	217
Game, high	26	Insalivation	122
Garden cress	91	Insects, as food	104
Garlic	89	Iron	27
Geese	103	Iron, cracked	215
Gelatin	45	Iron cooking utensils	215
German silver	217	Iron mold	217
Glue	46	Italian wheat	55
Gluten	45	Jam, cherry	211
Gooseberries	70, 204	Jar, filter	38
Gooseberry pie	181	Jelly	42
Graham bread	162	Jelly, animal	45, 46
Grains and seeds	186	Jelly, currant	190
Grains of starch	88	Jerusalem artichoke	198
Grapes	78, 205	Johnny cake	164
Grape sirup	211	Jujube	83
Grasshopper	104	Juvia	83
Grease	42	Jumballs	172
Green beans, boiled	187	Juniper berries	78
Green bean soup	192	Kidneys, as food	101
Green corn	54, 109	Kitchen miscellany	218
Green corn, boiled	188	Knives and forks	218
Green corn, roasted	188	Lacteals	141, 142
Green corn pudding	185	Lactic acid	43, 107
Green peas	56	Lactometer	106
Green peas, boiled	187	Lake water	29
Green peas soup	191	Lamb lettuce	91
Greens	199	Lard	42, 44, 98
Griddle cake	167	Lavender	94
Groat gruel	190	Leaden vessels	216
Groats	52	Leaven	157
Grouse	103	Leeks	89
Grub worm	104	Legumes	56
Gruels	189	Lemon	75

224   INDEX.

	Page
Lentils	22, 56
Leprosy	44
Lettuce	91
Lichens	95
Liebig criticised	26
Lignin	41
Lima beans	56, 109
Limes	83
Livers	44, 101
Liver disease	44
Lobster	104
Locusts	104
Love apple	76
Low diet	118
Lozenges	86
Macaroni snow pudding	183
Mackerel	104
Madeira-nuts	58
Magnesium	27
Maize	54
Maize-meal	22
Mamma	83
Mango	88
Mangostan	84
Manna	37
Marjoram	93
Marmalade	208
Marrow	42
Marrow pudding	44
Marsh water	20
Mastication	123
Meal, quality of	177
Medlar	60
Melons	77
Milk	48, 105
Milk, baked	212
Milk biscuit	169
Milk, concentrated	106
Milk, distillery	106
Milk, essence of	109
Milk porridge	176
Milk risings	158
Milk toast	171
Milk, vegetable	48
Millet	55
Mineral water	29
Mints	93
Moist rice bread	168
Molasses	37
Molasses cake	166
Molded farinaces	175
Molluscs	104
Morel	97
Mulberry	79
Muscle	99, 101
Mushes	178
Mushrooms	95
Musk	77
Mussels	104
Mustard	91
Mutton	98, 206
Nasturtium	96
Nectarine	61
New Zealand spinach	92
Nitrogen	26
Nuts	57

	Page
Nut oils	42
Nutriment in food	22
Nutrition	118
Oatmeal—oats	22, 52
Oatmeal cake	167
Oatmeal gruel	189
Oatmeal mush	174
Oatmeal porridge	176
Oil, as food	101
Okra	76
Oleaginous seeds	57
Olive—olive oil	42
Omnivorous animals	21, 97
Onions	59, 197
Orange	74
Organic acids	42
Organization and diet	21
Osmazome	105
Ostrich	108
Oven, new kind of	213
Oxalic acid	42
Oxygen	26
Oyster plant	200
Oysters	104
Painted wood	218
Papau	83
Papered walls	218
Parched corn	186
Parched peas	56
Parsley	91
Parsnep	86, 197
Partridge	102
Paste	218
Paste, water-proof	219
Pastry	44
Patent barley	58
Peach	60
Peaches, cooked	202
Peach leather	114
Peach pies	180
Peanuts	58, 187
Pea-meal	56
Pears	65, 202
Peas	22, 56
Pearl barley	58
Pepones	76
Pewter dishes	217
Pepper dulse	97
Philosophy of diet	15
Phosphorus	26
Pie crust	177
Pies	177
Pilchards	104
Pineapple	79, 205
Pineapple ice cream	210
Pistachio-nut	58
Plantain	84
Plums	61
Pomaceous fruits	63
Pomegranate	70
Population and diet	22
Pork	98
Pork cheese	viii
Porridges	173
Portland arrow-root	46
Potash, salts of	46

INDEX.

	Page
Potassium	28
Potato apple dumpling	185
Potatoes	22, 86
Potato bread	163
Potato cake	168
Potato cheese	214
Potatoes, cooked	194, 196
Potato flour	87, 195
Potato jelly	196
Potato pie	179
Potato rot	87
Potato scones	171
Potato starch	39
Potato shortening	195
Potato, sweet	87
Potato tops	91
Potato yeast	158
Pot cheese	210
Pot barley	58
Poultry	207
Prawns	104
Proximate elements	24, 25
Prepared fruits	201
Preservation of Foods	109
Pumpkin bread	163
Pumpkin pies	178, 179
Pumpkins	77
Puddings	177
Pure water	29
Quail	152
Quality of flour	154
Quinces	67, 208
Quince marmalade	208
Radish	68
Rain water	29
Raised bread	152, 161
Raised Indian cake	164
Raised pie crust	179
Rampion	69
Rape	91
Raspberries	81, 204
Raspberry ice cream	210
Rats and mice	215
Ready rat trap	219
Red beet root	23
Reducing diet	118
Refining sugar	36
Relishes	209
Reptiles	97
Revolving cask filter	33
Rhubarb	93
Rhubarb pie	180
Rice	22, 51
Rice and apple pudding	184
Rice and milk mush	175
Rice and sago porridge	176
Rice, boiled	186
Rice bread	163
Rice custard	209
Rice griddle cake	167
Rice gruel	191
Rice mush	175
Rice pudding	182
Rice soup	191
Rich corn cake	165
Risings, milk	158

	Page
River water	29
Roasting, in papers	216
Robin	103
Rosamble	89
Rosemary	94
Roots	194
Ruba, yeast	159
Rye	58
Rye and Indian bread	163
Rye drop cake	169
Rye-meal mush	174
Sage	93
Sago	22, 39, 40
Sago and apple pudding	52
Sago gruel	190
Sago porridge	176
Sago starch grains	39
Salad oil	68
Salads	91
Salmon	104
Salsify	200
Salt, table	27
Salt of lemons	98
Samp	54, 174
Samphire	94
Sap, of maple	36
Sausages	44
Savory	94
Savory herbs	93
Savoys	90, 199
Scalded bread	163
Scalds and burns	214
Scallops	4
Schwartzbrot	58
Scrofula	44
Scurvy	44
Sea-kale	89
Seasoning herbs	93
Sea-water	29
Sea-weeds	95
Seeds	48
Semina	48
Shad	104
Shallots	89
Sheep	97
Shell-fish	
Shepherdia	72
Shoots	89
Shortened biscuit	168
Shrimps	104
Silver, German	217
Sirup	87
Sirup, grape	211
Skirret	80
Slapjacks	168
Slappers	167
Smallage	91
Snails	104
Snipe	103
Snow-ball pudding	184
Snow cream	210
Snow pudding	188
Sodium	27
Soft water	29
Sole	104
Sorrel	92

10*

INDEX.

	Page
Soups	189
Sour milk biscuit	168
Sourkrout	91
Spanish-nut	58
Sparrow grass	89
Spiders	104
Spinaceous plants	90
Spinach	91
Spinach soup	192
Split peas	56
Split peas soup	191
Sponge, setting the	155
Sponge filter	80
Spots, iron and ink	217
Spirits	44
Spring water	29
Spurred rye	53
Squashes	77
Squash pie	179
Starch	37, 218
Steam-cooking	218
Stews	44
Stains, fruit	217
Stimulating food	118
Stone filter	30, 34
Strawberries	79, 204
Strawberry cream	210
Strawberry pie	281
Strawberry tart	281
String beans	200
Sweet almonds	57
Sweet apple pudding	184
Sweet brown bread	168
Sweet herbs	98
Sweet oil	63
Sweet potatoes	87, 196
Succory	91
Succotash	188
Suet	42
Suet puddings	44
Sugar	35
Sugar, refining	36
Sulphur	26
Swine	25
Tahiti arrow-root	40
Tallow	42
Tangle	97
Tansy	93
Tapioca	89
Tapioca gruel	190
Tapioca pudding	188
Tarrago	93
Tartaric acid	42
Theory of nutrition	118
Thyme	98
Tin cooking utensils	216
Toadstools	95
Toast	171
Tomatoes	76
Tomatoes, cooked	205
Tomato soup	191
Tonic diet	118
Treacle	37
Trays	218

	Page
Trout	104
Truffle	96
Turbot	104
Turnips	22, 64, 196
Turkey	102
Ultimate elements	24
Unbaked bread cake	170
Uncooked bread cakes	164
Uncooked fruit cake	170
Unleavened bread	150, 160
Utensils, cooking	215, 217
Vegetable acids	42
Vegetable albumen	44
Vegetable broth	192
Vegetable casein	44
Vegetable fibrin	44
Vegetable milk	48
Vegetable marrow	200
Vegetables	194
Vegetarian system	20
Venison	270
Vinegar	42
Vine training	74
Walls, papered	218
Walnut	57
Walnut oil	42
Water	29
Water cress	91
Water-cure waffles	170
Water melon	77
Water-proof cement	218
Wedding cake	172
Well water	29
Wheat	49
Wheat-meal	22
Wheat-meal bread	162
Wheat-meal crackers	164
Wheat-meal drop cake	169
Wheat-meal fruit biscuit	171
Wheat-meal griddle cakes	167
Wheat-meal, grinding of	51
Wheat-meal gruel	189
Wheat-meal sweet cake	166
Wheat-meal wafers	164
Wheat starch grains	40
White ants	104
White-fish	104, 207
Whiting	104
Whole grains and seeds	186
Whortleberries	71, 206
Whortleberry pie	180
Wild endive	21
Wild rice	51
Wood, painted	218
Woodcock	103
Wood sorrel	93
Yams	88
Yarn filtering	84
Yeast	157
Yeast cakes	159
Yeast, of peas	160
Yolk of eggs	44
Zeiger	107
Zinc vessels	216

Sent prepaid by first post at prices annexed.

A List of Works

PUBLISHED BY

SAMUEL R. WELLS, No. 389 BROADWAY.

The following List embraces most of our Books, save private Medical Works contained in our "SPECIAL LIST," and those on PHONOGRAPHY, which are given in separate Catalogues. For full Titles see Illustrated and Descriptive Catalogue, which may be had gratuitously on application, personally or by letter, inclosing stamp.

WORKS ON PHRENOLOGY.

Annual of Phrenology and Physiognomy for 1868. By S. R. Wells..25c.

Annuals for 1865-6-7 and 1868, in one volume, of over 200 pages, with 200 illustrative engravings.. ....60c.

American Phrenological Journal. A handsomely illustrated monthly. Edited by S. R. Wells, a year......$3 00

Combe's Lectures on Phrenology. A complete course. In muslin...$1 75

Combe's Moral Philosophy; or, the duties of Man. New Ed., revised and enlarged. By Geo. Combe.......$1 75

Chart for Recording various Developments. A Synopsis Designed for Phrenologists... ....10c.

Constitution of Man. By Geo. Combe. Authorized Ed. Illustrations.....$1 75

Complete Works of Dr. Gall on Phrenology. 6 vols (very scarce) net $15

Defence of Phrenology; Arguments and Testimony. By Boardman...$1 50

Domestic Life, Thoughts on, its Concord and Discord. By N. Sizer, 25c.

Education Complete. Embracing Physiology. Animal and Mental, Self-Culture, and Memory; one vol......$4 00

Education, founded on the Nature of Man. By Dr. Spurzheim.....$1 50

Illustrated Chart of Physiognomy, in map form for framing.... ... 25c.

Matrimony; or, Phrenology and Physiology applied to the Selection of Conjugal Companions for Life...........50c.

Memory and Intellectual Improvement; applied to Self-Education..$1 50

Mental Science, Lectures on, according to the Philosophy of Phrenology. By Rev. G. S. Weaver. Muslin...$1 50

New Physiognomy; or, Signs of Character—As manifested through Temperament and External Forms, and especially in the Human Face Divine, with more than 1,000 illustrations. By S. R. Wells, Editor Phrenological Journal. In one large volume, handsomely bound. In muslin.... ......$ 5 00
Heavy calf, with marbled edges.. 8 00
Turkey morocco, full guilt....... 10 00

The Treatise of MR. WELLS, which is admirably printed, and profusely illustrated, is probably the most complete Hand-book upon the subject.—*N. Y. Tribune.*

Phrenology Proved, Illustrated and Applied. Thirty-seventh edition. A standard work on the Science....$1 75

Phrenology and the Scriptures. Their Harmony. By Rev. John Pierpont 25c

Phrenological Guide. Designed for the use of Students...............25c

Phrenological Bust. Designed especially for Learners, showing the exact location of the Organs of the Brain fully developed. Price, including box for packing (not mailable,) $1 75

Phrenological Specimens for Societies and Private Cabinets, 40 cents, net, (not mailable)......... ....$30 00

Self-Culture and Perfection of Character. Muslin.....................$1 50

Self-Instructor in Phrenology and Physiology. Illustrated with one hundred engravings. Paper............50c.
The same in muslin................75c.

HYDROPATHY; OR, WAT[ER]

Children, their Hydropathic Management in Health and Disease. Dr. Shew..1 75

Consumption, its Causes, Prevention, and Cure. By Dr. Shew. Muslin..1 50

Cook Book, Hydropathic. With New Recipes. Illustrated. By Dr. Trall, 1 50

Diseases of the Throat and Lungs, including Diphtheria. By Dr. Trall, 25c.

Domestic Practice of Hydropathy, with 15 illustrations of important subjects. By E. Johnson, M.D........2 60

Family Physician, Hydropathic. By Dr. Shew, a large and valuable work for Home or Domestic Practice. Profusely illustrated..............4 00

Hydropathy for the People. With observations on Drugs, Diet, Air, and Exercises. Notes by Dr. Trall.....1 50

Midwifery and the Diseases of Women. A practical work. Shew ...1 75

Philosophy of Water-Cure. By J. Balbirnie, M.D. For beginners....50c.

Practice of Water-Cure. By Drs. Wilson and Gully.................50c.

Water-Cure Manual. A Popular work on Hydropathy. Muslin..........1 50

Hydropathic En[cyclopedia, Illust]rated. A Comple[te System of Hydro]pathy and Hygie[nic System of Anato]my, illustrated; [The Laws of the Hu]man Body; Hygi[enic Agencies and] Preservation of [Health; Hygienic] Cookery; Theory [and Practice of Treat]ment; Special P[athology and] Therapeutics, in[cluding the Nature,] Causes, Sympton[s, and Treatment of] all known Disc[ases;] Surgical Disease[s; Application of Hygiene] to Midwifery an[d the Nursery.] Three Hundred E[ngravings.] One Thousand P[ages. With Gloss]ary, Table of C[ontents and Index,] complete. By R. [T. Trall, M.D.]

Of all the numero[us works that] have attained such [popularity as those] issued by this Hou[se, none have been] more adapted to ger[ieral usefulness, or a] rich, comprehensive [work, than this] Encyclopedia.—*N. Y.*

Water-Cure in C[hronic Diseases.] an exposition of [the Causes, Progress,] and Termination [of various Chronic] Diseases. By Dr [James Manby Gully. An im]portant work. ..

Water and Veget[able Diet in Scro]fula, Cancer, A[sthma, etc. By Dr.] Lamb. Notes by [Dr. Trall.]

WORKS ON PHYSIOLO[GY]

Alcoholic Controversy. A Review of the *Westminster Review* on the Physiological Errors of Teetotalism......50c.

Anatomical and Physiological Plates. These Plates were arranged expressly for Lecturers on Health, Physiology, etc. By R. T. Trall, M.D., of the New York Hydropathic College.

They are six in number, representing the normal position and life-size of all the internal viscera, magnified illustrations of the organs of the special senses, and a view of the principal nerves, arteries, veins, muscles, etc. For popular Instruction, for families, schools, and professional reference, they will be found far superior to anything of the kind heretofore published, as they are more complete and perfect in artistic design and finish. Price for the set, fully colored, backed and mounted on rollers. By express (not mailable)........20 00

Combe's Physiology, applied to the Improvement of Mental and Physical Education. Notes. Illustrated. ..1 75

Digestion, Philosophy of. The Principles of Dietetics. By Dr. Combe, 50c.

Family Gymnasi[um. With numerous] illustrations; con[taining the most im]portant method o[f Gymnastic,] Calisthenic, Kin[esipathic, and Vocal] exercises to the [development of the] bodily organs, the [invigoration of their] functions, the pr[eservation of health,] and cure of dise[ases and deformities.] By R. T. Trail, M[.D.]

Family Dentist, A[Popular Treatise on] the Teeth. By D. [

Food and Diet, co[nsisting of the kinds] of every kind of [Food in use. By] Dr. J. Pereira. [

Fruits and Fari[nacea, the Proper] Food of Man. [With numerous en]graved illustratio[ns. By John Smith,] M.D. Muslin...

Hereditary Desc[ent; Its Laws and] Facts applied to [

Infancy; or, the Ph[ysiological and Moral] Management of [Children.] By Dr. Combe. [

Natural Laws of [Man. By Dr. Spurz]heim. A capital

Philosophy of Sacred History, considered in relation to Human Aliment and the Wines of Scripture. By Sylvester Graham............3 50

Physiology, Animal and Mental, applied to Health of Body and Power of Mind. Illustrated. Muslin.....1 50

The Story of a Stomach: an Egotism. By a Reformed Dyspeptic..........75c.

Sober and Temperate Life, with Notes and Illustrations by Louis Cornaro, 50c.

Tea and Coffee, their Physical, Intellectual, and Moral effects. Alcott......25c.

The Science of Human Life. By Sylvester Graham, M.D. With a Biographical Sketch of the Author,.......3 50

Teeth, their Structure, Diseases and Management, with Engravings..........25c.

Special List. We have, in addition to the above, Private Medical Works and Treatises on subjects which, though not adapted to general circulation, are invaluable to those who need them. This Special List will be sent on pre-paid application, or receipt of stamp.

MISCELLANEOUS.

Æsop's Fables. People's Pictorial Edition, beautifully illustrated........1 00

Aims and Aids for Girls and Young Women. By Rev. G. S. Weaver...1 25

Chemistry, applied to Physiology, Agriculture and Commerce. By Liebig, 50c.

Footprints of Life; or, Faith and Nature reconciled. A Poem in three parts. By Philip Harvey, M.D. Part 1st—The Body. Part 2d—The Soul. Part 3d—The Deity. Something new......1 25

Fruit Culture for the Million; or, Hand-Book for the Cultivation and Management of Fruit Trees. Illustrated with Ninety Engravings. By Thomas Gregg. Muslin.. ....1 00

Gospel Among the Animals; or, Christ with the Cattle. By Rev. Samuel Osgood, D.D. ....25c.

Human Rights, and their Political Guaranties. By Judge Hurlbut,...1 50

Home for All. The Gravel Wall, a New, Cheap, and Superior Mode of Building. With Engravings......1 50

Hopes and Helps for the Young of both Sexes. By Rev. G. S. Weaver. An excellent work. Muslin...... 1 50

Life in the West; or, Stories of the Mississippi Valley. By N. C. Meeker, of the New York Tribune.... . ..2 00

Notes on Beauty, Vigor and Development. Illustrated..............12c.

Oratory, Sacred and Secular; or, The Extemporaneous Speaker. With Sketches of the most Eminent Speakers of all Ages. By William Pittenger, Author of "Daring and Suffering. Introduction by Hon. John A. Bingham, and Appendix, containing a "Chairman's Guide" for Conducting Public Meetings according to the best Parliamentary Models. Tinted paper..1 50

Movement-Cure. Embracing the History and Philosophy of this System of Medical Treatment. Illustrated. By G. H. Taylor, M.D..................1 75

Pope's Essay on Man. With Phrenological Notes by S. R. Wells. Beautifully illustated. Gilt, bev. boards..1 00

Prevention and Cure of Consumption by the Swedish-Movement Cure. With Directions for its Home Application. By David Wark, M.D.:......30c.

Saving and Wasting; or, Domestic Economy. Ill. By Solon Robinson 1 50

Temperance in Congress. Speeches delivered in the House of Representatives on the occasion of the First Meeting of the Congressional Temperance Society. 1 small 12m volume.. ... 25c.

The Christian Household. Embracing the Christian Home — Husband, Wife, Father, Mother, Child, Brother and Sister. By Rev. G. S. Weaver 1 00

The Education of the Heart; or, The Necessity of Proper Moral Culture for Human Happiness. An Address recently delivered at the Commencement Exercises of the Aurora (Ill.) Seminary. By Hon. Schuyler Colfax, Speaker of the House of Representatives........10c.

The Good Man's Legacy. A Sermon by Rev. Samuel Osgood, D.D... ...25c.

The Right Word in the Right Place. A Pocket Dictionary of Synonyms, Technical Terms, Abreviations, Foreign Phrases, etc. . . ..75c.

Ways of Life. The Right Way and the Wrong Way. By Rev. G. S. Weaver. A capital Work. Muslin......... 1 00

Weaver's Works for the Young. Comprising "Hopes and Helps," "Aims and Aids," and "Ways of Life,"...3 00

Agents, Booksellers, and others, would do well to engage in the sale of these Works, in every State, County, Town, and Village throughout the country. They are not kept by Booksellers generally. The market is not supplied, and *thousands might be sold where they have never yet been introduced.* For Wholesale Terms, and "Special List," please address, **SAMUEL R. WELLS, 389 Broadway, New York, U. S. A.**

THE Phrenological Journal

AND

LIFE ILLUSTRATED,

Devoted to Ethnology, Physiology, Phrenology, Psychology, Sociology, Education, Art, Literature, with Measures to Reform, Elevate, and Improve Mankind, Physically, Mentally and Spiritually.

S. R. WELLS, Editor.

Terms.—A New Volume, the 49th, commenced with the January Number. Published Monthly, in quarto form, at $3 a year, in advance. Sample numbers sent by first post, 30 cents. Clubs of ten or more, $2 each per copy, and an extra copy to agent.

Please address, **S. R. WELLS, 389 Broadway, New York.**

OUR NEW HAND-BOOKS.

How to Write. A Pocket Manual of Composition and Letter-Writing. Invaluable to all who would write well. 75c.

How to Talk. A Pocket Manual of Conversation and Debate, with more than Five Hundred Common Mistakes in Speaking corrected. .... 75c.

How to Behave. A Pocket Manual of Republican Etiquette, and Guide to Correct Personal Habits, with Rules for Debating Societies and Deliberative Assemblies. .... 75c.

How to Do Business. A Pocket Manual of Practical Affairs, and a Guide to Success in Life, with a Collection of Legal and Commercial Forms, suitable for all........................75c.

Hand-Book for Home Improvement. Comprising "How to Write,"
"How to Talk," "How to Behave," and "How to Do Business." In one large volume. Indispensable.. ...2 25
[More than 100,000 copies of this work have been sold. A capital book for agents.]

Library of Mesmerism and Psychology. Comprising the Philosophy of Mesmerism, Clairvoyance, and Mental Electricity; Fascination, or the Power of Charming: The Macrocosm, or the World of Sense; Electrical Psychology, or the Doctrine of Impressions; The Science of the Soul, treated Physiologically and Philosophically. Complete in two illustrated volumes....4 00

The Emphatic Diaglott; or, The New Testament in Greek. With a Literal Interlinear Translation, and a New Version in English. An interesting and valuable work. Plain. 4 00
In fine binding.................. 5 00

We have all works pertaining to that subject to which we are especially devoted, namely, the "Science of Man;" including Phrenology, Physiognomy, Ethnology, Psychology, Physiology, Anatomy, Hygiene, Dietetics, Gymnastics, etc. Also, all Standard Works on PHONOGRAPHY, HYDROPATHY, and the Natural Sciences generally.

Enclose stamps for Illustrated Catalogues, Terms to Agents, and address,

S. R. WELLS, Publisher,
389 BROADWAY, NEW YORK.

www.ingramcontent.com/pod-product-compliance
Lightning Source LLC
Chambersburg PA
CBHW021826230426
43669CB00008B/881